Black Market Exchange Rate, Unification of the Foreign Exchange Markets and Monetary Policy

European University Studies

Europäische Hochschulschriften

Publications Universitaires Européennes

Series V

Economics and Management

Reihe V Série V

Volks- und Betriebswirtschaft

Sciences économiques, gestion d'entreprise

Vol./Bd. 1963

PETER LANG

Frankfurt am Main · Berlin · Bern · New York · Paris · Wien

Nolvia N. Saca

Black Market Exchange Rate, Unification of the Foreign Exchange Markets and Monetary Policy

The Case of El Salvador

PETER LANG
Europäischer Verlag der Wissenschaften

Die Deutsche Bibliothek - CIP-Einheitsaufnahme

Saca, Nolvia N.:

Black market exchange rate, unification of the foreign exchange markets and monetary policy : the case of El Salvador / Nolvia N. Saca. - Frankfurt am Main ; Berlin ; Bern ; New York ; Paris ; Wien : Lang, 1997
(Europäische Hochschulschriften : Reihe 5, Volks- und Betriebswirtschaft ; Vol. 1963)
Zugl.: Kiel, Univ., Diss., 1995
ISBN 3-631-49954-X

NE: Europäische Hochschulschriften / 05

D 8
ISSN 0531-7339
ISBN 3-631-49954-X
US-ISBN 0-8204-2990-2

To my Parents and Jon

Dank

Die vorliegende Arbeit entstand am Institut für Theoretische Volkswirtschaftslehre der Christian-Albrechts-Universität zu Kiel unter Leitung von Prof. Dr. H. Herberg. Für seine wohlwollende Förderung möchte ich mich bedanken.

Acknowledgements

This work has been concluded thanks to technical, moral and financial support from many people.

I would like to express my gratitude to Professor H. Herberg for many precise and constructive criticisms that improved my theoretical analysis.

Professor Hans Genberg has always been willing to read, comment and discuss the different versions of my dissertation. I feel deeply indebted to him for his intellectual support.

I feel also profoundly grateful to Professor Gerd Hansen for several discussions and comments that led to sustantial improvement of my econometric work.

Thanks are also due to Professor Harmen Lehment and Professor Manfred Willms for reading the last version of my dissertation.

In addition, there are other people of the Library and the Institute of World Economics that have contributed in a meaningful way, but I feel particularly grateful to Ms. Ingetraud Müller, Ms. Susanne Tobias, Ms. Kiesner, Ms. Baur, and Mr. Paul Kramer.

Financial support from the World Bank and DAAD is gratefully aknowledged. I feel particularly grateful to Dr. Eckhard Schmidt of DAAD for his support. Thanks are also due to Ms. Nünning for encouragements.

I would like to thank the Directive Council of the Central Reserve Bank of El Salvador for the permission to put aside my duties at the Bank in order to realize this study. I own special thanks to my colleges at the Central Bank who always were willing to provide the necessary data for this research. I feel particularly grateful to Anabella de Palomo.

Finally, I would like to express my gratitude to my parents and to Jon for their unconditional and incessant support and also to some of my friends, especially to Anabella, Birget, Elisabeth and Günter.

Table of Contents

List of Figures

List of Tables

Chapter I

Introduction

A. Some Stylized Facts

The last fifteen years have been a very turbulent period for the Salvadorean economy. The civil war imposed heavy costs which impeded economic development and caused major economic, social, and human damage. Real GDP fell by 24.29 percent between 1979 and 1982. The decline was halted in 1983, and since then, until the end of the decade, economic growth averaged only 1.6 percent per year. About 750,000 people emigrated during the 1980's, while another 500,000 were refugees within the country.[1] Inflation rates, which started rising in the 1970's, accelerated, reaching 32 percent by 1986.[2] The balance-of-payments in the early 1980's registered a huge deficit which threatened to exhaust the stock of foreign reserves of the Central Reserve Bank and to precipitate the collapse of the fixed exchange rate. Under these circumstances, the authorities intensified the exchange controls to prevent further losses of reserves. Consequently, a very active black market for foreign exchange developed. In August 1982, a dual exchange regime was adopted, setting up a legal parallel market which, in principle, was assumed to be a free market emulating price developments in the black market for foreign exchange. However, in practice, both officially created markets were controlled, a fact that prolonged the existence of the black market. In early 1986, the authorities undertook the unification of the officially created foreign exchange markets and adopted a uniform fixed exchange rate regime. The black market for foreign exchange, however, continued to exist as a result of restrictions and exchange controls not being removed; in fact, they were intensified.

The principal motivation of the Salvadorean authorities for maintaining a system of exchange controls with the black market for foreign exchange was to protect international reserves in a balance-of-payments crisis without resorting to a maxi-devaluation, which they felt could be inflationary. By maintaining this system, the authorities believed that domestic prices were partly insulated from

1 World Bank (1989a), p. i.

2 Such rates of inflation were rather high for El Salvador, which enjoyed almost complete price stability for about two decades, from the early 1950's until the early 1970's (see Figure III.1).

movements in the exchange rate, since most trade transactions took place at the official rate(s) which were fixed or gradually depreciated by the authorities.

On the other hand, the existence of a black market, despite the fact that it was officially tolerated, was of high concern to the Salvadorean authorities. Specifically, they considered that this dual exchange rate system with a black market had some adverse effects. First, there was a loss of tariff and export-tax revenues. Second, the existence of the black market and a high premium led to a diversion of export receipts from the official to the black market. Third, the expansion of the black market for foreign exchange weakened the effectiveness of capital controls, which accelerated capital flight. Fourth, the existence of a black market induced a dollarization of the economy. Fifth, the multiple exchange system generated distortions in production and consumption decisions. The unification of foreign exchange markets was thus an important objective of the macroeconomic policy of the Salvadorean authorities.

At the end of the past decade, the Salvadorean authorities began a comprehensive adjustment process in all economic areas. The unification of the exchange markets and the adoption of a flexible exchange rate as well as the removal of exchange controls and a financial liberalization were part of the overall adjustment process. This posed new challenges to the Central Reserve Bank in the conduct of monetary policy. Specifically, the Central Reserve Bank encountered serious difficulties in achieving its objectives of monetary policy (i.e., in controlling inflation and avoid exchange rate appreciation) as well as in achieving its monetary targets.

B. Goals and Organization of the Study

The purpose of this study is to examine theoretically as well as empirically the behavior of a small open economy, first, under a dual official-black market exchange rate regime, and then, under the process of unification that has as its ultimate objective to absorb and legalize the black market for foreign exchange, eliminating the inefficiencies and market fragmentation associated with a quasi-illegal activities.

In particular, the study focuses on four main issues: First, the determinants of the premium in the black market. Second, the effect of the black market on the domestic price level and on the real exchange rate. In particular, the issue is whether or not a dual exchange rate system with a black market is able to insulate domestic prices from movements in the black market exchange rate. Third, the issues that the authorities have to face in considering unification of the foreign exchange markets. The fourth and last issue to be analyzed is the monetary effects and implications for the conduct of monetary policy with the resulting changes in the exchange rate policy and financial and trade structure.

This study provides a modest insight into the difficulties of maintaining a system of dual exchange rates, on the one hand, and into the problems that a central bank may face in the conduct of monetary policy in the context of exchange rate and financial liberalization, on the other hand. It should also serve as a basis and motivation for continuing work on the design of the appropriate strategy of monetary policy for El Salvador. Additionally, it could serve as a guide for many developing countries which have a sizable black market and consider the unification of foreign exchange markets an important policy objective.

This study is organized as follows: after this introduction, Chapter II contains a brief survey of the Salvadorean economy. Institutional arrangements and the working of the foreign and monetary sectors are described so as to give a general idea of how this economy functions.

Next, the institutional framework and developments in the foreign markets are analytically examined. Detailed descriptions of the foreign exchange regimes in the 1980's and of the structure and the nature of the black market in El Salvador are provided. The linkage between the foreign exchange markets and the Central Reserve Bank's intervention in the foreign exchange market are also discussed (Chapter III).

The following chapter is devoted to discussing the black market for foreign exchange on a purely theoretical level. In so doing, causes, behavior, and economic effects of black markets as well as the various models of black market exchange rate determination are discussed. The chapter concludes with the macroeconomic effects of various economic policies and disturbances in the presence of a black market for foreign exchange (Chapter IV).

Chapter V is devoted to econometric work, starting out with the empirical estimation of the various models existing in the literature. Second, a simple portfolio model of black market premium determination that captures some special features of the black market for foreign currency in El Salvador is developed and estimated. The model takes into account leakages between the official and the black markets, central bank indirect intervention in the black market, and remittances of Salvadorean workers abroad, which was a major source of supply in the black market. This model attempts to provide an answer to the following questions: (a) What were the determinants of the black market premium in El Salvador? (b) To what extent was the foreign exchange acquired in the black market in El Salvador considered an asset, or was it a means of exchange used for carrying out international commodity transactions? (c) Are domestic prices insulated from black market exchange rate movements? The empirical evidence presented is based both on traditional estimations and on cointegration and vector autoregression analysis.

The last two chapters discuss issues related to the unification of the foreign exchange markets and the conduct of monetary policy with a flexible exchange rate and ongoing financial liberalization. Chapter VI analytically discusses the main issues that the policymakers have to face when they consider the unification of the foreign exchange markets, namely: (1) the pace of unification, (2) the choice of the uniform foreign exchange regime, and (3) the macroeconomic effects of exchange rate unification. Every issue is illustrated with the recent experience of El Salvador. The chapter concludes with some lessons from the experience of El Salvador in the 1990's.

Chapter VII examines the monetary policy under a uniform flexible exchange rate regime and in the wake of financial liberalization. The chapter starts out by outlining the general principles of the design of monetary policy in open economies. It serves as a background for the analysis of the monetary policy in El Salvador, as it provides the theoretical structure with which El Salvador's experience is interpreted. Thus, in the next section, the Central Reserve Bank's objectives of monetary policy and their feasibility are discussed. This section also discusses the Central Reserve Bank's operating procedure for implementing monetary policy, namely, policy formulation, targets, and instruments. Section D recounts some stylized facts of the recent economic experience of El Salvador. It focuses on the development of inflation, nominal and real exchange rates, transfers and capital flows, interest rates, monetary aggregates, and real economic activity. The last section (Section E) analyzes the implications for monetary policy of the exchange rate and financial liberalization. This section especially attempts to provide an answer to the following questions: Does the unification and exchange rate flexibility create any problems? What are the monetary policy implications of the exchange rate and financial liberalization? Has the exchange rate unification or financial liberalization made monetary control difficult? The chapter concludes with some policy recommendations concerning the new role of monetary policy, the objectives of the Central Reserve Bank, and the new strategy of monetary control.

A summary of the major findings of this study, general recommendations, and some suggestions for further research are reported in a concluding chapter (Chapter VIII).

C. The Theoretical Framework

1. Models of Black Market for Foreign Exchange

The black market for foreign exchange is analyzed in the context of a dual exchange rate regime, giving particular emphasis to the macroeconomic aspects, particularly its interaction with the economy and policy issues.

Analytical models of black markets for foreign exchange can be classified into the following categories: smuggling and real trade models, monetary models, and portfolio balance models. The real trade approach (see, for instance, Sheikh [1976] and Culbertson [1975]) is based on a partial equilibrium analysis, neglecting the interactions between the black market and macroeconomic developments in the economy. The monetary approach (Blejer 1978a) emphasizes the relationship between monetary policy and the behavior of the black market exchange rate. The portfolio balance or currency substitution approach, developed by de Macedo (1982, 1987), Dornbusch et al. (1983), and Frankel (1990), stresses the role of asset composition on the determination of the black market exchange rate.

The general approach adopted in this study to analyze the black market for foreign currency in El Salvador is the portfolio balance approach, into which some elements of the monetary approach are incorporated. This was considered appropriate especially for two reasons. First, the development of the black market for foreign currency in El Salvador was closely associated to the political instability there. Thus, portfolio diversification can be expected to prevail and represent a key determinant of the demand for foreign exchange on the black market. Second, the Central Reserve Bank's intervention was an important determinant of the behavior of the black market exchange rate.

2. Exchange Rate Unification

Existing analytical studies of exchange market unification concentrate on a number of macroeconomic effects of the exchange reforms. Pinto (1991) focuses on the fiscal effects of exchange rate unification, while Lizondo (1987) and Kiguel and Lizondo (1990) emphasize exchange-rate and balance-of-payments effects. Agénor and Flood (1992), which is the most complete study in this area, focuses, in addition, on the real effects of exchange rate unification.

This study, based on the Salvadorean experience of 1989-1993, examines the unification of foreign exchange markets as a process, namely, the dynamic effects on the black market exchange rate in the transition period (pre-reform period), at the moment of the reform (June 1, 1990), and post-reform period are analyzed. Other aspects of exchange-rate unification, such as the choice of the uniform exchange rate regime, the macroeconomic effects of the unification, and the monetary policy implications in the post-reform period, are also investigated.

In Chapters VI and VII the general principles regarding exchange-rate unification and financial liberalization are set out and used to interpret the particular experience of El Salvador. The general principles are based especially on the theoretical framework first developed by Poole (1970) for the optimal choice of monetary policy instruments. Although Poole's analysis was carried out in the context of a closed economy, it has been extended, with qualifications, to open economy models, for example, by Bryant (1980), Benavie (1983), and Gardner (1983). This framework has also been widely applied in the literature on the choice of exchange rate regimes. The principal prescriptions that emerge from all these studies are that rates (interest rates and/or exchange rates) should be targeted or pegged when monetary disturbances are dominant, whereas the targeting of monetary aggregates would be preferable when real sector disturbances are more important.

D. Empirical Analysis

The core of the empirical work is contained in Chapter V. This chapter focuses on two main issues: first, what were the determinants of the black market premium in El Salvador, and second, the question of whether or not domestic prices are insulated from black market exchange rate movements.

The analysis took place in four steps. First, a preliminary analysis of the data and tests for stationarity were performed to establish the order of integration of the data series. Second, having found that most variables under investigation are nonstationary, an error correction representation of the most representative models of every analytical framework of black market for foreign exchange determination was specified and estimated. Third, a simple portfolio model of the black market premium determination was developed and estimated that captures some special features of the black market for foreign currency in El Salvador and also measures the impact of the black market exchange rate change on domestic prices and on the real exchange rate. One of the most important findings of the last two steps is that none of the theoretical views of the black market for foreign exchange is entirely satisfactory in the empirical tests. Thus, in order not to impose a particular theoretical view in the empirical results, as is the case in structural models, in the fourth and final step, an empirical methodology was adopted that leaves the data relatively free to characterize the interrelationships between the variables of interest, namely a VAR model in vector autoregressive error correction form.

Chapter II

Introduction to the Salvadorean Economy

A. The Economic Structure

El Salvador is a small open economy.[1] Its most export-oriented sector is agriculture, which is of fundamental importance not only in terms of exports, but also in terms of income generation, employment, and fiscal revenue.

Traditionally, the economy has relied more on agriculture and a tertiary sector than on industry (Table II.2). In the 1970's and 1980's, about 24 percent of the gross domestic product in real terms was made up of agricultural and livestock production. In the 1990's this proportion has remained virtually unchanged (Table II.2). The economy has depended particularly on coffee production, which accounts for about 7 percent of GDP and about 50 percent of exported goods, although the later proportion has declined in the 1990's, but remains high (around 30 percent [see Table II.3]). This makes the economy extremely vulnerable to world prices of agricultural products.

The incipient industrial development has occurred in the past behind high rates of protection. Industrial production is heavily concentrated in consumer goods that are not competitive in world markets. Most of the production is oriented toward satisfying domestic demand; only 20 percent of this production is exported, of which about 17 percent was exported to countries of the Central American Common Market (CACM).[2,3] Thus, the manufacturing sector is mainly an import-competing-oriented sector; therefore, unlike the agricultural sector, the manufacturing sector's performance depends primarily on internal and

---

1 Small in the sense that it is a price taker in international markets, but it also meets other usual characteristics of smallness, such as population (5.4 million in mid-1992). With a total area of 21,000 square kilometers, El Salvador has one of the highest population densities in the world (estimated at 354 inhabitants per square kilometer of cultivable land in 1988). It has limited natural resources, but is one of the more developed Central American countries, with per capita GDP in 1992 estimated at 1,170 dollars, although with a very unequal income distribution (World Bank [1989a and 1994]). Indicators of the openness of the Salvadorean economy are presented in Table II.1.

2 World Bank (1989a), p. 52.

3 The Central American Common Market (CACM) comprises Costa Rica, El Salvador, Guatemala, Honduras, and Nicaragua.

Table II.1

Indicators of Openness
(percent of GDP, unless otherwise indicated)

	1970-1974	1975-1979	1980-1984	1985-1989	1990	1991	1992	1993
Exports/GDP	26.0	31.0	22.6	13.3	10.8	9.9	9.2	9.6
Exports and Imports/GDP	53.1	63.4	48.7	34.7	34.3	33.6	35.2	34.8
Imports of Capital/Gross Domestic Fixed Investment	32.9	38.4	24.2	38.0	37.1	40.4	42.2	37.7
Export Crops*/Agriculture Production	53.2	67.6	58.8	54.0	41.0	38.8	33.6	35.5

Source: Central Reserve Bank of El Salvador, *Quarterly Review*, various issues, and author's calculations.
*Includes: Coffe, cotton, and sugar.

Table II.2

Sector's Share in GDP
(percent of GDP)

	1970-1974	1975-1979	1980-1984	1985-1989	1990	1991	1992	1993
Agricultural Sector (Export-oriented Sector)	25.1	23.5	25.8	23.7	23.9	23.1	24.1	23.6
Coffee Production	8.2	7.3	8.8	6.8	7.0	6.6	7.1	6.9
Manufacturing Sector (Import- competing Sector)	18.6	18.8	17.2	17.7	18.0	18.2	18.5	18.9
Nontraded Goods Sector	56.3	57.7	57.0	58.6	58.1	58.7	58.0	58.0
Commerce	23.1	22.7	17.3	16.2	16.2	16.3	16.3	16.5
Pub. Adm. & Defense	8.1	8.5	12.0	14.3	14.1	14.1	13.3	12.1
Personal Services	8.2	7.5	7.2	6.6	6.5	6.5	6.5	6.6
Construction	3.3	4.1	3.2	3.4	3.1	3.3	3.4	3.6
Banking, Insurance and Real Estate	2.4	2.8	3.3	3.4	3.1	3.1	3.1	3.2
Housing	3.7	3.5	4.6	4.8	4.9	4.8	4.8	4.7
Public Utilities	2.1	2.6	3.5	3.8	3.9	4.0	4.1	4.6
Transport	5.3	5.9	5.8	5.9	6.1	6.3	6.4	6.6
Mining	0.1	0.1	0.1	0.1	0.1	0.1	0.2	0.2

Source: Central Reserve Bank of El Salvador, *Quarterly Review*, various issues, and author's calculations.

regional demand incentives and not on international price trends. As demand fell, output in the manufacturing sector declined by 34.6 percent from 1978 to 1982, even more than the rest of the economy. However, since 1983 this sector has also recovered faster than the rest of the economy. The share of manufactures in total output has increased slightly in the 1990's, and in 1993 it reached its relative position of the 1970's again (Table II.2).

The nontraded goods sector, in which commerce, personal services, and public administration and defense are the largest subsectors, has maintained a share in real GDP close to the levels of the pre-crisis period despite a substantial increase in the share of public administration and defense in real GDP, reflecting the increased role of the public sector in the economy.[4]

The Salvadorean economy is fundamentally a market economy, although during the 1980's the participation of the public sector was heavy. In 1980 the Salvadorean financial system, including commercial banks and the savings and loans associations, were nationalized. Moreover, state-owned institutions completely controlled the country's international trade in coffee and sugar, the most important export crops. The State was the only authorized agent to export coffee and sugar through the National Coffee Institute (INCAFE) and the National Sugar Institute (INAZUCAR).

In mid-1989, El Salvador undertook a mid-term program which sought to change the role of the public sector, to transform it into an entity in conformance with a market-oriented economy. The program included institutional reforms as well as privatization of most state-owned financial institutions and some state enterprises.

B. Foreign Sector

1. Trade Structure

As mentioned above, El Salvador is a small open economy with high export concentration in relatively few agricultural commodities.

Table II.3 shows the relative importance of the different components of exports. Exports of four products (coffee, sugar, cotton, and shrimp) accounted for over 60 percent of the total in the 1970's and 1980's. In the 1990's, this structure

---

4 The increase in public administration and defense can be explained by the increase in security expenditures due to the civil war, but also by an increase in the bureaucracy as a result of the nationalization of the banking system and other financial institutions, as well as some enterprises (see further on in this chapter).

has changed toward a relatively higher importance of nontraditional exports which consist mostly of manufactured products (e.g., food products, tobacco, clothing, and footwear) and which are still primarily directed toward the Central American Common Market (CACM). As will be discussed in section B.2, the previous trade policy favored regional trade.

The structure of imports is another aspect of the openness of the Salvadorean economy: it is dependent on imports of intermediate goods for domestic assembly, as shown in Table II.3. The structure of imports reveals the incipient industrial development of the economy noted above.

Table II.3

Trade Structure
(percent of the totals)

	1970-1974	1975-1979	1980-1984	1985-1989	1990	1991	1992	1993
EXPORTS								
Traditional	62.4	69.6	69.0	68.4	50.8	46.2	36.4	37.3
i. Coffee	43.9	54.1	58.1	61.9	44.6	37.2	25.3	30.2
ii. Cotton	10.6	9.5	6.0	1.2	0.2	0.1	0.3	0.0
iii. Sugar	5.7	4.7	2.7	3.0	3.5	5.4	7.5	4.1
iv. Shrimp	2.2	1.3	2.2	2.3	2.5	3.4	3.3	2.9
Nontraditional	37.6	30.7	31.0	31.6	49.2	53.7	63.6	61.5
i. Foodstuff	4.5	3.5	2.6	2.1	3.7	4.8	3.8	2.5
ii. Chemicals	5.7	4.7	4.2	5.5	7.8	8.8	10.9	10.1
iii. Manufactures	22.1	17.7	16.8	10.8	19.4	20.7	22.1	21.0
iv. Others	5.3	4.7	7.3	13.3	18.3	19.4	26.8	27.8
IMPORTS								
i. Consumer Goods	26.9	25.2	30.2	24.9	31.6	26.5	28.8	26.7
ii. Intermediate Goods	54.3	50.6	58.2	50.9	49.8	50.5	45.8	47.2
iii. Capital Goods	18.7	24.2	11.6	23.1	18.6	23.0	25.4	24.2
Memorandum Items								
Nontraditional Exports								
i. CACM	24.0	24.7	24.6	19.3	29.8	32.9	43.1	43.0
ii. Rest of the World	13.7	6.0	6.4	12.3	19.4	20.8	20.6	18.4

Source: Central Reserve Bank of El Salvador, *Quarterly Review*, various issues, and author's calculations.

El Salvador's main trading partners are the United States, Germany, Japan, Guatemala, and Costa Rica, which account for about 70 percent of total trade (Table II.4).[5] More recently, trade with Mexico increased from 0.85 percent of the total in 1980 to 4.1 in 1993.

Table II.4

El Salvador's Major Trading Partners
(percent of the total)

	1980		1993	
Countries	Exports to	Imports from	Exports to	Imports from
Central America				
Costa Rica	6.3	5.8	9.0	3.6
Guatemala	16.2	26.4	22.0	10.8
Others countries				
Germany	13.9	2.5	7.2	3.5
Japan	4.0	3.9	1.5	5.1
United States	41.2	20.1	29.9	44.2
México	0.5	1.2	2.2	5.9
Total*	81.6	58.7	69.9	67.2

* Excluding México

Source: Central Reserve Bank of El Salvador, *Quarterly Review,* October/December 1982 and April/June 1994, pp. 50-51 and 64-65, respectively.

2. Trade Policy

This section provides an overview of the trade policy in El Salvador prior to the trade liberalization, as well as of the current trade system.

5 Trade with the other Central American countries Honduras and Nicaragua has been reactivated in the 1990's. However, they are not included in Table II.4 because no trade between El Salvador and Honduras took place in the 1970's and part of the 1980's, after a border conflict between those countries; and there was very little trade with Nicaragua during the 1980's, since the political and economic crisis in this country began in 1978. In 1993, if these countries were included, the percentage of total trade would increase to 75.6 percent.

a. Preliberalization Trade System

Prior to mid-1989, El Salvador's trade and exchange rate systems were instruments of an inward-oriented development strategy.[6] The trade system was very complex, including a large number of instruments: tariffs, exchange controls, and quantitative import restrictions[7], export taxes and subsidies, and the exchange rate system was also an instrument of commercial policy.[8]

Tariffs and exchange controls represented the most important trade barriers. Other non-tariff barriers have played a relatively minor role since 1986 and they often changed. Most important were licenses and prior deposits.

Export taxes were levied on most traditional exports, namely coffee, sugar, and shrimp. The most important was the coffee tax, which was charged at a marginal rate of 30 percent.[9] By contrast, nontraditional exports to non-CACM countries received a subsidy (e.g., honeydew melons, and clothing). Exporters of these products enjoyed custom duty exemption for the import of machinery, equipment, fuel, and lubricants, and full exemption from income and wealth taxes over a period of ten years.

As a member of the Central American Common Market (CACM), El Salvador had a tariff system which favored regional imports over those from the rest of the world. The legal tariff structure of El Salvador comprised 1,902 tariff positions, about 90 percent of which were common to the countries participating in the CACM: Common External Tariff (CET).[10] The tariff structure also favored domestic industries producing final consumer goods at the expense of those producing capital and intermediate goods. The highest rates were applied

---

6 In the World Development Report (1987), El Salvador was classified among the countries that followed a "moderately inward-oriented" trade strategy. This category is defined as follows: The overall incentive structure distinctly favors production for the domestic market. The average rate of effective protection for home markets is relatively high and the range of effective protection relatively wide. The use of direct import controls and licensing is extensive, and although some direct incentives to exports may be provided, there is a distinct bias against exports. Moreover, the exchange rate is clearly overvalued (see *World Development Report,* 1987, p. 82).

7 Quantitative import restrictions included: (a) a list of prohibited items (e.g., imports of luxury goods), (b) import-licensing schemes (e.g., a number of agricultural products and fertilizers required previous authorization by the Ministry of Agriculture).

8 For details of the exchange rate systems in El Salvador during the last decade, see Chapter III.

9 The coffee tax was not a simple ad valorem tax of 30 percent. The tax was $6.75 per quintal (i.e., 100 pounds) plus 30 percent on the price exceeding $45 per quintal. Thus, depending on the price, the ad valorem equivalent of the tax could vary.

10 For details of the trade policy in the Central American countries, see World Bank (1989b).

to final consumer goods, while intermediate and capital goods received a lower rate of protection (Table II.5).

The disparity in nominal protection led to a very high effective protection (protection on value added). Table II.6 presents nominal and effective rates of protection which are calculated not only on the basis of legal tariffs, but also take into account the effects of non-tariff barriers such as prior deposits, quantitative restrictions, exchange controls, and multiple exchange rates.

The consequences of such a trade regime have been extensively analyzed in the literature and have also been examined for the case of El Salvador.[11] Thus, it is not necessary to describe those effects here.

b. Trade Liberalization during the 1990's.

The trade reforms have been consistent with the philosophy of the economic program undertaken in mid-1989 (i.e., excessive controls and regulations were viewed as inappropriate for efficient resource allocation and the attainment of rapid economic growth),[12] and have been motivated by the need to improve export performance. The past system of a dual official-black market exchange regime with exchange controls and high tariffs was considered to be inadequate to reduce the external imbalances.

The trade liberalization can be summarized in four types of measures: (i) removal of exchange controls and all quantitative restrictions, including all prohibitions and licensing requirements, and prior deposits; (ii) elimination of all exemptions and exonerations from import duties; (iii) reduction of the level and dispersion of import tariffs;[13] (iv) elimination of export taxes (on shrimp and sugar) and reduction of the export tax on coffee.[14] Later, in March 1993, the coffee export tax was replaced by an income tax on coffee producers.[15]

11 For a general review of the consequences of protection in terms of production efficiency and the distribution of income, see, for example, Clements and Sjaastad (1984) and Bhagwati (1978); for the particular case of El Salvador, see Genberg, Sjaastad, and Rodriguez (1985).

12 Consistent with the philosophy outlined in Harberger and Wisecarver (1989).

13 The range from import duties was gradually narrowed from 0-290 percent to 5-20 percent in 1993 (see Table II.5).

14 For details of the measures on the trade reform in El Salvador, see World Bank (1991) and Loehr (1991).

15 International Monetary Fund (1994a), p. 39.

Table II.5

Average Unweighted Nominal Protection Rates*

Sectors	1988		September 1989		April 1990		July 1993		July 1994	
	Mean	St.Dev.	Mean	St.Dev.	Mean	St.Dev.	Mean	St.Dev.	Mean	St.Dev.
WHOLE ECONOMY	36.9	42.8	20.4	17.4	17.8	13.6	11.7	8.8	11.6	8.7
Agriculture	39.0	38.9	20.4	18.6	17.2	13.2	12.1	5.9	12.1	5.9
Mining	10.4	4.6	6.9	3.7	6.9	3.7	6.3	2.5	6.3	2.5
Manufacturing	37.2	43.2	20.6	17.4	18.0	13.7	11.8	9.0	11.7	8.9
Consumption	59.2	53.4	29.5	18.5	24.2	13.6	19.1	9.2	19.0	9.1
Intermediate	21.8	24.9	14.4	13.1	13.8	11.8	7.8	5.4	7.8	5.4
Capital	21.5	22.2	14.0	13.9	13.3	12.6	6.4	4.3	6.4	4.3

* Nominal protection rates granted through legal tariffs, plus other duties.

Source: World Bank and Ministry of Planning of El Salvador calculations; data provided by the Ministry of Planning of El Salvador, October 1994.

Table II.6

Nominal and Effective Rates of Protection in 1987

Sectors	Nominal	Effective
Coffee	- 25.0	- 28.0
Cotton	0.0	- 9.8
Other agriculture and mining products	4.8	- 0.5
Foodstuffs	29.7	93.7
Beverages and tobacco	88.5	301.5
Textiles	40.5	84.8
Clothing, leather and footwear	41.7	75.1
Wood and furniture	43.8	87.1
Paper and printing	27.3	43.7
Chemical products	12.2	7.9
Rubber, plastic, and nonmetallic products	23.8	38.6
Basic metal industries	14.2	14.1
Machinery and equipment	21.7	38.6
Oil and electricity	6.1	2.3
Nontradeables*	12.0	10.7
Nontraditional exports	0.0	- 2.6

*Change in the price of nontradeables induced by import and export taxes.
Source: IBRD calculations; World Bank (1989a), p. 31.

C. The Monetary and Financial Sector

1. Institutions of the Financial System

The main institutions of the Salvadorean money market are: (a) the Superintendency of the Financial System, (b) the Central Reserve Bank, (c) five commercial banks, (d) four savings and loans associations, (e) other financial institutions of development and public character, and (f) the Stock Exchange Market.

a. Superintendency of the Financial System

In many countries, banking supervision and regulation are part of the functions of the central bank. In El Salvador these responsibilities are entrusted to the Superintendency of the Financial System.

In this regard, the Superintendency of the Financial System's main objective is to promote the maintenance of a healthy and efficient financial system and to maintain public confidence in the country's financial institutions. In fulfillment of this mission, the Superintendency of the Financial System supervises all financial institutions for compliance with legal regulations.[16,17]

In general, the main supervision tasks are monitoring registration requirements, procedures of credit analysis, bank portfolios, and the enforcement of prudential ratio.

b. The Central Reserve Bank

The Central Reserve Bank formulates and implements the monetary and exchange rate policy of the country. The new Organic Law of the Central Reserve Bank of El Salvador of May 3, 1991 grants the Central Reserve Bank the status of being the highest authority in monetary and exchange rate matters in the country and authorizes its Directive Council to formulate and execute the monetary and exchange rate policy.[18] Previously, the highest authority in those matters resided in the Monetary Board, founded in 1973 and integrated by the Ministers of Planning, Finances, Economics, and Agriculture and the President of the Central Reserve Bank.

The Organic Law of the Central Reserve Bank of 1991 stipulates that the fundamental objective of the central bank is to promote and maintain monetary and exchange conditions to assure the stability of the national economy, that is,

16 Organic Law of the Superintendency of the Financial System (Ley Orgánica de la Superintendencia del Sistema Financiero), Art. 2, published in the Diario Oficial No. 278, December 10, 1990.

17 The new Organic Law of the Superintendency of the Financial System (Ley Orgánica de la Superintendencia del Sistema Financiero) grants this institution the legal standing and resources to supervise and control the financial system, including the Central Reserve Bank, commercial banks, and other private and public financial institutions. Its Directive Council has four members: (a) a member appointed by the Central Reserve Bank; (b) a member appointed by the Finance Minister from three candidates proposed by the Association of Professionals of Economic Sciences; (c) a member appointed by the Minister of Economics from three candidates proposed by the Public Accounting Council (Consejo de Vigilancia de la Contaduría Pública y Auditoría); and (d) a member appointed by the Court of Justice from three candidates proposed by the Association of Lawyers (Federación de Asociaciones de Abogados de El Salvador).

18 This Council has seven members: one president, two vice presidents, and four directors. The President of the Directive Council is, by tradition, the President of the Central Reserve Bank, and the vice presidents are usually the first and second vice president of the Central Reserve Bank. The four Executive Directors are: a representative of the Ministries of Finance, Planning, Economics, and Agriculture; a representative of the private sector in the area of agriculture, industry, and commerce; a representative of the Association of Professionals of Economic Sciences; a representative of the Banking and Financial Institutions.

(a) to maintain the internal and external value of the colon and its convertibility, and (b) to prevent inflationary and deflationary tendencies.[19] These are to be achieved by regulating the volume of money and credit in the economy as well as the level of interest rates. This can be interpreted in several ways. Chapter VII discusses the way this has been interpreted in practice and the difficulties that the Central Reserve Bank may encounter in achieving both objectives.

c. Commercial Banks

The largest and most important of the financial intermediaries are the commercial banks and the savings and loans associations (Financieras).[20] The commercial banks are responsible for the handling of most current, saving and time deposit accounts (about 75 percent of total deposits in the financial system in 1993).[21]

The commercial banks and the savings and loans associations are subject to the Central Reserve Bank regulations in the form of minimum reserve requirements. The reserve requirements are the same for both types of institutions, but vary by type of deposit.[22] As of December 1993, the reserve requirements are 30 percent on demand deposits and 20 percent on savings and time deposits; 10 percentage points of the latter are remunerated.[23,24]

The commercial banks in El Salvador, as in many less developed countries, mainly provide credit to landowners, exporters, merchants, and in general borrowers who are creditworthy. The rest of the economy must borrow from some institutions of development character and from what is considered the informal sector, which includes cooperatives, enterprises, and moneylenders.[25]

---

19 Organic Law of the Central Reserve Bank (Ley Orgánica del Banco Central de Reserva de El Salvador), Art. 3, p. 21, Diario Oficial No. 80, Tomo 311, May 3, 1991.

20 There are several commercial banks (five national and two foreign banks) and the Mortgage Bank. The latter bank will be also privatized and considered to be as any commercial bank.

21 Central Reserve Bank of El Salvador, *Quarterly Review* April-June 1994, pp. 31-33.

22 Before July 1991, the reserve requirements also varied by the type of institution. The reserve requirements were lower for savings and loans associations than for commercial banks.

23 The Central Reserve Bank pays interest on part (50 percent) of the reserves resulting from the reserve requirements of savings and time deposits.

24 International Monetary Fund (1994a), p. 7.

25 In a recent study by Cuevas et al. (1991) it was found that in El Salvador the informal financial sector is not as big as in other Latin American countries such as the Dominican Republic, Costa Rica, and Chile, and that the informal financial intermediaries mainly finance their own business, clients, and related activities and less

d. Other Financial Institutions

There are other institutions with a developmental orientation, such as the Agricultural Development Bank. The purpose of this institution is to finance the activities of medium and small landowners. In contrast, the Federation of Credit and Workers Bank extends loans to small farmers and enterprises and others low-income sectors.

In the industrial and commercial sectors there are two financing institutions: the Industrial Development Bank (BANAFI), which channels financial resources to encourage industrial development, and the Fondo de Financiamiento y Garantía para la Pequeña Empresa (FIGAPE), which grants credit to small enterprises.

In the housing sector there are two financing institutions: the Financiera Nacional de la Vivienda finances medium-size housing, and the Fondo Social de la Vivienda, a type of social security scheme, finances low-cost housing projects.

Recently (in August 1994), an official development bank, the Multisector Investment Bank (Banco Multisectorial de Inversiones) was created, which aims at substituting the rediscount window at the Central Reserve Bank and allowing the Central Reserve Bank to concentrate effectively on its essential functions. The private sector portfolio of the Central Reserve Bank, estimated at about 1,600 million colones, was passed on to the Multisector Investment Bank.[26] This bank provides credit through commercial banks, nonbank financial institutions, and financial official institutions to the private sector to finance investment projects.

All these institutions operate with an interest rate structure for loans very similar to that of the commercial banks.

e. The Stock Exchange Market

Before 1992, a formal capital market did not exist in the Salvadorean financial system. The Stock Exchange has been operating since April 1992 and the level of transactions is still not very significant. The total volume of transactions was 197.2 million colones (0.4 percent of the GDP) and 7,009.1 million colones (10.6 percent of the GDP) in 1992 and 1993, respectively. Most transactions involve trading of stabilization bonds (Certificados de Estabilización Monetaria) issued by the Central Reserve Bank that have original maturities of up to one

---

speculative activities. Moreover, the study also concludes that El Salvador does not experience the duality of the financial markets of some African countries (for example, Cameroon), where most monetary circulation is from the informal financial sector. However, it was found that in El Salvador 30 percent of the debt in the clients' portfolio represents informal credit (pp. 98-102).

26 International Monetary Fund (1994a), p. 52.

year. Other transactions involve trading of investment certificates issued by the private sector with maturities of up to three years.

2. *Preliberalization Financial System*

The financial system in El Salvador shared the characteristics of the financial systems in many developing countries. These included controls on interest rates and domestic credit, an important role of the Central Reserve Bank in the allocation of credit, and controls on international capital flows, segmented financial markets, and underdeveloped capital markets.

Controls on the interest rates took the form of fixing the ceiling of deposit and loan interest rates of the commercial banks and of the savings and loans associations. The lending rates varied by the type of activities. The structure of the interest rates was motivated to provide low-cost funds to encourage production, particularly some agricultural activities, and for manufacturing products exported to outside the CACM.

Direct controls and sectoral allocation of credit included central bank lending to priority sectors (rediscount credit), preferential central bank refinancing, and credit lending ceilings for the commercial banks and nonbank financial institutions. The preferred sectors were agriculture and manufacturing. Within them, exporters, artisans, and small enterprises received special credit facilities.

The rediscount credit was used as an instrument of monetary policy aimed to affect both the level of money supply and to direct credit to priority sectors.[27] This was complemented by the lending ceiling schemes for the commercial banks discussed below.

Preferential central bank refinancing was very important during the 1980's owing to economic deterioration caused by the armed conflict, to problems with the implementation of the agrarian reform, and to the decrease in productivity of the reformed lands as well as to adverse external developments that affected exports which led to a high level of borrowers' insolvencies that threatened that of the banks themselves and which the Central Reserve Bank attempted to prevent by providing a rediscount credit for refinancing.

Rediscounting was traditionally the main instrument of monetary policy; the rediscount credit of the Central Reserve Bank represented about 22 percent of the total commercial bank credit in the 1970's and 1980's. This proportion dropped to 8.5 percent in 1993.[28]

---

27 The Interamerican Management Consulting Corporation (1989).

28 Central Reserve Bank of El Salvador, *Quarterly Review*, several issues.

Sectoral credit allocation schemes also included a credit lending ceiling for the state-owned commercial banks. These schemes had the objective of providing credit to sectors considered to be of priority and of controlling bank credit. In this context, all state-owned financial institutions had a particular sectoral credit allocation program for every year.

The interest rates charged on preferential credit were in some cases substantially lower than the rates on nonpreferential credit, especially the rediscounts from the Central Reserve Bank financed with external sources. For example, the interest rate charged on refinancing credit for coffee was 6 percent when the rate on nonpreferential credit was about 17 percent.[29]

The effectiveness in allocating credit of the directed credit programs has been questioned, arguing that they fail to reach their intended beneficiaries.[30] A study of the financial sector in El Salvador concluded that directed credit is an inefficient mechanism to channel credit to priority sectors. The distribution of credit was skewed in favor of larger firms.[31]

Moreover, international capital flows were strictly controlled to support relative fixed exchange rate arrangements (see Chapter III).

3. Financial Liberalization during the 1990's

In mid-1989, El Salvador began a process of financial reforms aimed at bringing about a more liberal financial system. The measures included the gradual liberalization of interest rates, lifting controls on capital movements, rehabilitation and privatization of state-owned banks and nonbank financial institutions, reforming the Banking Superintendency, elimination of direct controls on commercial bank lending, elimination of the barriers to opening new domestic and foreign banks, reduction in central bank lending, and, in July 1994, closure of the rediscount window at the Central Reserve Bank and creation of an official development bank (the Multisector Investment Bank), which assumed the function of directing credit to priority sectors. In August 1994, the private sector portfolio of the Central Reserve Bank was transferred to the Multisector Investment Bank. Most of these reforms were gradually implemented over a period of five years. Each will be briefly commented on.

---

29 The Interamerican Management Consulting Corporation (1989), pp. 23-26.
30 World Bank (1989a), p. 59.
31 The Interamerican Management Consulting Corporation (1989), pp. 18 and 25.

a. Liberalization of Interest Rates

The liberalization of interest rates took place gradually. During the first period, beginning in March 1991, the basic deposit interest rate (TIBP), which is the minimum rate of interest on time deposits with maturity of 180 days, was adjusted every six months in line with the inflation rate prevailing over the preceding six months, while the basic lending rate (TIBA), which is the maximum rate of interest on credit with maturities of up to one year, was adjusted in order to keep it at least 4 percentage points above TIBP.

In November 1991, the Central Reserve Bank authorized the financial institutions to set a negotiated interest rate within a band. Finally, in March 1992, the interest rates were completely liberalized.

The immediate impact of the full interest rate liberalization in March 1992 was to move nominal rates downward. The decrease of interest rates was due to the excess of liquidity resulting from capital inflows.[32]

In spite of the downward tendency of the nominal interest rate, the real interest rate during the first six months of full deregulation was still positive due to a substantial reduction on the inflation rate (see Figures II.1a, II.1b and II.1c).[33] At the end of 1992, the inflation rate accelerated and subsequently the nominal interest rates rose, but their increase was not sufficiently large and resulted in negative real interest rates during the first seven months of 1993. Then the inflation rate declined and nominal interest rates experienced a slight decline, resulting in a positive real interest rate for the rest of the period.

Positive real interest rates contributed to curbing the falling tendency of the ratio of M2 to gross domestic product (GDP), which is used as a measure of financial depth (Figure II.2).

---

32 The Central Reserve Bank intervened to prevent a further downward tendency in 1992.

33 The real interest rate is calculated as the nominal interest rate minus the change in the consumer price index over the past 12 months. This assumes that inflation expectations can be approximated by actual inflation over the past 12 months.

Figure II.1a
EL SALVADOR: NOMINAL INTEREST RATES

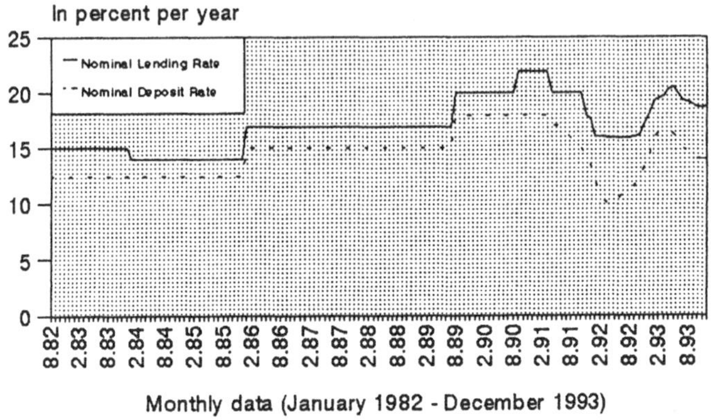

Source: International Monetary Fund, *International Financial Statistics*.
Lending rate: loans up to one year (line 60p), deposit rate: 180-day time deposits (line 60l).

Figure II.1b
EL SALVADOR: INFLATION RATE*

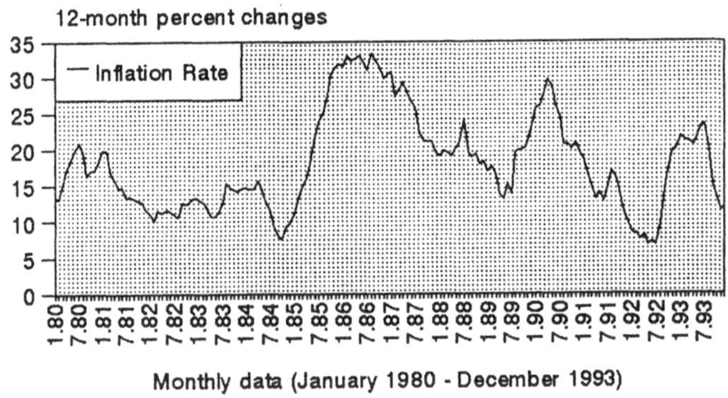

Source: International Monetary Fund, *International Financial Statistics*.
*Inflation rate is 12-month percent changes in Consumer prices (CPI) from the corresponding month in the previous year.

Figure II.1c
EL SALVADOR: REAL INTEREST RATES

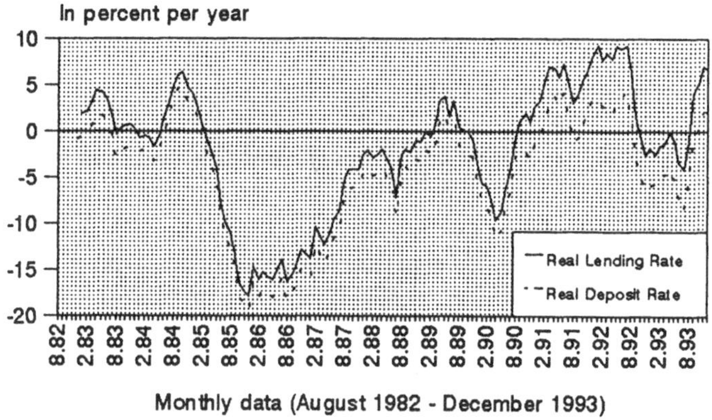

Source: International Monetary Fund, *International Financial Statistics*; and author's estimates. Real interest rates are the nominal interest rates deflated by 12-month percent change in CPI.

Figure II.2
BROAD AND NARROW MONEY

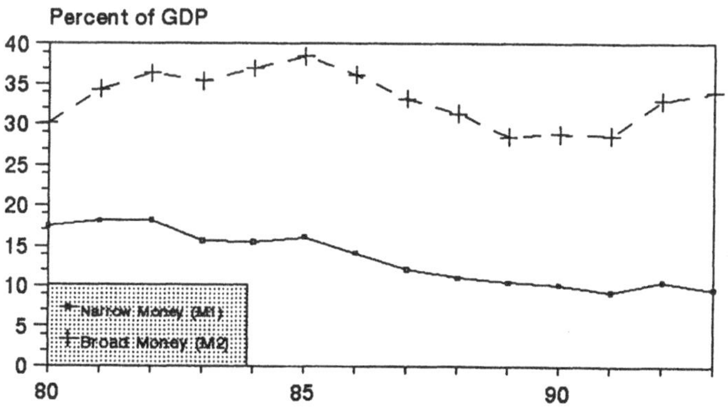

Source: Central Reserve Bank of El Salvador, *Quarterly Review*, various issues

b. Reduction in Credit Controls

Substantial reforms in the context of financial liberalization were introduced in the area of credit policy in the 1990's. Direct controls on commercial banks' lending were eliminated, direct lending through rediscount credit to the commercial banks was reduced.[34] Direct lending was realized only through the rediscount window (Ventanilla Unica de Redescuento) to the banks, which provides working capital to the agricultural sector, and through the liquidity window (Ventanilla de Liquidez Automática), which provides credit to solve liquidity problems of financial institutions.[35] With the first type of rediscount window (VUR), the Central Reserve Bank sets the quotas for each bank and the funds are used at the bank's discretion to finance eligible activities. The total rediscount credit is determined in the annual monetary program and adjusted in response to actual monetary conditions. The interest rate applied to this type of central bank lending is the 180-day time deposit rate of the previous month to the credit's application date plus one percentage point. The maturity period of these loans is 360 days.

As noted above, this rediscount window was closed in July 1994, and the Central Reserve Bank transferred this task to the Multisector Investment Bank (see above).

The second type of rediscount window, VLA, is for short-term loans extended by the Central Reserve Bank to the commercial banks and financial institutions to help them to meet temporary liquidity needs. These funds are available in an amount of up to 5 percent of their average daily reserve requirement, which is determined on the basis of the legal reserve requirement corresponding to the previous month to the credit application.[36] The time period of the credit is up to 30 days and the interest rate charged is equal to the previous month's interest rate on 180-day time deposits plus four percentage points.

c. Institutional Financial Reforms

To improve the efficiency of the financial system, most state-owned commercial banks and savings and loans associations have been restructured and privatized. This process was gradual and included a series of previous measures: assessment

34 The rediscount credit of the Central Reserve Bank as a proportion of the total credit of the commercial banks dropped from a peak level of 28.8 percent in 1989 to 8.5 percent in 1993.

35 These two windows were authorized in Directive Council Act of December 30, 1991 (CD-51/91) and went into effect as of April 1992.

36 International Monetary Fund (1992), p. 17.

of the solvency of the bank and nonbank financial institutions, recapitalizing six of the nine commercial banks (of which two were merged), and liquidating the rest.[37] The same process was followed to privatize the savings and loans associations.

This process was accompanied by a strengthening of the supervisory framework. As noted above, the Banking Superintendency obtained independent legal standing from the Central Reserve Bank under its new law as well as financial independence.[38]

d. Money and Capital Markets Development

The financial reforms also have the aim of stimulating the development of money and capital markets. In that context, a series of measures has been undertaken to strengthen the money market and to encourage the development of capital markets to improve the supply of long term credit, including the creation of new institutions (e.g., a Stock Exchange), development of new financial instruments (central bank bonds, investment certificates, repurchase agreements) and freeing the entry of new banks.

The government presented a draft of a securities law to the National Assembly in August 1993 to facilitate the use of government securities in open market operations and to contribute to the development of more active secondary markets.[39]

e. External Financial Policy

Financial reforms in the domestic financial markets were accompanied by measures to encourage foreign participation in those markets. On August 1, 1991, restrictions on capital flows were eliminated and a floating exchange rate regime was adopted in June 1990.[40]

37 World Bank (1991), p. 15.

38 Organic Law of the Superintendency of the Financial System, Art. 1, published in the Diario Oficial No. 278, Vol. 309, December 10, 1990.

39 International Monetary Fund (1994a), p. 40.

40 Foreign direct investment and capital inflows with a maturity of more than one year need to be registered with the Ministry of Economy but are not restricted. Payments of interests and amortization of external loans are made without any restriction (see IMF, *Annual Report on Exchange Arrangements and Exchange Restrictions*, 1993, p. 163).

Appendix II.1

Economic Reforms and Policies in El Salvador in the 1990's - Summary

I. EXCHANGE RATE POLICY

Exchange Rate Arrangement: Uniform floating exchange rate system under which commercial banks and exchange houses are free to purchase and sell foreign exchange at rates determined by supply and demand conditions. The Central Reserve Bank establishes daily the exchange rate applicable to its transactions with the public sector and to foreign exchange surrendered by coffee exporters to the Central Reserve Bank.[41] This rate is the arithmetic average of the exchange rates set by commercial banks and the exchange houses during the previous working day.

Central Bank intervention in the foreign exchange market: The Central Reserve Bank intervenes to smooth out short cyclical fluctuations in the exchange rate.

Exchange controls: No exchange restrictions on current account and on capital account transactions. By December 1990, current account restrictions were completely eliminated. The capital account transactions were liberalized later, in August 1991.

II. TRADE SYSTEM REFORMS

Tariff System: Gradual reduction of the level and dispersion of import tariffs. In 1992 most import tariffs were reduced to a range of 5-20 percent, with exceptions for motor cars and a few selected luxury goods. In May 1994 all items were brought into a range of 5-20 percent.

Quantitative Restriction: All quantitative restrictions were eliminated.

III. MONETARY POLICY REFORMS

Open Market Operations: Main instruments are sales and purchases of foreign exchange and sales of central bank stabilization bonds (Certificados de Estabilización Monetaria). The government plans to develop a security market, which will facilitate the sales of government securities in open market operations.

41 In August 1993, the surrender requirements on coffee export receipts were reduced from 100 to 50 percent and in May 1994 they were eliminated.

Reserve requirements: On July 1, 1991 reserve requirements were unified for saving and time deposits in commercial banks and in saving & loans associations. The reserve requirements for saving and time deposits were 20 percent and for demand deposits 30 percent. From March 1993, 5 percent of the reserve requirements on savings and time deposits were remunerated.[42]

Central Bank credit: In July 1994, the rediscount window of the Central Reserve Bank was closed and created an official development bank (Banco Multisectorial de Inversiones).

Credit Controls: They were eliminated.

Liberalization of Interest rate: Interest rates were liberalized in March 1992.

IV. FINANCIAL REFORMS

Commercial Banks Privatization: In mid-1989 the process of restructuring and privatizing the state-owned commercial banks and of savings and loans associations began. Through a series of mergers the number of state-owned savings and loans associations was reduced from seven to four. The privatization of the commercial banks was completed by May 1993 and of the savings and loans associations by May 1994.

Financial Market Development: From April 1992 a stock exchange market began to perform where mainly Central Reserve Bank's stabilization bonds and agrarian reform bonds are traded. More recently private firms have issued commercial papers.

Deregulation and Competition: From July 1993 the prohibition on the establishment of new financial institutions was lifted, and foreign banks have been allowed to operate since 1990.

Supervision: The supervisory capacity of the Banking Superintendency was strengthened with its new Organic Law of December 10, 1990.

V. FISCAL POLICY AND PUBLIC SECTOR REFORMS

Revenue Policies: A fiscal package was introduced with the objective of establishing a new tax system that permits an increase in tax collections, which are among the lowest in Latin America. This package included the introduction of value added tax (VAT) of 10 percent, extension of income tax for coffee pro-

42 This portion increased to 10 percent in July 1994.

ducers to replace the coffee export tax, etc. as well as administrative measures to improve the supervision of tax collection and reduce tax evasion.

Expenditure Policies: Measures aimed to reduce the size of the public sector have been implemented (e.g., in December 1992 four thousand vacant positions in civil services were frozen). Moreover, mechanisms such as the National System of Public Investment has been introduced to promote more efficient utilization of public sector resources.

Privatization Program: Several state-owned enterprises have been sold to the private sector.

Chapter III

Institutional Framework and Developments in the Foreign Exchange Market in El Salvador

A. Foreign Exchange Regimes in El Salvador

During the 1980's El Salvador adopted different foreign exchange regimes; common to all was that they used exchange rate controls as a complementary method to adjust the balance-of-payments.

Exchange controls were established in the country by the Law of Controls of International Transactions on May 30, 1962. The law established major obstacles to obtaining foreign exchange for capital transactions. All foreign exchange resulting from capital transactions, including direct and indirect investment, had to be surrendered to the monetary authorities. For example, payments abroad representing capital movements required exchange control licenses; amortization payments on external loans had to be authorized by the Central Reserve Bank.[1]

However, El Salvador enjoyed a long period of domestic price and exchange rate stability until 1973. The inflation rate was even lower than the United States' inflation rate (see Figure III.1). From 1973 to the end of that decade, the inflation rate in El Salvador could be substantially explained by a sharp increase of international prices, particularly the rise in international oil prices.[2] In the 1980's, the situation changed dramatically. The deterioration of the political climate in the country caused a significant increase in the budget deficit which was partly monetized. The disequilibrium in the money market produced tensions on the exchange rate, and the level of international reserves dropped. As a result, in the early 1980's the monetary authorities extended exchange restrictions to current account transactions. These restrictions included import licenses, prior deposit requirements, and foreign exchange allocations established by the Central Reserve Bank.

On two occasions during the last decade (in August 1982 and July 1989), the authorities have officially adopted a dual exchange rate regime with the purpose of a gradual devaluation, as a devise for correcting serious balance-of-payments

---

1 For details on exchange arrangements and capital movements restrictions, see the IMF, *Annual Report on Exchange Arrangements and Exchange Restrictions,* 1983.

2 See de Sebastian (1979) for empirical evidence on the determinants of the inflation rate in El Salvador in the 1970's.

difficulties. Moreover, during the periods of both the dual exchange regime and the officially unified fixed exchange rate regime, the country had a black market for foreign exchange, which emerged as a response to the imposition of restrictions to operate in the officially created foreign exchange markets for certain trade transactions and especially for capital transactions, thus operating on a de facto multiple exchange rate regime.

Figure III.1
INFLATION RATES

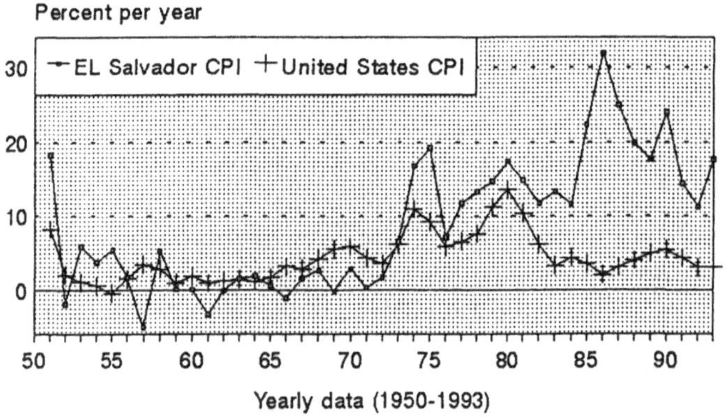

Source: International Monetary Fund, *International Financial Statistics*. Annual Changes in consumer prices (line 64).

For a clear presentation of the exchange rate policy of El Salvador during the last decade, the analysis can be divided into three periods, starting in 1982.

It will be useful, before beginning our discussion, to review conceptual distinctions among different foreign exchange regimes and markets used in this study.

A Uniform Fixed Exchange System can be defined as a system under which the same exchange rate applies to all transactions and there is a single market for foreign exchange. It is a system with full intervention by the authorities and changes in the exchange rate are policy-determined. According to the IMF classification (*Annual Report on Exchange Arrangements and Exchange Rate Restrictions,* 1993), pegged exchange rate arrangements include: (a) pegged to a single currency (i.e., U.S. dollar, French franc, pound sterling), and (b) pegged to a currency composite (SDR or currency basket). In this study, and for the particular case of El Salvador, fixed exchange rate regime refers to the category of the arrangement pegged to the U.S. dollar.

A Uniform Flexible Exchange Rate System as in the case of uniform fixed system the same exchange rate applies to all foreign exchange transactions but under this system the exchange rate varies relatively freely. Flexible exchange rate arrangements include the following categories: (a) limited flexibility vis-à-vis single currency, (b) cooperative arrangements (e.g., EMS), (c) adjusted according to a set of indicators, (d) managed floating, and (e) independently floating. The one recently adopted in El Salvador is managed floating, under which the Colon's value fluctuates freely against the dollar according to supply and demand conditions, subject to official intervention to resist exchange rate movements that may seem unjustified in the light of economic fundamentals (e.g., export competitiveness, balance-of-payments equilibrium).

A Dual Exchange Rate System is a system created by the authorities under which there are two officially accepted exchange rates: an official rate, usually for current account transactions (commercial exchange rate), and a parallel market exchange rate usually for capital account transactions (financial exchange rate). In this typical arrangement usually presented in the literature, the official exchange rate is usually pegged or managed while the parallel market rate is market determined.[3] In other cases, current account transactions are carried out at both the official and the parallel market rates which is the most common arrangement adopted in developing countries in recent years (for example, in Mexico, in El Salvador and in Costa Rica in August 1982, in Guatemala in November 1984, and in Sudan in 1981).[4]

A Dual Official-Black Exchange Rate System is a system which is not directly created by the authorities, but is the result of economic agents' behavior trying to evade some official restrictions. This system emerges primarily due to foreign trade restrictions and capital controls. Typically, the official exchange rate is pegged by the central bank and the sale of foreign currency is restricted to use judged by the authorities to be "essential" for economic development reasons. As a consequence, the restricted users will search for an alternative market to carry out their transactions. In this market, in general, foreign exchange will be sold above the controlled rate, which would be an incentive for foreign exchange holders to divert some of the supply and sell it illegally.

---

3 This is the arrangement most commonly assumed in the literature, for example, in Swoboda (1974), Gardner (1985), Cumby (1984), Flood (1978), Guidotti and Vegh (1988), and Kiguel and Lizondo (1990).

4 For details of different dual exchange rate arrangements adopted in developing countries in recent years, see *World Currency Yearbook* 1988-1989, and the IMF, *Annual Report on Exchange Arrangements and Exchange Restrictions,* (particularly the issues of the 1980's).

Legal parallel market and black market: The terms "black," "parallel," "unofficial," and "grey" have been used interchangeably in the exchange rate literature. "Black market" is the term of common usage for "parallel market." However, Lindauer (1989) provides analytical distinctions between these descriptions of market structure based on the degree of legal enforcement (e.g., expected cost of those who violate the rules, the foreign exchange regulations). He uses the term "parallel" to cover a broad heading of markets that develop in response to government intervention in the official market that limits participation in some way. But, as Lindauer pointed out, "black market" is not just a synonym for "parallel." First, the term "black market" has the distinct implication of illegality, and not all parallel markets are illegal, for example, some governments adopt a dual or multiple exchange regime. The parallel market concept includes both legal and illegal markets. Second, not all black markets are parallel: "black" can refer to the market for prohibited goods, such as cocaine, for which there is no legal market, hence no parallelism. In this study, however, the term "black market" refers to the market illegally created by the behavior of economic agents trying to evade exchange restrictions, and the term "parallel market" refers to the second market created by the authorities when adopting a dual system. As will be clear further on in this chapter, in the particular case of El Salvador the parallel market was not a free foreign exchange market functioning side by side with an official market like the one described in the literature; rather, it was a market established with arbitrary rules about who may transact in the market, and when and for what purpose. Consequently, a black market coexisted with this market.

1. Dual Exchange Rate Regime, 1982-1985

The dual exchange rate regime adopted in August 1982 consisted of an official market (central bank market), in which the domestic currency, the colon, was pegged to the U.S. dollar, and a legal parallel market (commercial banks market) in which, even though in principle the colon was allowed to float, in actual fact the exchange rate was managed by the Central Reserve Bank together with the system of publicly owned commercial banks. The exchange rate in the parallel market was depreciated relative to the official rate.[5]

---

5 The exchange rate is defined as the amount of domestic currency (colones) equivalent to one unit of foreign currency. Thus, depreciation (appreciation) means an increase (decrease) in the exchange rate.

Only commercial banks and the Mortgage Bank were allowed to buy and sell currency in the parallel market; however, certain firms and individuals[6] were allowed to open foreign currency deposit accounts in the commercial banks and the Mortgage Bank and use funds for certain authorized transactions settled in the parallel market.[7]

In contrast to the usual arrangement of the dual regimes presented in the economic literature, in which the official market clears through changes in international reserve or by official depreciation in the exchange rate, and the parallel market, in which normally the exchange rate is allowed to float freely, clears through a depreciation of the parallel exchange rate, the Salvadorean regime was characterized by the lack of convertibility on current and capital account transactions at the official and legal parallel market rates. The rationing of foreign exchange on both markets explains why the black market did not disappear upon the adoption of a dual exchange rate regime.[8] Moreover, the premium in the black market was high and showed large fluctuations during the period of dual regime even though a gradual devaluation of the official exchange rate took place since the introduction of the dual exchange rate regime (see Figure III.2).

Thus, during the period from August 1982 to January 1986, three foreign exchange markets existed. The official market handled the external transactions of the public sector (current and capital account transactions), traditional exports (coffee, cotton, sugar, and shrimp), "priority" imports and certain service account payments of the private sector. The parallel market, which had a more depreciated exchange rate than the official market, handled nontraditional exports, the remainder of authorized imports, labor remittances, and the rest of the service account transactions. International capital market transactions of the private sector were, in practice, excluded from both markets.[9] The black market handled **all** other transactions not effected in the other two markets because of rationing.[10] The exchange rate in this third market was determined by supply and demand conditions.

---

6 They included exporters of specified nontraditional products, industrial enterprises that exported part of their production to outside the Central American Common Market, agents with income from tourism, foreign companies, embassies, and international organizations.

7 IMF, *Annual Report on Exchange Arrangements and Exchange Restrictions* (1983-1986).

8 Note that the adoption of a legal dual exchange rate regime was motivated by the existence of a widespread black market.

9 For details of the allocation of current account and capital transactions between the two markets, see El Salvador pages of IMF, *Annual Report on Exchange Arrangements and Exchange Restrictions* 1983-1986, Washington, D.C.

10 For example, the black market handled unauthorized external transactions (smuggle)

Figure III.2
BLACK MARKET PREMIUM*

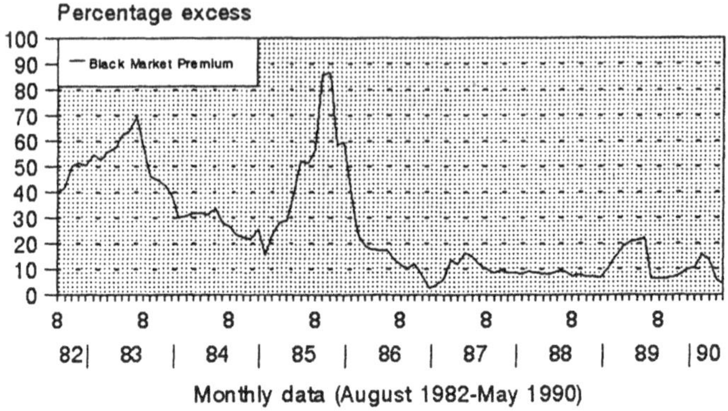

Source: Data provided by the Department of Exchange, Central Reserve Bank of El Salvador.
*Black market premium is:((black market rate/volume-trade-weighted average of the official and parallel market rates)-1)*100

Examining the basic institutional framework of the Salvadorean dual regime (see El Salvador pages, IMF *Annual Report on Exchange Arrangements and Exchange Restrictions* 1983-1986) reveals the following facts: (a) Under this system there is no market separation of current and capital transactions. Many current account transactions, both merchandise and service account items, were **officially** assigned to the parallel market, and capital transactions of the public sector were assigned to the official market. (b) Examination of the official allocation of transactions between the two markets reveals that proportions of exports and imports of the same product could be officially assigned to both markets. For example, exporters of nontraditional products to Central America had to surrender 50 percent of the proceeds to the official market, and the rest was authorized to be sold in the parallel market with the exception of proceeds from exports of medicines, fertilizers, fungicides, insecticides, herbicides, and other goods using imported inputs which were payable at the official rate. However, exporters were allowed to sell in the parallel market all the proceeds from nontraditional exports with a destination outside the Central American markets. (c) Another important feature of the Salvadorean dual system is that the proportion

or transactions that were not illegal but were at the bottom of the priority list (e.g., payments abroad representing capital movements), and normally they did not obtain foreign exchange in any of the official markets).

of current account transactions allocated between the two markets changed over the period of the dual exchange regime. The initial arrangement of the dual regime adopted in August 1982 changed over time until the unification of the officially created exchange markets in January 1986. In agreement with the policy of gradual devaluation, the Monetary Authority continuously transferred transactions from the official to the parallel market.

It is clear, therefore, that the type of dual exchange regime arrangement adopted in El Salvador involved various types of "leakages" between the foreign exchange markets: A first type of leakages was determined by the official allocation of transactions between the two markets created by the authorities ("administrative fiat").[11] As noted above, specified proportions of current transactions were officially assigned to the official and/or to the parallel market. The economic literature on dual exchange rate regimes emphasizes that an important condition for effective separation of the two markets is that **all** current and **only** current transactions are effected through the official market.[12] Moreover, in El Salvador these proportions changed over time by monetary authority decree. An increase in the exchange rate differential over time was accompanied by an increase of the proportions of exports and imports officially settled in the parallel market. This implied a devaluation of the average-official exchange rate through both (a) depreciation of the parallel market rate and (b) through increasing the proportion of transactions handled in the parallel market.

A second type of leakages resulted from illegal cross-transactions motivated by the exchange rate differential. Exporters would find it profitable to sell foreign receipts at the higher rate (parallel rate) and importers to buy foreign exchange at the lower rate (official rate). Given the type of institutional arrangement of the Salvadorean dual exchange rate regime, agents presumably found it easier to circumvent the regulations under that system than in a system where current account transactions were assigned to one market. Recent literature on dual exchange rate regimes has analyzed the latter type of leakages between the exchange markets.[13]

The practical functioning of the Salvadorean dual regime involved a third type of leakage specifically between the two legal markets and the black market.

---

11 This type of leakage determined by administrative fiat has not been examined thoroughly in the literature on dual exchange markets. The only studies that specifically introduce this type of leakage in the analysis are Bhandari and Decaluwe (1987) and Bhandari (1988).

12 Fleming (1971), and Swoboda (1974).

13 Examples are Gros (1988), Guidotti (1988), Bhandari and Vegh (1990). In some of the earlier work, Fleming (1971) and Lanyi (1975) have recognized that, in practice, this type of arbitrage activities is hard to evade.

The black market financed a proportion of imports, which were eligible for payment at the official or the parallel rate, during periods when the Central Bank and the commercial banks could not instantaneously satisfy the demand for foreign exchange corresponding to the official allocation for current account transactions. Normally, the Central Bank and/or the commercial banks provided the requested foreign exchange with a lag of about two to three months. Consequently, producers obtained foreign exchange for imports of raw materials on the black market. When they obtained the foreign exchange at the official or parallel rate, the possibility existed of selling it at the black market rate. This established a link between the two legal markets and the black market, creating large profit opportunities through arbitrage.

Under these circumstances, most probably, the dual exchange rate regime was not effective in insulating the goods markets from movements in the black market exchange rate. Hence, as is demonstrated in Chapter V, the black market exchange rate was also relevant in the domestic price determination process.

2. *Uniform Fixed Exchange Rate Regime, 1986-1989*

In early 1986, the Monetary Authority undertook the unification of the officially created exchange markets and adopted a uniform fixed exchange rate regime. The exchange rate was settled at 5.00 colones per 1 U.S. dollar, which was very similar to the legal parallel market rate, but it was below the black market rate which averaged 6.65 colones per 1 U.S. dollar at the end of December 1985. The black market for foreign exchange continued to exist as a result of restrictions and exchange controls not being removed; rather, they were intensified. The exchange controls on current account transaction consisted of import licensing, prior deposits requirements, and a system of foreign exchange allocation established by the Central Reserve Bank which favored imports of essential foodstuffs, medicines, raw materials, and capital goods in a declining order of priority. Manufactured goods were last on the priority list and, when they could not acquire foreign exchange from the official market, these imports were financed through the black market.

However, the authorities were able to maintain a relatively narrow spread between the black market and the official exchange rate (around 10 percent) during this period (see Figure III.2) through indirect intervention in the black market.

The policy intervention aimed at stabilizing the black market exchange rate. In periods of instability in the black market, the Central Reserve Bank satisfied the demand for current account transactions at the official rate. This policy reduced the demand for foreign currency in the black market, which in turn helped to maintain the low premium in this market.

The *de facto* dual exchange rate regime that existed in El Salvador from 1986 to mid-1989 operated with an incomplete market separation. The demand for foreign exchange in the black market was the residual from the official market. As long the Central Reserve Bank supplied more foreign exchange for current account transactions at the official rate, the demand in the black market declined, as importers did not need to buy foreign exchange in the black market.

With this policy the Central Reserve Bank stabilized the black market exchange rate and sterilized excess liquidity which also contributed to stabilized prices.

3. Dual Exchange Rate Regime, July 1989-May 1990

The new administration that came into power in June 1989 undertook major exchange rate and trade reforms as well as reforms in other economic areas (see Chapter II).

As an initial step and as a temporary policy, in July 1989 a dual exchange rate regime was again adopted. The arrangement involved an official market in which the exchange rate was pegged at 5.00 colones per 1 U.S. dollar and a parallel market operated by commercial banks in which the exchange rate was jointly settled by the Central Reserve Bank and commercial banks, but followed the development of the black market exchange rate very closely. Between 75-80 percent of the current account transactions were transferred to the parallel market. The official market handled only proceeds from coffee, foreign exchange from loans and transfers to the Government, petroleum imports, public sector debt services payments, and other imports of goods and services of the public sector.[14]

With the introduction of a dual exchange rate regime the authorities gradually removed most of the exchange controls on current account transactions.[15]

This time, the premium in the black market was lower than during the first occasion that a dual exchange rate regime was adopted. The spread between the black market and the legal parallel market was narrowed, in fact close to zero, from July to December 1989 (see Figure VI.1, p. 159). However, political events in late 1989, as well as the easing up of monetary policy and adjustment in cer-

---

14 International Monetary Fund, *Annual Report on Exchange Arrangements and Exchange Restrictions,* 1990, p. 147.

15 The capital account transaction was later liberalized, in August 1991.

tain public sector services prices, led to an acceleration of inflation and a depreciation of the colon in the black market during the first quarter of 1990.[16] Consequently, by mid-March 1990 the authorities devalued the official exchange rate and modified the dual exchange rate system, which afterwards consisted of an official rate fixed at 6.90 colones per U.S. dollar for official transactions and for imports of petroleum and certain other essential products, and a parallel rate (commercial banks' rate) determined jointly by the Central Reserve Bank and the commercial banks,[17] and a combination of these two rates for payments of certain imports and receipts from coffee exports.[18]

This dual arrangement was different from the one adopted in 1982-1986. First, this time it was adopted merely temporarily (less than one year). Second, as under the dual regime of 1982-1986, the parallel market rate was jointly determined by the Central Reserve Bank and the commercial banks, but this time the parallel rate was set very close to the black market rate, at least during the first six months of this system. Third, this time the dual arrangement was adopted as a transitional regime from the pegged exchange rate with exchange controls to a unified flexible regime; during this transitional regime a series of measures to simplify the exchange rate and trade system were undertaken, including a gradual removal of current account restrictions, import tariff reduction from a range of 0-290 percent to 5-35 percent, and elimination of the restrictions to open foreign currency deposit accounts.[19]

Subsequently, in preparation for the unification of the exchange rate, the authorities permitted the operation of exchange rate houses, thus legalizing the black market. On April 10, 1990, the regulations on the establishment of exchange houses were announced and they were effectively permitted to operate by the end of May 1990. Also by the end of May greater flexibility in the commercial bank market was granted.[20]

---

16 The black market exchange rate depreciated by about 23 percent between December 1989 and March 1990; the inflation rate accelerated from an average 1.5 percent per month during the last months of 1989 to an average of 2.70 percent per month from December 1989 to March 1990.

17 At the end of March 1990, the parallel market rate averaged 7.78 colones per U.S. dollar.

18 International Monetary Fund, "El Salvador-Staff Report for 1990 Article IV Consultation and Request for Stand-By Arrangement," August 8, 1990, p. 9. Also see IMF, *Annual Report on Exchange Arrangements and Exchange Restrictions*, 1991, p. 158.

19 For details of the measures undertaken in 1989-1990, see IMF, *Annual Report on Exchange Arrangements and Exchange Restrictions*, 1991.

20 International Monetary Fund, *Annual Report on Exchange Arrangements and Exchange Restrictions*, 1991, pp. 157-158.

On June 1, 1990, the process of unification concluded with the establishment that the Central Reserve Bank's official exchange rate would henceforth be determined on a weekly basis as a simple arithmetic average of the exchange rates between the commercial banks and the exchange houses during the previous week.[21] This rate was applied to coffee export proceeds, public sector transactions payments and petroleum imports.

4. Uniform Floating Exchange Rate Regime, from June 1990

Since June 1990, El Salvador has maintained a unified floating interbank exchange rate system in which commercial banks and exchange houses are free to purchase and sell foreign exchange at rates determined by supply and demand conditions. The exchange rate is determined in negotiations between banks and exchange houses and their clients and is free to vary from day to day. The Central Reserve Bank establishes the exchange rate daily to be applicable to its transactions. This exchange rate is the arithmetic average of the exchange rates set by the commercial banks and the exchange houses for the previous working day. The system is basically a market-determined exchange rate with central bank intervention limited to smoothing out cyclical fluctuations.

B. Black Market for Foreign Exchange in El Salvador

1. The Emergence of the Black Market

Since 1962, a black market for foreign transactions developed in El Salvador as a result of the imposition of exchange controls.[22] However, the black market came into prominence only in the 1980's when the country faced a serious deficit in the balance-of-payments that resulted from political and economic policy instability and more basic macroeconomic imbalances.

In this regard, the emergence of the black market is related to the imposition of the exchange controls, but its development has been closely associated with the political and economic policy instability that prevailed in the 1980's in El Salvador. Under exchange and capital controls, the black market became the

---

21 From July 18, 1992, the Central Reserve Bank began to establish its exchange rate daily (see IMF, *Annual Report on Exchange Arrangements and Exchange Restrictions*, 1993, p. 163.

22 *Pick's Currency Yearbook*, 1986-1987, p. 301.

source of financing imports considered non-essential by the authorities as well as capital flight and portfolio transactions (i.e., foreign currency being a hedge against adverse political uncertainty and against inflation).

Thus, the black market exchange rate operated as the marginal cost of foreign exchange for a probably significant range of transactions, affecting the economy in a similar way as a multiple exchange rate system in which certain transactions take place at a floating rate. This analogy between dual and black market system has also been noted in the literature.[23]

The Salvadorean black market did not have a specific location and dealers did not advertise their services. According to anecdotal information, dealers were well organized, capable of performing fairly large transactions and acting more like legal exchange houses. In some cases, they had offshore locations, courier agencies (agencias de encomiendas) in the United States, which is the country of the major source of workers' remittances. Small transactors were to be found in the streets (near the main post office).

In principle, the black market in El Salvador was illegal, but officially tolerated, and in fact alleviated the pressures on the Central Reserve Bank (see section B.4); it was not clandestine since there was no penalty for trading in currency in it. In this context a black market exchange rate existed alongside an official pegged (managed) exchange rate(s).

The most reliable figures available on the black market exchange rate exist since 1982. Using monthly data, Figure III.2 plots the black market premium. The premium was calculated as the percentage excess of the black market exchange rate over the official rate during the period of uniform fixed exchange rate, and as a percentage excess of the black market rate over the volume-weighted average of the official and parallel market rates during the period of the dual exchange rate regime.[24] Two aspects appear to be interesting from the figure. First, during the period of dual exchange rate regime (August 1982 to January 1986), the premium showed large fluctuations, with an average premium of about 45 percent. This high and volatile premium was due to various reasons: (a) In the legal parallel market the value of the colon was not determined by supply and demand conditions; rather, it was set by agreement between the Central Reserve Bank and the commercial banks at rates which were below the free market rate (i.e., black market exchange rate). (b) Since the dual exchange rate systems are in general considered as temporal regimes, they probably generated expectations of unification and future devaluation of the two official exchange

23 See, for example, Kiguel and Ghei (1992) and Lizondo (1990).

24 See Chapter V, for details on the calculation of this average exchange rate.

rates.[25] (c) Uncertainty about macroeconomic policy and rumors of policy reforms. A second interesting aspect, observed from the figure, is that during the period 1986-1988, the black market premium was relatively low, around 10 percent, due in part, as already mention to indirect official intervention in the black market,[26] and in part to a large flow of workers' remittances. As Banuri (1989) pointed out, remittances and tourism differ from commercial sources of foreign currency in that they necessitate no additional illegal transactions. Smuggling of exports, by contrast, required illegal transportation across the country's borders. This raises the costs of supplying at the black market rate because of the need for payoffs to officials and the risk of confiscation and other legal penalties (Agénor, 1992).

2. *Supply of and Demand for Dollars in the Black Market*

There is no reliable estimate of the volume of transactions handled in the black market in El Salvador, as is the case in most countries where such markets exist, due to the illegal or semi-illegal nature of the transactions. This precludes the collection of detailed and reliable data. Therefore, the magnitudes mentioned here come from more indirect information and should be treated with caution.

Examining the likely sources of supply and demand of the black market during the 1980's, it seems that the volume of foreign exchange transactions was sizable.

The *supply* of dollars in the black market probably came from four main sources: workers' remittances, underinvoicing of exports, overinvoicing of imports, and foreign visitors. However, workers' remittances have been considered the key source.[27] Thus, estimating private transfer receipts could give an idea of the amount transacted in the black market.

---

25 Although the dual regime lasted for over three years, with a gradual devaluation in the process, the system was perceived as temporary for at least two reasons: (a) both official and parallel markets were controlled and, as a consequence, the black market premium was high (45 percent on average during the whole period); (b) there was pressure from international organizations, especially from the U.S. Agency for International Development, to make a corrective adjustment of the exchange rate.

26 The Central Reserve Bank, with the double aim of controlling inflation and the depreciation of the black market exchange rate, satisfied the demand for foreign currency at the official rate as much as possible, which reduced the demand in the black market, thus reducing the premium in the black market.

27 World Bank (1989a), pp. 86-90; see also Comisión Económica para América Latina y el Caribe (1991), pp. 9-10.

Until 1979, the official figures of remittances were measured directly using banks' foreign exchange receipts, but with the development of a black market these receipts began to fall and estimates were developed. However, official estimates were very conservative and they were considered too low.[28]

TABLE III.1

Private Transfers Receipts Estimates*
(millions of U.S. dollars)
1980-1993

Years	Central Reserve Bank	World Bank	CEPAL
1980	17.4	203.0	73.8
1981	65.7	265.0	114.3
1982	94.2	325.0	169.7
1983	107.4	382.0	201.3
1984	141.7	441.0	263.6
1985	125.5	477.0	231.5
1986	165.9	532.0	306.7
1987	201.6	557.0	451.1
1988	225.8	583.0	795.3
1989	237.4	597.0	759.4
1990	346.0	608.0	na
1991	543.5	611.0	na
1992	708.0	611.0	na
1993	823.0	610.0	na

* The Central Reserve Bank figures are estimates until 1990; from 1991 on they are actually recorded figures

Sources: Central Reserve Bank of El Salvador, *Quarterly Review*, several issues; World Bank (1989a) p. 89; and Comisión Económica para América Latina y El Caribe (CEPAL), 1991, p. 62.

Table III.1 presents estimates for the 1980's of private transfer receipts from different sources: (a) official estimates;[29] (b) World Bank estimates, based on a sample survey undertaken by the Universidad Centroamericana José Simeón Cañas (UCA) in 1986-1987;[30] (c) CEPAL estimates, which are based on a recent

28 See World Bank (1989a), pp. 86-87.

29 Only 8-9 percent of the officially estimated volume passed through the banking system in the 1980's (World Bank, 1989a).

30 In this sample survey it was found that the average total monthly amount received by each Salvadorean family that has emigrant relatives in the United States was around U.S.$128. Using an estimate of 328,000 recipient families, presented in the same study, this results in a total estimated remittance of about U.S.$589 million. This is approximately equal to the total of merchandise exports in the late 1980's.

study undertaken in El Salvador, Guatemala, and Nicaragua to evaluate the socio-economic impact of the remittances in those countries (CEPAL, 1991).

Both the World Bank and CEPAL estimates differ substantially from the Central Reserve Bank estimates and, as was noted above, the latter were considered underestimated. Looking at the actual official figures of private transfers in the post-black market period (1991-1993),[31] it seems to be that other sources were closer to reality than the official estimates. Although the World Bank's *ex ante* forecast for the last two years (1992 and 1993) they are lower than actual figures.[32] This means that over U.S.$400 million per year, only from one source of black market supply, were probably flowing into that market in the late 1980's.

Underinvoicing of exports, especially of nontraditional exports, and overinvoicing of imports were probably other important sources of foreign exchange in the black market. To estimate the scale of under-and overinvoicing of trade transactions, there are indirect procedures. The most widely used method has been to examine discrepancies in the data concerning trade between partners after accounting for insurance and freight. For example, one can compare exports to major partners countries, as shown by domestic data, with the corresponding imports recorded by the partner country. When, after taking into account insurance and freight, the latter are larger, the discrepancy could reflect to a significant extent underinvoicing of exports. A similar procedure can be applied to estimate illegal imports. This approach was adopted in some studies reprinted in Bhagwati (1974). For more recent analyses, see McDonald (1985), and Arslan and van Wijnbergen (1993). McDonald (1985) presents estimates on trade data discrepancy for ten countries, including El Salvador. According to this study, the average trade data discrepancy in El Salvador was 15 percent of reported exports during the period 1962-1979; it varied between a minimum value of less than 1 percent and a peak value of 35 percent. However, that issue is beyond the scope of the present study.

The *demand* for foreign exchange in the black market probably arose from three main motives: (a) for legal current account transactions (namely, imports that were allowed and were not on a list of prohibited items, but did not obtain foreign exchange at the official or parallel rate), and for smuggling. Unsatisfied legal demand for foreign exchange emerged when the Central Reserve Bank (even the commercial banks, in periods of the dual regime) could not provide

31 Central Reserve Bank's figures (column 1).

32 Note that the Central Reserve Bank figures are actually recorded figures for the post-black market period from 1991 to 1993, which were measured directly from commercial banks' and exchange houses' foreign exchange receipts.

enough foreign exchange at the established exchange rate(s). As was explained in Part A, the available volume of foreign exchange was allocated on a priority basis for the imports considered essential. When the prospective applicants for foreign exchange received less than their demand from the official sources, or they received it with a lag of two to three months, they had to acquire the foreign exchange for their imports in the black market. Thus, the demand in the black market was not independent of the supply of foreign exchange in the official markets. This established a link between the official market(s) and the black market. (b) An additional demand for foreign currency arose from the needs of the Salvadorean in excess of the limit established by the Central Reserve Bank for traveling abroad and other payments of services. (c) The demand for foreign currency may have arisen for portfolio diversification motives as a hedge against inflation, which was relatively high during the 1980's (see Figure III.1) and for capital flight purposes as hedge against the political and economic policy instability that prevailed in El Salvador during the 1980's. This demand may have been high in periods of high political uncertainty or when rumors of policy reforms surfaced. As noted above, during the period that a dual exchange rate regime was in effect, the black market premium was high and showed a large fluctuation, as a result of expectations of future devaluation and economic policy reforms.

3. Leakages between the Black Market and the Official Market(s)

An important aspect of this dual regime of official-black markets is the incomplete segmentation of its markets. The demand in the black market was not independent of the supply in the official market(s). A decline in the official supply would divert a greater unsatisfied demand to the black market and would be reflected in the price at which the black market cleared. Thus, black market demand was related to the official market(s) supply.

Another type of leakage across markets resulted from transactions motivated by the exchange rate differential. As noted earlier, exporters would have found it profitable to sell foreign receipts at the higher rate (black market rate) and importers to buy foreign exchange at the lower rate (official rate). However, in this type of regime, because the foreign exchange was rationed in the official market(s), these flows did not lead to a gradual automatic convergence of two exchange rates.[33] Unification of the foreign exchange markets only occurred when

33 Although the premium in the black market was low during the last years of the black market's existence, probably due to those flows and the Central Reserve

the authorities legally recognized the black market, along with authorizing the exchange houses and relaxing of exchange controls.[34]

Thus, as long as the exchange controls were imposed, there coexisted a black market with the official market(s) with at least two different prices for seemingly homogeneous goods.[35]

The parallel market literature gives some explanations for the coexistence of more than one market and for price disparity. Specifically, it explains why all foreign exchange does not flow from the official to the unofficial market when, as in most cases, the price in the latter is higher.

The first explanation was formally introduced and developed in a model of smuggling by Pitt (1981 and 1984). Pitt (1981) developed an alternative theory of smuggling observing Indonesia's experience. He introduced the possibility that the risk of being caught may not only increase with illegal sales (smuggled goods in his case, and sales of foreign exchange in the black market in our case), but could also decrease with legal sales. Some legal sales are necessary to hide the illegal ones. Selling through legal channels provides legitimacy and reduces suspicion by officials about sales in the black market. Thus, both official and black markets will coexist if the risk and costs of dealing in black markets is reduced by engaging in legal sales which hide the more profitable but illegal transactions.[36] This explanation does not fit in the case of El Salvador, since, as noted earlier, the black market was officially tolerated.

Bank's indirect intervention in the black market.

34 Recent literature on dual exchange rate regimes has analyzed the latter type of leakages between official exchange rate markets. However, this literature concludes that these arbitrage flows lead to a gradual convergence of the two exchange rates. The explanation of different conclusions is straightforward. Most of the literature on dual exchange rates assumes the two markets clear. The common assumption is that the official market clears through changes in international reserves, and that the central bank is committed to sell all foreign exchange demanded for current account purposes at fixed exchange rates. The parallel market clears through changes in the exchange rate. Thus, under this type of regime the arbitrage flows will lead to an increase in the demand for foreign exchange in the official market and in the supply of foreign exchange in the parallel market, which in turn leads to a gradual convergence of the two exchange rates. However, in the dual regime of official-black markets, the official market does not clear, instead rationing is implemented (see Chapter IV). Of course, these arbitrage flows could occur, but would be limited by the foreign exchange rationing in the official market.

35 They were seemingly homogeneous, since no penalties existed for trading in foreign currency in the black market.

36 See Pitt (1981 and 1984), Lindauer (1989), and Roemer and Jones (1991). Also in the early literature of black markets, Gönensay (1966) has recognized that a monopoly operating in a black market will sell part of its production in the official

The second explanation has been derived from the analysis of financial markets (McKinnon, 1981), and of labor markets (Lindauer, 1987). They show that government controls of supply of some key input – foreign exchange in this case – enable the central bank to maintain an overvalued official rate. The resulting excess demand for foreign currency spills over into a black market that clears at a depreciated rate. Given the central bank's ability to capture and ration foreign exchange, there will not be an automatic convergence of both markets. This second explanation fits El Salvador's experience with the black market quite well. The Central Reserve Bank had substantial control over the foreign exchange supply: the foreign exchange proceeds from official external grants and loans were exchanged on the official market and the same was true with respect to the proceeds from coffee and sugar exports, since state-owned institutions completely controlled the international trade in both products.

4. Importance of the Black Market

The relevance of the black market exchange rate in El Salvador was especially due to its relation to labor remittances, since the latter were exchanged almost exclusively in the black market. The labor remittances from abroad are an important aspect of El Salvador's economy, since they are higher than merchandise exports (see Tables VI.2a and VI.2b). If most of that volume of trade in currency took place in the black market, events in this market must have had important repercussions on other segments of the economy. At least three effects can be mentioned:

1. The black market financed a considerable proportion of imports and capital outflows, including both allowed and nonallowed transactions, especially during periods when the official markets could not satisfy the demand for foreign exchange for current account transactions at the official rate(s). This relieved the foreign exchange constraint and accelerated economic growth, since the country's manufacturing industry depends heavily on imports of raw materials.

2. The black market rate influenced the rate of domestic inflation, since, as was mentioned above, producers were not certain of obtaining foreign exchange at the official or parallel market rates. Thus, the black market exchange rate could be expected to play an important role in the domestic price determination process.

---

market because of the risk which may realistically be greater, the smaller the quantity that is available in the official market (p. 221).

3. As will be discussed in Chapter VI, the fiscal effects of the black market in the case of El Salvador were negative for two reasons: (a) there was a loss of tariff and export tax revenues as a result of smuggling, and (b) the government gave a subsidy on foreign exchange to the private sector (see Chapter VI), since the government was a net seller of foreign exchange during the period of the black market.

C. Some Remarks

Before concluding this chapter, it would be useful for the issues analyzed in the next two chapters to summarize the most important features of the Salvadorean black market for foreign exchange:

The first feature is the practical functioning of the dual or multiple exchange rate regime, which may have involved various types of leakage between the foreign exchange markets: (a) Leakages that resulted from cross-transactions motivated by the exchange rate differential. (b) The black market financed a proportion of imports which were eligible for payments at the official or parallel market rate during periods when the Central Reserve Bank and the commercial banks could not instantaneously satisfy the demand for foreign exchange corresponding to the official allocation of current account transactions. As noted above, sometimes the Central Reserve Bank and/or the commercial banks provided the requested foreign exchange with a lag of about two to three months. Consequently, some producers obtained foreign exchange for imports of raw materials on the black market. This established a link between the official market(s) and the black market.

A second interesting feature is that during the period 1986-1988, the black market premium was relatively low, around 10 percent due to indirect official intervention in the black market.

A third interesting feature of the black market is that workers' remittances constituted the major source of supply in the black market, which could be an additional reason for explaining why the premium was relatively low.

Chapter IV

Theoretical and Policy Issues of Dual Official-Black Market Exchange Rate Systems

A. Introduction

Analysis of black markets dates back to Boulding (1937), Bronfenbrenner (1947), Michaely (1954), and Gönensay (1966). These authors laid the microeconomic foundation of the behavior of black markets. But it was not until the 1970's that this literature was applied to analyzing foreign exchange markets; see the seminal studies by Culbertson (1974) and Sheikh (1976). Since then, the literature on black markets for foreign exchange has focused on three type of economic issues: the origin of these markets and their impact on the local economy, determinants of the black market exchange rate premium, and policy issues for economies where a black market for foreign exchange exists.[1]

This chapter discusses the macroeconomic aspects of black market exchange rates on a purely theoretical level, paying particular attention to the similarities of (1) an official-black market dual exchange rate regime (dual exchange market regime with reserve rationing) to (2) a legal dual exchange market regime (dual exchange market regime with reserve adjustment).[2] The two regimes share a series of similarities, but they are also different in some important aspects. In addition to the fact that the origins of both regimes are different, they are different in another important aspect, namely, the clearing mechanisms in the markets for foreign exchange. Both regimes are described briefly in the following.

1. Dual Exchange Market Regime with Reserve Rationing

This type of regime has been examined in the black market literature and is the focus of the analysis of this chapter. It is generally assumed to correspond to a dual exchange rate regime with an official market in which the exchange rate is determined by the authorities, and a black market which develops in response to

1 The first two issues, especially the second, have received considerable attention in the literature, while the third one has been relatively neglected.

2 The terms "dual exchange rate regime with reserve rationing" and "dual exchange rate regime with reserve adjustment" are borrowed from Lizondo (1991).

the imposition of restrictions to operate in the official market for certain trade and capital transactions. The black market exchange rate is determined by market forces. Under this regime the official market does not clear. The authorities implement a rationing scheme to allocate all the surrendered foreign exchange between public and private importers, so as to protect international reserves. Thus, there is an excess demand which is satisfied at a premium in the black market.[3]

2. Dual Exchange Market Regime with Reserve Adjustment

The alternative regime is the one assumed in most models of dual exchange rate markets. It corresponds to the legal dual exchange rate regime, and is one of the reference systems in the analysis of this chapter. Under this regime, the official market clears through changes in international reserves, so the authorities specify the types of imports that have access to foreign exchange at the official exchange rate, and the central bank is committed to selling all the foreign exchange demanded at that price.

In this type of regime a variety of assumptions have been made regarding the assignment of different types of transactions between the markets. The typical arrangement assumed in most theoretical models involves an official market for all current account transactions in which the exchange rate, fixed or crawling, is determined by the authorities, and a second (parallel) market for all capital account transactions in which the exchange rate is determined by market forces.[4] Some models allow some current account transactions in the parallel market, which is the most typical arrangement in developing countries.[5,6] Under this arrangement the official market channels public sector transactions and some private sector trade transactions, e.g., priority imports and traditional exports. The parallel market channels the remaining private trade and capital transactions.

3 Examples of models assuming this type of regime are Nowak (1984), Pinto (1986, 1991a, and 1991b), and Kharas and Pinto (1989).

4 This is the assumption, for example, in Swoboda (1974), Flood (1978), Cumby (1984), Gardner (1985), and Guidotti and Vegh (1988).

5 For models that allow some current account transactions in the parallel market, see, for example, Lizondo (1987a, 1987b, and 1991), Macedo (1982), and Nowak (1984).

6 The developing countries that have adopted this type of arrangement include, among others, Mexico in 1982, Costa Rica in 1980, Syria in 1972, and El Salvador in 1982 and 1989.

The analysis in this chapter focuses on four main aspects: first, reasons for the emergence of black markets for foreign exchange; second, macroeconomic effects of black markets for foreign exchange, particularly the effects on the domestic price level; the question of whether or not a dual system of official-black market is able to insulate domestic prices from movements in the black market exchange rate is also addressed; third, the determinants of the black market premium; fourth, policy issues for economies with black markets for foreign exchange.

B. Emergence of Black Markets for Foreign Exchange

Black markets typically emerge when governments establish and control the price at which a commodity, asset, or service is traded, thus generating excess demand or supply. Government controls on access to foreign exchange create excess demand that need to be satisfied at a premium in a second market, giving incentives for the emergence of a black market for foreign currency. Under a pegged exchange rate regime with exchange controls, there is no mechanism to ensure that the demand for foreign exchange is met and the official exchange rate market clears. Thus, black markets play the role of clearing transactions that are not allowed or simply not effected in the official market.

Thus, black markets originate as a result of authorities' inability to enforce the exchange restrictions. In contrast, official dual regimes originate as a decision of the authorities to apply different exchange rates to different transactions.

Sheikh (1976) developed a model in the same tradition of Michaely (1954) and Brofenbrenner (1947) and showed how exchange controls generate conditions that may lead to the development of black markets for foreign exchange. He asserts that a black market for foreign exchange can exist only if there are controls in the foreign exchange market. He notes that a tariff (in the absence of exchange control) creates incentives for smuggling but does not create incentives for the creation of a black market for foreign exchange.

Note that part of the transactions that may take place on the black market may not be prohibited transactions, but the authorities just refuse to sell foreign exchange from official reserves for those purposes; thus, in this regard, the second market that develops would be legal. Therefore, in this context the dual official-black market exchange rate system would be like the one officially adopted by the authorities. However, additional demand and supply will arise from some illegal activities motivated by the exchange rate differential. Exporters will find it profitable to sell foreign receipts at the higher rate (incentives to underinvoice exports) and importers to buy foreign exchange at the lower rate (overinvoice imports) and sell the excess at the black market.

A second reason for the development of black markets for foreign exchange is the existence of an underground (or informal) economy in the country.[7] Pitt (1984) argues that a black market for foreign exchange may exist even in the absence of import quotas or foreign exchange rationing. Tariffs and import quotas may induce smuggling as well as a black market for foreign exchange transactions. Importers who underinvoice in order to avoid tariffs will need to illegally obtain an amount of foreign exchange equal to the difference between the actual and the declared value of their shipments. Exporters who underinvoice to avoid export taxes will possess illegally-earned foreign exchange which they will be willing to sell. The market formed by these illegal traders is referred to as the black market for foreign exchange.[8] In other words, the existence of contraband markets whose participants could not use the official foreign exchange market could be a sufficient condition for development of a black market.

In Colombia, for example, the black market is especially important for facilitating operations of narcotraffic business and tax evasion. Thus, it is likely that a black market may exist even after the removal of exchange rate controls.[9,10]

This section can be concluded by noting that black markets for foreign exchange are not created by the authorities, in contrast to the case of the adoption of a dual exchange rate system, but are the result of economic agents' behavior when trying to evade some official restrictions and regulations; and one of the main reasons for the emergence of such markets is the existence of foreign exchange controls.

C. Macroeconomic Effects of Black Market for Foreign Exchange

The existence of black markets for foreign exchange has important implications for the functioning of an economy, as compared with an economy with an uni-

7 This idea was first developed by Pitt (1984). See also Grosse (1992).

8 See Pitt (1984), p. 247.

9 See Grosse (1992) for details of the reasons for the existence of the Colombian black market.

10 Note that this reason assumes that the foreign exchange used in illegal trade activities cannot be channeled through the official market because it increases the probability of being caught in those activities. However, this is not always the case, assuming, for example, that there is free access to the official market and that the participation in that market does not increase the risk of being caught in an illegal activity. In this case there is no demand for and supply of foreign exchange in the black market.

fied exchange rate regime. Black markets have an impact on the determination of a number of macroeconomic variables, especially on the fiscal deficit, inflation rate, the real exchange rate, balance-of-payments, and economic welfare.

1. Fiscal Effects

Multiple exchange rate regimes are sometimes adopted as a method of subsidization and taxation. These systems imply a structure of implicit subsidies and taxes for activities that need and produce foreign exchange. Since there is more than one price at which foreign exchange is bought and sold, imports that are assigned to the official market at a relatively low exchange rate are subsidized relative to other imports. Similarly exports, whose proceeds must be exchanged at the lower rate, are taxed. The same applies to capital flows.[11]

In principle, the fiscal effects of a dual official-black market regime are similar to the fiscal effects described above of an official dual or multiple exchange rate regime, but some additional effects as well as some differences should be highlighted. There are two effects on government revenues associated with the existence of a black market for foreign exchange. First, a black market will deprive the government of revenues that could otherwise be captured through trade taxes (e.g., taxes are not paid for smuggled exports or imports). In addition, as the black market exchange rate depreciates, the fraction of exports that is channeled through the official market keeps falling. This also implies that the amount of official imports is being cut. For most developing countries, trade-related taxes are an important source of government revenues; thus, a high black market premium may significantly reduce government revenues in developing countries. Second, black markets also could cause an increase in revenues or a reduction in government expenditure. The basic idea has been developed by Pinto (1990 and 1991) in analyzing the experience of African countries, and by Kharas and Pinto (1989) in explaining the Bolivian experience. In these papers it is assumed that the central bank buys foreign exchange from private exporters, sells part of that foreign exchange to the public sector for imports, and sells the rest back to the private sector for imports. All these transactions are carried out at the official exchange rate, which is lower than the market-clearing exchange rate. But, because of the rationing scheme implemented in the official market, there is a black market for foreign exchange where proceeds from underinvoiced exports and foreign exchange needed for illegal imports or imports for which

11 On the fiscal effects of multiple exchange rate regimes, see, for example, Sherwood (1950) and Adams and Greenwood (1985).

foreign exchange cannot be obtained from the official market are exchanged at a higher exchange rate. Thus, the black market exchange rate is the marginal price for foreign exchange used in imports, and it is the relevant one for pricing those imports in terms of domestic currency.

The fiscal effects depend on whether, on balance, the government sells foreign exchange to the private sector (for example, El Salvador) or buys foreign exchange. In the case of the net seller, there is a subsidy on foreign exchange to the private sector, which increases the fiscal deficit. In the net buyer case, there is an implicit tax which increases government revenues or reduces government expenditures, reducing the fiscal deficit. Most papers concentrate on the net buyer case.[12] In this context, the conclusion of those papers is that the black market premium functions as an implicit tax on export production and as a source of hidden fiscal revenues. Fiscal revenues that arise from the government's purchase of foreign exchange with the overvalued domestic currency, specifically the positive fiscal effect, arise because the government's foreign transactions are made at an official exchange rate that is lower than the market-clearing rate.[13]

The second fiscal effect should be very similar in both types of regimes, but it could be stronger under a dual official-black market exchange rate regime because the fiscal effect of this system arises because the government foreign exchange transactions are at an official rate that reflects a lower price of foreign exchange than the market-clearing rate, rather than because foreign exchange is bought and sold at a multiple rate where all exchange rate markets, including the official market, clear.

2. *Insulation Properties of the Dual Official-Black Market Regimes on Domestic Prices*

Dual exchange rate regimes are sometimes adopted as a device for insulating the domestic economy from foreign and domestic disturbances. Flood and Marion (1982) and Marion (1981) have shown that, under complete market separation, the dual exchange rate regime provides insulation from most foreign disturbances as well as from domestic monetary disturbances. The basic idea is that foreign disturbances and domestic monetary disturbances will be absorbed by

---

12 See, for example, Pinto (1990 and 1991), and Kharas and Pinto (1989).

13 Part of that tax revenue is returned as a subsidy on imports to the private sector by the central bank selling foreign exchange to the private importers at the official exchange rate.

changes in the financial exchange rate (parallel market rate). Since this exchange rate is not applied to trade transactions, it is expected that the domestic real sector will be insulated from those disturbances.

Similarly, the principal motivation for maintaining a system of exchange controls with official-black markets is to protect international official reserves in a balance-of-payments crisis without resorting to a maxi-devaluation, which can be inflationary. By maintaining this system, the authorities believe that the domestic prices are partly insulated from movements in the exchange rate, since most trade transactions (at least those judged by the authorities to be "essential") take place at the official rate, which is pegged or gradually depreciated by the authorities.

The insulation properties of the dual exchange rate systems have been examined in the literature and the overall conclusion is that they are very limited. In Cumby (1984) the lack of insulation comes from the presence of the wealth effect of changes in the financial rate. In Guidotti (1988) the lack of insulation arises from the incomplete segmentation of the foreign exchange markets as well as the existence of nontraded goods.[14] Although these papers include a variety of assumptions, they generally conclude that the ability to insulate domestic prices from short-term changes in the parallel exchange rate depends crucially on the complete segmentation of the official and parallel markets. However, it has been demonstrated in the dual exchange rate literature that complete segmentation of these markets is hard to achieve.[15] The typical arrangement assumed in most models of dual exchange rate markets is one in which there exists an official exchange for current account transactions which is pegged by the authorities, and a floating exchange rate (parallel or financial rate) for capital account transactions which is determined by market forces. Under this arrangement, the official market clears through changes in official international reserves, while the parallel market clears through exchange rate changes. In this type of arrangement, incomplete separation will result from illegal cross-transactions motivated by the exchange rate differential.

In recent practice, the most common arrangement in most developing countries is one in which some trade transactions are officially assigned to the parallel market.[16] Under this type of arrangement, in addition to the leakages noted

---

14 The analysis of the insulating properties of the dual exchange rate regimes includes the effects on other domestic variables in addition to domestic prices, such as domestic output and the domestic interest rate. However, only the effects on domestic prices will be focused on here.

15 See, for example, Gros (1988), and Bhandari and Decaluwe (1987).

16 The developing countries that have adopted this type of arrangement are, among others, Costa Rica, El Salvador, the Dominican Republic, Sudan, Syria, and Egypt

above, there are other leakages created by the official allocation of trade transactions between the two markets.[17]

Under these circumstances, domestic prices will be affected by the parallel market exchange rate, and the insulation property provided by such systems will be small. How small will it be? That depends on the type of arrangement assumed. In dual exchange rate models which assume that some trade transactions are channeled through the parallel market, or models that take inter-market leakages into consideration, the domestic prices depend on the exchange rates in both markets.[18]

Likewise, under a dual official-black markets regime, the complete separation of markets is even harder to achieve. Since the foreign exchange is rationed in the official market, the demand for foreign exchange in the black market depends on the supply of foreign exchange in the official market.

In models with foreign exchange rationing and a black market for foreign exchange, the domestic price will be more closely affected by the black market exchange rate, to the extent that the black market exchange rate becomes the marginal cost for imports, and the insulation will be smaller than in a legal dual exchange rate system. Pinto (1986 and 1991) assumes that prices of all traded goods are likely to reflect the exchange rate in the black market.[19] However, the relevant exchange rate for the price of traded goods determination is mainly an empirical question which is addressed for the case of El Salvador in Chapter V.

Prices of nontraded goods vary according to changes in demand and cost conditions, which are sometimes partly determined by the behavior of one or more of the exchange rates (i.e., the exchange rate applied to the imported input used in this sector). Additionally, the black market exchange rate may also have an indirect effect on the price of nontraded goods. For example, a black market exchange rate depreciation will raise the price of importable goods. This shifts resources from the nontraded goods sector and probably from the exportable sector (assuming underinvoicing of exports is difficult and it is not a substantial amount) into the import-competing industry, and shifts demand away from im-

---

(see Country Pages, IMF, *Annual Report on Exchange Arrangements and Exchange Restrictions*, 1983 and 1984).

17 See the description of the dual exchange rate arrangement adopted by El Salvador in 1982-1986, in Chapter III.

18 For the first type of models, see Lizondo (1987a and 1987b); for the second type see Guidotti (1988).

19 Also see Lizondo (1991).

portable goods in favor of nontraded and exportable goods.[20] The reduction in supply and increase in demand for nontraded goods results in an upward pressure on the price of those goods, a pressure that will not abate until their prices have risen sufficiently to eliminate the excess demand.

Thus, the domestic price level has been expressed in different models in the literature as some weighted average of the price of nontraded goods and the price of traded goods, where the price of traded goods is also a weighted average of the various exchange rates. The specific weights depend on the assumptions about the channeling of transactions through the various foreign exchange markets.[21] Formally, the domestic price level is expressed as:

$$P = P_N^{\,1-a}\, e^{a(1-v)}\, be^{av},$$

where:

P:	the domestic price level
P_N:	the price of nontraded goods
e:	the official exchange rate
be:	the black market exchange rate
a:	the share of the traded good prices in domestic price level
(1-a):	the share of nontraded good prices in domestic price level
(1-v) and v:	the share of tradables channeled through the official and the black market, respectively.

3. Balance of Payments Effects [22]

In contrast to the cases of uniform exchange rate regimes (pegged or flexible), the determination of the balance of payments under dual or multiple exchange rate regimes depends on the demand and supply conditions and clearing mechanisms in the various markets for foreign exchange. To understand the balance-of-payments determination of dual exchange rate systems it would be useful to first examine the different mechanisms of adjustment under uniform exchange rate regimes, and then under a dual official-black markets system.[23]

---

20 Although in developing countries the domestic consumption of exportable products is very small, thus the change on domestic demand in favor of exportable goods could not be significant due to the nature of export goods.

21 See Lizondo (1991) and Agénor (1991).

22 This section is based upon the analysis of Lizondo (1990).

23 The balance of payments is defined as the change of international reserve of the central bank.

Under a uniform pegged exchange rate, all excess demand and supply is reflected in the balance-of-payments, and the clearing mechanism is through movements of central bank reserves. Under a uniform floating regime the balance-of-payments is zero, and the clearing mechanism is changes in the exchange rate. Under a managed float, the clearing mechanism is a combination of reserve movements and changes in the exchange rate. Whatever the clearing mechanism under uniform exchange rate regimes is, the mechanism is the same regardless of the type of transactions. In contrast, in a dual official-black market exchange rate regime or in a legal dual exchange rate regime, different types of transactions may have at least two clearing mechanisms, depending on which market they are assigned to and on the clearing mechanism of those markets. In models of black markets for foreign exchange, it has been assumed that some rationing schemes in the official market are implemented and that official international reserves remain constant. The balance-of-payments, in this case, is necessarily zero, since the black market clears through changes in the exchange rate.[24] However, this assumption that the official international reserves remain constant has been questioned by Kamin (1993), who argues that it would be more realistic to assume at least some disaccumulation of official international reserve for economies with black markets and balance-of-payments problems due, for example, to central bank indirect intervention in the black market as an instrument of controlling black market activities.

In practice, as was the case in El Salvador, the authorities may probably implement some rationing scheme in the official market to avoid excessive losses of reserves, but also intervene in the official market to keep the black market premium low. Thus, the foreign exchange market clears through reserve movements and a depreciation of the black market exchange rate.

But, on the other hand, official reserves are not unlimited amounts and a high black market premium would increase the diversion of export receipts from the official to the black market and weaken the balance-of-payments. If the authorities insist on defending an officially fixed exchange rate, the final result could be a balance-of-payments crisis and the collapse of the official regime in a way similar to that which would occur under a uniform fixed exchange rate regime. This suggests that a dual official-black markets exchange rate regime does not "save" an otherwise unsustainable system.

24 See, for example, Nowak (1984), Pinto (1991a), and Kharas and Pinto (1989).

4. Effects on Resource Allocation and on Welfare

As noted in the section on fiscal effects, a system of dual official-black markets is actually equivalent to a system of taxes and subsidies. Since there are two prices at which foreign exchange can be bought and sold, exporters whose proceeds are surrendered at the official exchange rate are taxed relative to other exporters for whom underinvoicing is easier; importers who obtain foreign exchange at the official rate receive a subsidy that they could collect by selling the imported goods at the black market exchange rate, which is the real cost for other potential competitors who obtain the foreign exchange at the black market rate.

Thus, such a system acts as an implicit tax on exports which is equal to the black market premium. Exporters will also be penalized by the increase of the price of importable goods resulting from the rationing of foreign exchange discussed above.

Following Clements and Sjaastad (1984), there are at least three ways in which exporters will be hurt by the resultant higher prices of imports:

(i) Exchange controls increase the domestic price of imported inputs that are utilized in producing exports, which obviously will increase the cost for exporters.

(ii) As in the case of tariffs, exchange controls will increase the price of domestically produced inputs and thus also increase the cost for exporters.

(iii) Finally, higher prices of importable and nontraded goods will increase the cost of living, resulting in labor demanding higher wage rates.

As was pointed out above, this will encourage, on the one hand, a reallocation of resources away from the production of exports towards the production of nontraded and import-competing goods and, on the other hand, a shift in consumer preference in favor of imports. The consequence will be a change in the pattern of production and consumption towards goods which do not generate or save foreign exchange. The change in the pattern of production and consumption will involve costs for the economy in terms of lower real national income and welfare.

In addition, the expansion of a black market weakens the effectiveness of exchange controls, increasing the payments imbalance which motivated the implementation of exchange control regulations. High black market premia have represented a strong incentive in many developing countries to divert export receipts from the official to the black market.[25]

---

25 Kamin (1993) found empirical evidence that there is a negative relationship between black market premium and officially recorded exports.

Thus, instead of increasing official reserves, exchange controls have caused the creation of a black market and the diversion of part of the available foreign exchange to the black market.

However, the literature has advanced some potential gains from black markets for foreign currency. First, a number of authors have concluded that to the degree that black market activities circumvent foreign exchange controls, black markets mitigate the adverse effects of exchange controls on the allocation of resources.[26] Nowak (1985) pointed out that black markets provide the possibility to exporters who do not sell foreign currency to the official market to exchange their proceeds at a higher price[27] and allow importers to purchase goods which they could not otherwise obtain at prices they are willing to pay. In this way, the black market provides a mechanism by which the domestic currency effectively undergoes a depreciation in its external value, while the official rate is fixed.[28] Second, the existence of black markets increases employment by raising the domestic availability of imported inputs (McDermott, 1989). Third, it actually raises the flow of foreign currency to the central bank. This latter, somewhat paradoxical, effect arises because the increased availability of inputs allows total exports to be increased, and so much so that foreign currency flows in increased amounts, both legal and illegal.[29]

D. Models of Black Market Exchange Rate Determination

Another important issue that the literature has focused on is the determination of the black market exchange rate. Many models of black market exchange rate determination have been developed and empirically analyzed using different theoretical frameworks. Models of black market exchange determination can be classified into the following categories: smuggling and real trade models, monetary models, and portfolio models.

1. Smuggling and Real Trade Models

These models emphasize the factors that create supply and demand for foreign exchange in the black market. Sheikh (1976) used supply and demand analysis

26 See, for example, Greenwood and Kimbrough (1987) and Nowak (1985).
27 Increasing international competitiveness of domestic exports, which in turn, would increase production of goods for export.
28 Nowak (1985), p. 21.
29 McDermott (1989), p. 261.

to model the black market for foreign exchange. The supply of foreign exchange in the black market depends on: (a) the black market exchange rate, (b) the degree of risk involved in the black market transactions, and (c) the extent of underinvoicing of exports and overinvoicing of imports due to the overvaluation of the official exchange rate. The demand for foreign exchange in the black market arises from the unsatisfied demand for current account and capital account transactions.

Real trade models of determination of the black market premium focus solely on the parallel market and neglect its interactions with the rest of the economy (Agénor, 1992). In these models the sole motive for dealing in black market foreign currency would be to enable smuggling to take place.[30] Specifically, the black market exchange rate is modeled as reflecting the demand for foreign currency to purchase illegal imports and the supply of foreign currency derived from illegal sources (e.g., underinvoicing of exports). These models emphasize the effect of trade taxes on smuggling and on the black market premium (de Macedo, 1987). A rise in tariffs will increase the demand for foreign currency in the black market, and increase the premium, whereas a rise in export taxes will generate excess supply in the black market and a decline in the black market premium.

In contrast, Culbertson (1975) emphasizes the resale of officially allocated foreign exchange. He assumes that underinvoicing exports and overinvoicing imports enables recipients of foreign exchange to divert part of the officially rationed quantity to higher-valued alternatives. This quantity of foreign exchange forms the supply to the black market and commands a price in excess of the official exchange rate.[31]

Culbertson's model assumes that the black market essentially reallocates some portion of the quantity of foreign exchange disbursed by the authorities. In this regard, the black market exchange rate premium will depend on (a) the divergence between the official exchange rate and the equilibrium rate, and (b) the supply of foreign exchange at the black market, which in turn depends on the penalties for reallocating foreign exchange in the black market. Thus, in this model, movements in the black market rate are closely associated with changes in relative price levels (purchasing power parity doctrine),[32] the official exchange rate, and the level of foreign exchange held by the government. An increase in the relative prices of domestic to foreign goods and/or an increase in

30 See, for example, McDermott (1989), Pitt (1984), and Sheikh (1976).

31 Culbertson (1975), p. 289.

32 Purchasing power parity calculation is used as a proxy of the equilibrium exchange rate.

the level of reserves held by the government will depreciate the black market rate, while the effect of an increase in the official exchange rate (a devaluation of the official exchange rate) is ambiguous. On the one hand, it will produce a positive foreign exchange supply response in the official market, increasing the ability of the central bank to supply the foreign exchange demanded, thereby reducing the demand in the black market, but, on the other hand, it will reduce the black market supply.

2. *Monetary Models*

Blejer (1978a) has developed a model in which the behavior of monetary variables is the main factor of the black market exchange rate determination. In this model, an increase in the domestic money stock, say by a rise in domestic credit, results in a disequilibrium in the money market.[33] This increases domestic prices, which would reduce the demand for domestic goods, raising the demand for foreign goods and foreign currency, and entails a depreciation of the black market exchange rate. This in turn increases the black market premium, which raises the incentives to underinvoicing exports or to diverting remittances through the black market. Although the increase in the supply of foreign exchange in the black market tends to reduce the initial upward pressure on the black market exchange rate, an increase in the money stock will, in general, be associated with a depreciation of the black market exchange rate.[34]

In Blejer's model, the rate of depreciation of the black market exchange is a function of monetary disequilibrium and the world rate of inflation. The black market rate will depreciate faster, the higher the domestic credit expansion relative to the demand for the domestic real cash balances is and it will depreciate more slowly, the higher the world rate of inflation relative to the domestic inflation is (Blejer 1978a, p. 123). This model was tested by Blejer using annual data for Brazil, Chile, and Colombia. He concludes that almost all flow disequilibria created in the money market are transmitted to the black market exchange rate within a period of two years (Blejer 1978a, p. 127).[35]

---

33 In Blejer's model, monetary disequilibrium is measured as the difference between the expansion of the domestic credit component of the base and variations of the money multiplier, and the changes in the demand for real cash balances.

34 See Agénor (1991), p. 5.

35 Blejer's model has also been tested for India (Biswas and Nandi, 1986) with basically good results. Agénor (1991) extended this model dealing with some of the limitations mentioned below. He tested it for 12 developing countries, confirming

Blejer's model provides an important insight into the relationship between monetary policy and the behavior of the black market exchange rate (Agénor, 1991). For example, the model indicates that a tight monetary policy is the key instrument for preventing official reserve losses and black market exchange rate depreciation. However, his formulation suffers from an important limitation (Gupta, 1980, and Agénor, 1991). He conceived of the black market as an outlet for capital transactions barred from the official market. In other words, foreign exchange is bought and sold in the black market because of the private agents' desire to alter the composition of its portfolio of financial assets, and not for the purpose of carrying out current account transactions. Thus, he assumed that all current account needs are satisfied in the official market. This assumption may be inadequate in the case of El Salvador in view of the exchange controls in both the current account and capital transactions and foreign exchange rationing for current account transactions on the official market during the period that the black market existed.

Gupta (1980) extended Blejer's model. His model considered monetary and real factors applied to the case of India. In his model, the demand for money is the main vehicle of analysis. The principal determinants of the black market exchange are the official exchange rate, the nominal quantity of money, the level of real income, the nominal interest rate, the world price of gold and silver, and the world price level. A devaluation of the official exchange rate will reduce the incentives for underinvoicing exports or overinvoicing imports. Since the demand for foreign exchange in the black market is not independent of the supply of foreign exchange in the official market, an increase of foreign exchange receipts in the official market would lower the demand for foreign exchange in the black market. Monetary growth will depreciate the black market exchange rate. By contrast, an increase in real income, in the world price of silver and gold, or in the world price level would increase the demand for domestic money and cause the black market rate to appreciate.

Gupta's model differs from Blejer´s in several respects. Gupta extended the analysis considering monetary and real factors and, contrary to Blejer, took into account the relationship between the black market and smuggling. Thus, the black market also provides foreign exchange for current account transactions. Therefore, some of the conclusions in Gupta's study differ from those in Blejer´s study, especially in that the relationship obtained between the official exchange rate and the black market rate is reversed. According to Gupta, a devaluation of the official exchange rate would appreciate the black market rate, while Blejer

---

the role of monetary disequilibria as one of the main determinants of the behavior of parallel market exchange rates.

concludes that depreciation of the official rate would induce a depreciation in the black market exchange rate. This is because Blejer assumes a complete separation between the official market and the black market.

Canto (1985) develops and estimates a monetary model for the Dominican Republic which accounts for currency substitution and for indirect government intervention in the black market for foreign exchange through the imposition of restrictions, i.e., the transaction cost of using U.S. dollars in domestic transactions, which reduce the convenience of holding foreign currency in order to prevent erosion of the inflation tax.

The basic hypothesis of his model is that excessive money creation, say, because of monetization of the budget deficits, may give rise to inflation tax revenues and to a depreciation of the domestic currency. This, in turn, leads to a shift away from the domestic currency into a foreign currency (e.g., the U.S. dollar, hence the term "dollarization"). From the domestic authorities' point of view, "dollarization" is an unwelcome phenomenon; thus the monetary authorities will attempt to arrest this phenomenon while maintaining the excessive money growth.

Canto (1985) considers two alternative hypotheses of government intervention in the foreign exchange market: One is the imposition of transaction costs on the use of foreign money in order to prevent the erosion of the inflation tax base. To the extent that the transaction costs are imposed to increase the demand for domestic money to absorb the excess domestic money creation, one would expect a causal relationship going from the money supply to the exchange rate.

The second hypothesis of intervention is that the central bank/government sector dominates the foreign exchange market by its own reserve demand behavior. In that case the foreign exchange market is not really a market in the sense that the price is determined by private supplies and demands. In effect, the central bank pegs the foreign exchange rate or changes it from time to time, allowing the domestic money stock to respond endogenously. This suggests a causal relationship going from the exchange rate to the money supply.[36]

Canto's results are supportive of the view that currency substitution is large in the Dominican Republic, and his results also suggest that as monetary expansion is planned by the domestic authorities they will increase the transaction costs of using the U.S. dollar in domestic transactions in anticipation of the increase of the domestic money supply, thereby inducing a shift toward the Dominican peso. To the extent that they are successful, the depreciation of the currency will be less than proportional to the money supply growth. The evidence presented in

36 See Canto (1985), p. 515.

his paper also suggests a causal relationship going from the money supply to the exchange rate rather than the opposite.

Canto's model provides important insights for an analysis of the impact of monetary policy on currency substitution and on the black market exchange rate, particularly the effect on the black market exchange rate of the central bank's intervention in the foreign exchange market.

3. Portfolio Balance Models

Additional studies have examined this issue using a different framework. Braga de Macedo (1979, 1982), Dornbusch et al. (1983), and Frenkel (1990), using a theoretical framework along the lines of the portfolio balance approach to exchange rate determination[37] have developed models of black market exchange rate determination. In these models, relative asset supplies and expectations of future exchange rate developments play a crucial role in determining the black market exchange rate.

The basic idea of this type of model is that foreign exchange is viewed as an asset. Fears about inflation, low domestic interest rates in relation to foreign interest rates, as well as political and economic policy instability give rise to demand for foreign currency in the black market, both as a store of value[38] and as a means of acquiring and hoarding imports.

Dornbusch et al. (1983) developed a model of the black market premium in Brazil. The model assumes that the black market in Brazil is of minor importance to policy making with no effect on the domestic interest rate or the official exchange rate, so that the black market for foreign exchange is analyzed in a partial equilibrium fashion,[39] emphasizing portfolio decisions on holding black market dollars versus domestic assets. The model explains how changes in financial and real variables, and expectations of future exchange rate developments lead to a depreciation/appreciation of the black market exchange rate. A restrictive monetary policy, for example, increases the attractiveness of domestic assets (through interest rate increases) relative to the foreign currency leading to

37 Rodríguez (1980), Branson (1976), Mussa (1985), and Kouri (1976 and 1983).

38 In countries with trade and exchange restrictions and a black market for foreign exchange, the black market constitutes the only channel through which the public can change its stock of foreign assets.

39 This assumption is warranted for the case of Brazil where the daily black market turnover is negligible compared with the total financial market trade. This might not be applicable to the case of El Salvador where the black market for foreign exchange was a major concern of policymakers (see Chapter III).

a decline in the black market premium. Similarly, a real depreciation of the official exchange rate leads to a decline in the premium. Expectations of future official devaluation initially lead to a depreciation of the black market rate and subsequently to a decline in the premium when the expected official depreciation actually occurs. A gain in competitiveness (i.e., real depreciation of official exchange rate) reduces the relative cost of domestic goods and services and, therefore, lowers the demand for black market dollars by import smugglers and tourists, giving rise to an increased net inflow of black market dollars.[40]

The application of this model to the case of Brazil also includes seasonal factors which capture the seasonal patterns of net inflows due to tourism, especially from Argentinean visitors to Brazil. Thus, in this model, the main determinants of the black market premium are the real official exchange rate, the official depreciation-adjusted interest rate differential and seasonal factors associated with tourism.

In the same spirit, Braga de Macedo (1982) developed a model for regimes of currency inconvertibility, emphasizing the relationship between the exchange rate and the current account. Unlike Dornbusch et al. (1983), Braga de Macedo (1982) treated the black market as if it were part of a dual exchange rate regime, with current account transactions through the official market and capital account transactions through the black market. Contrary to the general assumption of the literature on dual exchange rate regimes, he assumes that the two markets are linked by smuggling. This model emphasizes general equilibrium interactions between the black market and the rest of the economy.

For easy reference, the reduced form equations and variables of the most representative models of each approach discussed above are listed in Table IV.1.

E. Macroeconomic Effects of Various Economic Policies and Disturbances under the Presence of a Black Market for Foreign Exchange

In the literature on exchange controls, several economists have recognized that the standard models of a uniform exchange rate (pegged or flexible) and dual market models which assume currency convertibility may not be applicable to economies with a dual exchange rate regime with official and black markets in which the latter appears because of rationing in the official foreign exchange market and because of foreign exchange controls.[41]

40 Dornbusch et al. (1983), p. 29.
41 See, for example, Krueger (1978 and 1983) and Bhagwati (1978).

Table IV.1

Models Equations and Variables

Culbertson (1975 and 1989)

$$be = a_o + a_1\, e + a_2\, P/P^* + a_3\, IR + u$$

Blejer (1978a)

$$be = a_o + a_1\, Z + a_2\, P^* + u$$

Gupta (1980)

$$be = a_o + a_1\, e + a_2\, Ms + a_3\, P^* + a_4\, i + a_5\, Y + u$$

Dornbusch et al. (1983)

$$x = a_o + a_1\, r + a_2\, (i^* + d_o - i) + a_3\, DU + u$$

Endogenous Variables:

be	=	black market exchange rate.
x	=	black market premium.

Exogenous Variables:

e	=	official exchange rate.
P	=	domestic prices.
P^*	=	foreign prices.
IR	=	level of international reserves held by the central bank.
Z	=	monetary disequilibrium, defined as the difference between the expansion of the domestic-credit component of the monetary base and the changes in the demand for real cash balances.
Ms	=	domestic money supply.
i	=	domestic interest rate.
i^*	=	foreign interest rate.
d_o	=	rate of depreciation of the official exchange rate.
Y	=	real income.
r	=	real official effective exchange rate.
i^*+d_o-i	=	expected official depreciation-adjusted interest rate differential
DU	=	dummy reflecting seasonal factors associated with tourism.
u	=	error term.

However, very little has been done to develop a theoretical model to analyze policy issues for this type of economies. To my knowledge, the most complete theoretical frameworks of analyzing policy issues of this type of economies were developed by Nowak (1984) and by Agénor (1990).[42] The analysis here is based on those studies to a certain extent, and it will focus on the effects of monetary policy, of a nominal devaluation of the official exchange rate, and of an inflow of capital in the context of an economy with a dual official-black market exchange rate regime.

1. Expansive Monetary Policy

Assume an economy with an officially adopted fixed uniform or dual exchange rate regime, and also assume that there exists a black market for foreign exchange, because of exchange controls and of rationing of foreign exchange in the official market(s). Let us consider the case of an increase in domestic credit to the private sector. With constant international reserves, this will produce an increase in the money supply, which will lead to depreciation of the black market exchange rate, increasing the domestic price of imported goods.[43] As was discussed in section C, this price rise shifts resources from the nontraded sector into the import-competing industry, and shifts demand away from importable goods in favor of nontraded goods and exportable goods. The reduction in supply and the increase in demand of nontraded goods result in an upward pressure on their prices, a pressure that will not be abated until their prices have risen sufficiently to eliminate the excess demand. Thus, the real exchange rate defined as the relative prices of traded to nontraded goods falls as a result of an increase in the domestic credit. This change in relative prices is due to the fact that the price of exports will be held fixed by conditions in the official market and in international markets, while prices of other goods are free to vary.[44] This implies that under a dual exchange rate regime with rationing in the official market, the

42 Partial equilibrium analyses include Dornbusch et al. (1983), Kharas and Pinto (1989) and Pinto (1990) and Kamin (1993).

43 By contrast, if it is assumed some movements in official international reserves (e.g., central bank's intervention in the foreign exchange market), there will be some offsetting effect on the money supply coming through the balance-of-payments. In this case, the rate of depreciation of the black market exchange rate generated by an expansionary credit policy will be lower.

44 Clearly, this assumes that no substantial amounts of exports are exchanged in the black market.

neutrality properties associated with uniform fixed exchange and dual exchange rate regimes are not achieved.

To aid the understanding of adjustment in a dual regime of official and black market exchange rates, which is the issue of this section, the effects of monetary policy under uniform fixed, flexible, and official dual exchange rates regimes will be summarized briefly below.

Under a uniform fixed exchange regime and the assumption of perfect international capital mobility, an increase of money stock has no impact, even in the short run.[45] The adjustment process can be described as follows: The increase in money stock puts downward pressure on the domestic interest rate and causes a capital outflow, which puts pressure on the exchange rate to depreciate. To maintain the exchange rate, the central bank must sell reserves, thereby decreasing the money stock. The pressure on the exchange rate would continue until the money stock is reduced to the original level. Thus, an increase in the money stock is immediately offset and has no impact other than reducing the central bank's international reserves.[46]

Under a flexible exchange rate regime, the exchange rate will depreciate and prices of all goods will increase in the same proportion, maintaining real variables constant in the long run (Dornbusch, 1976). The adjustment process is as follows: At the initial level of prices, the monetary expansion reduces the interest rate and also leads to expectations of a depreciation of the exchange rate. Both factors serve to reduce the attractiveness of domestic assets, leading to an incipient capital outflow, and thus cause the spot exchange rate to depreciate. The extent of that depreciation has to be sufficient to give rise to the anticipation of an appreciation to compensate for the reduction on domestic interest rates and equalize the yields on domestic assets to the yields on foreign assets. It is in this sense that in the short run the exchange rate is determined in the asset markets.[47]

Thus, in the short run, the effect of monetary expansion is to induce an immediate depreciation in the spot rate, and one that exceeds the long-run depreciation (overshooting), since only under these circumstances will the public anticipate an appreciation of the exchange rate and then be compensated for the reduced interest rate on domestic assets.

Over time, the price level will rise to match the expansion in the nominal quantity of money until the monetary expansion is exactly matched by a price increase, so that real balances and interest rates return to their initial levels and the spot and forward rate depreciate in the same proportion as the increase in the

45 See Mundell (1968), Ch.18, pp. 254-255.
46 Mundell (1968), Ch. 18.
47 See Dornbusch (1976), p. 1168.

nominal quantity of money. The dynamics of the adjustment process will depend on the speed of price adjustment process. According to Dornbusch's analysis, there will be two channels that contribute to the price adjustment: first, the traditional effect of a reduction in interest rates on aggregate spending, and, second, the exchange rate depreciation will make domestic goods cheaper than foreign goods and therefore induce world demand toward domestic goods. Both channels serve to drive domestic prices up and cause the real effects of a monetary expansion to be transitory.[48]

Dornbusch's analysis is based on the following assumptions: First, that domestic and foreign assets are perfect substitutes, implying that a reduction in domestic interest rates has to be matched by a forward discount on foreign exchange in order to equalize the net yields on domestic and foreign assets. Second, the dynamic aspects of exchange rate determination (overshooting) in Dornbusch's model are based on the assumption that exchange rates and asset markets adjust relatively faster than the goods markets. Third, prices adjust freely in the long run. If prices do not adjust freely, changes in the money stock will lead to changes in the interest rate that will have real effects in the long-run. Fourth, expectation formation is consistent with perfect foresight.

Finally, consider a dual exchange rate regime with a fixed commercial rate (official rate) for current account transactions and a flexible financial rate (parallel market rate) for capital account transactions under which the official market clears through changes in international reserves and the parallel market clears through changes in the exchange rate.[49] In this type of regime, an increase in the money stock has also a transitory impact, but not an impact in the long-run. The adjustment will occur with a falling stock of international reserves and a depreciation of the financial exchange rate. The process of adjustment is as follows: Immediately following the increase in domestic credit, the domestic interest rate falls and the financial exchange rate depreciates and there is no immediate change in reserves, as a dual exchange rate regime prevents a net outflow of private capital. The financial exchange rate depreciation has no direct effect on domestic prices and on the current account, since these papers[50] assume a complete separation of both markets. It influences them through the wealth effect of the depreciation, which raises aggregate demand and moves the current account into a deficit; the wealth effect on internal aggregate demand is reduced by the increase in domestic prices resulting from the monetary expansion. This,

48 See Dornbusch (1976), p. 1171.

49 This is the typical arrangement found in the literature of dual exchange rate. See, for example, Cumby (1984), Gardner (1985), Flood (1978), Lanyi (1975), Swoboda (1974).

50 See footnote 49.

in turn, moves demand away from domestic goods. Over time, reserves decline and the financial exchange rate appreciates relative to the depreciated level initially induced by the monetary expansion. The decline in wealth associated with the exchange rate appreciation reduces absorption and therefore reduces domestic price over time. The price decline continues until the original domestic price level is restored. Monetary policy is therefore able to influence domestic price in the short run but not in the long run.[51]

Thus, under the dual exchange rate the adjustment is much more complicated, but the long-run response to changes in monetary variables is identical to that of the uniform fixed rate regime.[52]

By contrast, under a dual official-black market regime, no mechanism such as reserve movements exists to ensure that all prevailing demand for foreign exchange at the official rate is met and the official market clears. Thus, the system clears through a depreciation of the black market rate and an increase in domestic prices that can freely vary (nontraded and importable goods), while the price of exportable goods is dominated by the conditions in the official market and in international markets.[53] This implies that relative prices will change and that a monetary expansion will have real effects.

2. *Devaluation of the Official Exchange Rate*

A devaluation of the official exchange rate has an ambiguous effect on the black market rate and on relative prices, depending crucially on the assumptions of the theoretical analysis. Nowak (1984) showed that an official devaluation will result in an appreciation of the domestic currency in the black market. He assumes that the central bank retains a fixed level of reserves and does not disaccumulate reserves before the official devaluation takes place, and also does not accumulate reserves after a devaluation has taken place. In contrast, Kamin (1993) argues that reserve losses, which typically motivate devaluation, and reserve accumulation, which often follows a successful devaluation, are more adequate assumptions and concludes that a devaluation of the official rate will depreciate the black market rate.

The effect of an official devaluation on the black market rate should be regarded as an empirical question. The reason is that a devaluation produces a

---

51 See Cumby (1984) and Gardner (1985).

52 For details, see Gardner (1985), pp. 329-335.

53 As mentioned earlier, this assumes that most export earnings are exchanged in the official market(s).

reduction of the black market supply, but it also reduces the black market demand. As long as the second effect is stronger than the first one, an official devaluation will appreciate the black market rate. The result depends on the assumptions mentioned above concerning reserves and on the assumptions relating to the penalty cost of transacting in the black market.

The effect on prices would depend on the resulting effect of devaluation on the black market exchange rate. If the black market rate appreciates, the price level will probably decline as a result of a fall in the price of imported goods or, at least, there will be no inflationary effect in the current and subsequent periods. Nowak (1984) showed that the deflationary effect of a devaluation of the official rate is stronger if expectations are taken into account and devaluation of the official rate is pre-announced or widely anticipated. The reason is that, because under rational expectations, all market participants are presumed to know in the pre-devaluation period that this devaluation will involve an appreciation of the black market rate. Therefore, the demand for foreign currency will decline, which in turn implies a rise in the demand for domestic currency and, for equilibrium to be maintained, there must be a drop in both the black market exchange rate (that is, it appreciates) and in the price level at the time of the announcement.[54]

These predictions stand in sharp contrast to those obtained from the standard models for uniform fixed or flexible regime or the models for official dual regime which predict that a devaluation will raise all domestic prices proportionally.

In contrast, if a devaluation further depreciates the black market exchange rate, as Kamin argues, the price of imported goods will increase and a further increase in the price level will take place.

As was pointed out above, the way in which a devaluation of the official rate affects the black market rate and the price level seems, then, to be an empirical question that can only be answered for each particular country, taking into account the specific circumstances concerning the way in which the government handles its reserves and the degree of risk and costs of dealing in black markets.

3. Exogenous Exchange Rate Receipts

The last disturbance to be considered here is an exogenous increase in exchange rate receipts, for example, an increase in private and official transfers. The

54 Nowak (1984), p. 418.

analysis of this type of disturbance is considered important in view of the surges in capital inflows experienced in El Salvador during the last few years.

Recent studies have analyzed the effects of an inflow of capital in terms of *Dutch disease* economics,[55] concluding that capital inflows may cause *Dutch-disease*-type effects in the same way that a boom in an enclave export sector does (Younger, 1992, and Bautista, 1988).[56]

The *Dutch disease* framework has more commonly been applied to export booms, primarily in the oil exporting economies.[57] However, as Corden (1982) has pointed out, the analysis can be applied to other situations. He suggests the *Dutch disease* analysis can also be applied to the inflows of American gold in the sixteenth century, capital inflows to Switzerland, and the growth in the technologically advanced manufacturing industry in Japan. Similarly, capital from workers' remittances, repatriations, aid, and external borrowing received by El Salvador during the last few years could be analyzed in terms of *Dutch disease* economics.

Before proceeding, it may be useful to summarize the salient features of the *Dutch disease* framework.[58] The basic framework is essentially the dependent economy model of Salter (1959), assuming a small open economy producing three goods: two traded goods and one nontraded good. The price of tradables is determined exogenously in the world market (small country assumption), while the price of nontraded goods is set by domestic supply and demand.

Corden and Neary (1982), and Corden (1984) separate the effect of the export boom into two effects: the "resource movement effect" and the "spending effect." The first refers to the movement of labor out of the manufacturing sector and the nontraded goods sector into the booming sector due to the increased productivity in the latter, which raises marginal revenue product of labor bidding up their wages, and causing other sectors to contract. In the present case, this effect does not occur or it could occur only indirectly. The second effect, the "spending effect", refers to the fact that the increase in real income in the booming sector raises domestic spending, raising consumption of both traded and nontraded goods (assuming positive income elasticity for them).

---

55 This term originated after the decline in the Netherlands' export competitiveness after the discovery of the Groningen gas field in the 1970's.

56 The short-run adjustment of an economy to capital inflows was first analyzed by McKinnon (1976). He also used a dependent economy model, most commonly known as the Australian model.

57 See, for example, Enders and Herberg (1983), Benjamin, Davarajan, and Weiner (1989), Neary and van Wijnbergen (1986), and Pinto (1987).

58 See Corden and Neary (1982), Corden (1982 and 1984), and Enders and Herberg (1983).

Thus, following the terminology of Corden and Neary (1982) and Corden (1982 and 1984), an increase in inflows of foreign exchange gives rise only to a "spending effect" and there is no direct "resource movement effect."[59] As already mentioned, this results in a greater consumption of both traded and nontraded goods, assuming that all of them are not inferior in total absorption. The increase in demand for nontraded goods will result in an upward pressure on the price of those goods until their prices have risen sufficiently to eliminate the excess demand, while the increased demand for traded goods will be satisfied, as the Australian model assumes, by imports at constant world prices and a fixed exchange rate. Thus, the price of nontraded goods relative to traded goods rises, causing appreciation of the real exchange rate. In this context, one of the standard results of the Australian model is that the nontradable sector expands and the tradable contracts. However, for economies with exchange controls on current account transactions, this result may not necessarily be true. The import-competing sector may expand its output with a large infusion of foreign exchange. The explanation of this result is as follows:

In developing countries with exchange control regimes, the foreign currency price of tradable goods is determined in the world market. Their domestic prices are different because they also depend upon the different exchange rates (official and black market rates) and upon commercial policy.

The presence of foreign exchange controls implies that the market for importable goods behaves partly in the same manner as the market for nontraded goods. An increase in demand for importable goods, say, because of receiving a transfer, cannot be freely satisfied by imports because of the exchange controls. Thus, in order to clear the market, the domestic price of these goods must rise to equate the domestic demand for imports and the governmentally determined supply of imports.[60] However, part of the excess demand for imports could be satisfied through the black market at a higher exchange rate than the official one.[61]

59 The mechanism of the resource reallocation in this case is the real appreciation caused by an increase in spending that puts upward pressure on the price of nontraded goods, inducing in turn a resource reallocation from the traded goods sector to the nontraded goods sector.

60 Greenwood and Kimbrough (1987), pp. 277.

61 The black market exchange rate is subject to two opposing influences when there is an inflow of foreign exchange. On the one hand, the excess supply of foreign exchange, would appreciate the black market exchange rate, and on the other hand, the demand for foreign exchange in the black market may increase, leading to a depreciation of this rate.

In this case, the import-competing sector will contain both tradable and nontradable elements, so it could benefit from the spending effect when there is an inflow of foreign exchange.

To sum up, in developing economies with exchange controls and a black market for foreign exchange, the nontraded goods sector will certainly benefit and the import-competing sectors may also benefit from an inflow of foreign exchange. Output in both sectors will expand by drawing resources out of the exportable sector. Since agriculture in developing countries is usually the most export-oriented sector, agriculture, rather than manufacturing, would be the sector most likely to be hurt. Thus, despite the real exchange rate appreciation, some tradable sectors may expand their output.

This section can be concluded by recalling that conventional macroeconomic prescriptions under uniform exchange rates or dual exchange market regimes with reserve adjustment can, in fact, be reversed in situations where the black market for foreign exchange is important. For example, monetary expansion has no impact under uniform exchange regimes or under dual exchange market regimes with reserve adjustment in the long run. In contrast, under a dual official-black market regime, a monetary expansion may increase the price of nontradable goods, appreciating the real exchange rate. Moreover, the inflationary impact of a devaluation of the official exchange rate could be smaller than it would be in an economy without foreign exchange rationing.

Chapter V

Empirical Evidence on the Black Market for Foreign Exchange in El Salvador

A. Introduction

The purpose of this chapter is to examine empirically for El Salvador the determinants of the black market premium as well as the ability of the dual system of official and black markets to insulate domestic prices from movements in the black market exchange rate. Particularly, an attempt is made to give an answer to the following questions: (a) What were the determinants of the black market premium in El Salvador? (b) To what extent was the foreign exchange acquired in the black market in El Salvador considered an asset, or was it a means of exchange used for carrying out international commodity transactions? (c) Are domestic prices insulated from black market exchange movements?

The chapter proceeds in four steps. First, a preliminary analysis of the properties of the data is performed. Second, the most representative empirical models of every analytical framework existing in the literature are estimated for El Salvador using monthly data to see how well they explain the behavior of the black market premium. Third, a simple portfolio model of the black market premium determination which captures some special features of the black market for foreign currency in El Salvador is developed and estimated. Fourth, additional evidence using vector autoregression analysis is provided.

B. Empirical Issues

1. Estimation Issues

Recent econometric theory and practice have focused more attention on the time-series properties of the data used in empirical analysis. Many macroeconomic time series are not stationary in their levels (i.e., they have a persistent tendency to increase or decrease over time).[1]

---

1 That is, formal statistic tests cannot reject the null hypothesis of a unit root. The results of these tests, however, are sensitive to the manner in which the tests are per-

Nonstationarity gives rise to the possibility of the so-called *spurious* relationship among the levels of the economic variables and leads to incorrect statistical inferences.[2] The nonstationarity problem can be resolved by first differencing the data,[3] but in doing so potentially interesting information about long-run equilibrium relationships between economic variables is lost.

Engle and Granger (1987) found a way to resolve the *spurious* relationship problem by using Error Correction Models (ECMs) which have the important advantage of explicitly modeling the short-run dynamics jointly with the long-run relationships. This approach is based on the notion of cointegration. Cointegration means that one or more linear combinations of these variables are stationary even though individually they are not. The linear combination is called the *cointegrating equation* and is interpreted as an economic long-run equilibrium relationship. If these variables are cointegrated, they can be used in an error correction model.

There are several limitations to doing time-series analysis, such as testing for stationarity and cointegration of the time series of the macroeconomic variables under investigation. The main limitation of this type of analysis is the short time period of the reliable available data on the black market exchange rate, which is the main variable under investigation in the empirical work of this chapter.

On the other hand, the period of the available data on the black market exchange rate (August 1982 to May 1990) is included in the period of 12 years of civil war in El Salvador.[4] Thus, it is possible that the data on the series of interest were affected by structural changes, increasing the possibility of nonstationarity.

Despite these limitations, some general conclusions of practical use can be drawn, but care must be taken in interpreting the results of this exercise.

---

formed: whether the test assumes a zero mean, a non-zero mean, or a time trend, and the number of lagged differences in test equation.

2 The "spurious" regression problem was first introduced by Granger and Newbold (1974), who analyzed the case where a random walk variable (y_t) is regressed on an independent random walk (x_t). Since these variables are not cointegrated, the residuals are I(1) and this results in low values of Durbin-Watson statistics.

3 This means that the variables under investigation are integrated of order one and are denoted as I(1).

4 As noted in Chapter III, the black market came into prominence in the early 1980's and its development has been closely associated with the political and economic policy instability that prevailed in the 1980's in El Salvador.

2. *Data and Econometric Methodology*

a. Data

The theoretical models of black market exchange rate determination presented in Chapter IV were tested using monthly data for El Salvador from October 1982 to May 1990 (Culbertson, 1975 and 1989, and Dornbusch et al., 1983) and from October 1982 to July 1989 (Blejer, 1978, and Gupta, 1980). The reason for using a shorter period for the latter models is the availability of monthly data for gross domestic product at constant prices, which is included in those models. The data for all variables of El Salvador's economy were obtained from the Central Reserve Bank of El Salvador. The data for other countries were taken from the IMF's *International Financial Statistics*.

The dependent variable (*be*) is expressed as the price of one U.S. dollar in terms of colones in the black market or the black market premium (x), which is defined as the black market rate divided by the volume-trade-weighted average of the officially established exchange rate (e).[5] Thus, e is the volume-trade-weighted average of the Central Reserve Bank exchange rate (e_{CB}) and the legal parallel market rate (e_{LP}):

$$e = w_{CB}\, e_{CB} + w_{LP}\, e_{LP}$$

w_{CB} is the proportion of transactions officially assigned to the Central Reserve Bank's market.

w_{LP} is the proportion of transactions officially assigned to the parallel market.

During the period of uniform official fixed exchange rate regime (from January 1986 to June 1989) w_{LP} equals zero, thus $e = e_{CB}$.

The reasons for considering a weighted average of both exchange rates as a proxy of the official exchange rate are the following:

1. During the periods of dual official regime (from August 1982 to January 1986 and from July 1989 to May 1990) both exchange rates (the central bank rate and the parallel market rate) were determined by the authorities and rationing of foreign exchange was implemented in both markets (see Chapter III). This was especially true during the first occasion of the dual exchange rate regime, namely from August 1982 to January 1986.

2. The adoption of dual exchange rate regime had as an objective to implement a gradual devaluation of the official exchange rate through transferring transactions from the official to the legal parallel market.

---

5 This is actually one plus the premium.

3. In many cases, proportions of exports (imports) of the same product were officially assigned to both markets and these proportions changed over time (from August 1982 to January 1986).[6] Therefore, it is more appropriate to use a weighted average of both exchange rates as a proxy of the official exchange rate, i.e., the exchange rate applied to transactions that took place through official channels.

The ratio of domestic to foreign prices is the ratio of El Salvador's consumer price index (*P*) to a trade-weighted average of the same index of El Salvador's major trade partners outside the Central American Common Market (P^*).[7] As a measure of international reserves held by the government, the Central Reserve Bank Net International Reserve (*IR*) was used.

As a measure of real income, the gross domestic product at constant (1962) prices was also used. Since monthly GDP figures were not available, they were estimated from the quarterly figures, using a geometric interpolation available in the *AREMOS* program of the Wharton Econometrics. Both narrow money (*M1*) and broad money (*M2*) were used as a measure of money supply (M_s).

The real effective exchange rate is calculated as in Appendix V.1. The domestic interest rate (i) is the 180-day commercial bank time deposit rate. The foreign interest rate (i^*) is the U.S. Treasury bill rate. The definitions of the variables and source of the data used in the estimation of the various empirical models of this chapter are reported in detail in Appendix V.1.

b. Testing for Stationarity

Tests for unit roots were performed on all data using the augmented Dickey-Fuller (ADF) test with three lagged differences. The tests were performed in levels and first differences under three different assumptions of the test equation from the most restrictive to the least restrictive (Table V.1). The first column of Table V.1 reports tests of the stationarity of the time-series under investigation about zero mean (t_o), the second column assumes nonzero mean (t_μ), and the third column assumes nonzero mean and a deterministic time trend (t_τ). Critical values of the test statistic are reported at the bottom of Table V.1. The null hypothesis is that the variable under investigation has a unit root, against the alternative that it does not. The reported test statistics indicate that the null hypothesis cannot be rejected for any variables in levels, except for the black market premium and the money supply defined as *M1*.

---

6 See Chapter III.

7 El Salvador's major trading partners outside the Central American Common Market included are the United States, Germany, and Japan.

TABLE V.1

Augmented Dickey-Fuller Test for a Unit Root

	t_o	t_μ	t_τ
VARIABLE	3 lags	3 lags	3 lags
In level (logarithm)			
Log *be*	0.779	-1.266	-2.684
Log *x*	-1.827	-2.343	-3.878*
Log *e*	2.885	0.261	-1.384
Log *P*	3.240	0.592	-2.478
Log P_T	2.698	-0.177	-1.982
Log P_N	3.240	0.592	-2.478
Log *M1*	1.736	-0.620	-3.497*
Log *M2*	3.304	-0.627	-1.837
Log *X*	2.519	0.906	-1.301
IR	0.480	-0.910	-2.368
i	1.410	-0.183	-2.346
Log *Y*	0.095	-3.896	-5.953
Log *r*	-0.463	-1.186	-1.383
Log P_{us}	1.737	0.365	-0.873
*i**	-0.298	-1.344	-1.518
Log *P**	5.320	0.891	-0.964
Log *Pco*	-0.666	-1.544	-2.537
In first differences			
dLog *be*	-3.623**	-3.757**	-3.758*
dLog *x*	-4.100**	-4.135**	-4.109**
dLog *e*	-3.738**	-4.886**	-4.908**
dLog *P*	-0.994	-3.153*	-3.208
dLog P_T	-3.260**	-4.334**	-4.309**
dLog P_N	-0.994	-3.153*	-3.208
dLog *M1*	-5.953**	-6.328**	-6.320**
dLog *M2*	-3.716**	-5.251*	-5.191**
dLog *X*	-4.845**	-5.626**	-6.045**
d*IR*	-5.337**	-5.639**	-5.593**
d*i*	-4.610**	-4.861**	-4.949**
dLog *Y*	-4.879**	-4.840**	-4.809**
dLog *r*	-4.802**	-4.834**	-4.821**
dLog P_{us}	-3.421**	-3.834**	-4.043*
d*i**	-4.558**	-4.545**	-4.544**
dlog *P**	-4.725**	-8.262**	-9.182**
dLog *Pco*	-4.638**	-4.674**	-4.758**

Numbers of observatios: 90

** Indicate statistically significant at the 1 percent level

* Indicate statistically significant at the 5 percent level

Critical values

	t_o	t_μ	t_τ
1 percent	-2.589	-3.504	-4.063
5 percent	-1.944	-2.894	-3.460
10 percent	-1.618	-2.584	-3.240

Table V.1 also reports results for the augmented Dickey-Fuller test on first differences of the variables. The null hypothesis of the unit root is rejected for all of the time series using differenced data. This indicates that individual time series are I(1).

C. Application of the Theoretical Models of Black Market Exchange Rate Determination to the Case of El Salvador

1. Empirical Specification

Error correction models have become very popular in recent years and they have been proposed as a very convenient specification of stable relationships of non-stationary variables.[8] The error correction representation of the black market exchange rate models of Table IV.1 can be written as in Box V.1.

Box V.1. Error Correction Representation of Models of Table IV.1

Culbertson Model

$$\Delta be_t = a_0 + a_1\, be_{t-1} + a_2\, e_{t-1} + a_3\, \Delta\, e_t + a_4\, (P/P^*)_{t-1} + a_5\, \Delta\, (P/P^*)_t + a_6\, IR_{t-1} + a_7\, \Delta\, IR_t$$

Blejer Model

$$\Delta be_t = a_0 + a_1\, be_{t-1} + a_2\, (CBDC - M_d)_{t-1} + a_3\, \Delta\, (CBDC - M_d)_t + a_4\, P^*_{t-1} + a_5\, \Delta\, P^*_t$$

Gupta Model

$$\Delta be_t = a_0 + a_1\, be_{t-1} + a_2\, e_{t-1} + a_3\, \Delta\, e_t + a_4\, M_{St-1} + a_5\, \Delta\, M_{St} + a_6\, P^*_{t-1} + a_7\, \Delta\, P_t^* + a_8\, i_{t-1} + a_9\, \Delta\, i_t + a_{10}\, Y_{t-1} + a_{11}\, \Delta\, Y_t$$

Dornbusch et al. Model

$$\Delta be_t = a_0 + a_1\, be_{t-1} + a_2\, r_{t-1} + a_3\, \Delta\, r_t + a_4\, (i^* + d - i)_{t-1} + a_5\, \Delta\, (i^* + d - i)_t + a_6\, DUCR$$

where the symbol Δ denotes a first difference of a variable.

8 Engle and Granger (1987). See also the papers collected in Engle and Granger (1991).

2. Estimation Results

The error correction parameter estimates for the four models of the black market exchange rate determination are presented in Table V.2a. However, significant support for the use of an ECM specification was not found.[9] If cointegration is rejected, the data do not support the existence of stable long-run relationships between the variables. This means that *be* is weakly exogenous (in the statistical sense).[10] Moreover, in the Dornbusch model the error correction term is positive, which means that the estimated equation is dynamically unstable.

Additionally, since most short-run coefficients were not statistically significant, a reduced form of ECMs without contemporaneous differences was estimated (Table V.2b), but again cointegration was rejected.[11] Thus, it seems to be that none of the theoretical models of the black market for foreign exchange is entirely satisfactory in the empirical test.

Under these circumstances, the models were reestimated in first differences, even though this loses valuable long-run information in the data. However, this is valid in the case presented here, not only because cointegration was rejected, but also because one of the purposes of this section is to find out particularly the determinants of the black market premium, which was found to be a stationary variable. Since a stationary variable cannot be combined with nonstationary variables, then the equations are more adequately represented by first differences.

Tables V.3 to V.6 summarize the ordinary least squares estimates for the four models of the black market exchange rate. The models were estimated using both the level of the black market exchange rate (*be*) and the premium (*be/e*) as dependent variables and for two different functional forms. In the following the estimation results of each model will be commented upon briefly.

a. The Culbertson Model

The regression results based on the model reported in Table IV.1 showed some degree of autocorrelation, even though in the first differences functional form as indicated by the Durbin Watson statistic. The serial correlation might be ac-

9 According to the critical values in Banerjee, Dolado, and Mestre (1992), which are reported at the bottom of Table V.2a.

10 On weak exogeneity in ECMs, see Urbain (1993). Also see Hansen (1993) for a review of the main concepts.

11 Note, however, that a failure to find cointegration does not necessarily mean that there is no stable long-run relationship between the variables. It only suggests that there is no stable, long-run linear relationship between them.

counted for by the exclusion of some potentially significant variables or the inclusion of irrelevant variables. To correct this problem without changing the theoretical specification of the model, a lagged dependent variable is included. The corrected results are presented in Table V.3.

The response of the black market rate with respect to the official exchange rate is positive, implying that a devaluation of the official rate leads to a depreciation of the black market exchange rate.

The coefficient of the purchasing power variable has the expected positive sign, but it is statistically not significant.

Contrary to Culbertson's assumption, the sign of the coefficient of the black market exchange rate with respect to official reserves is negative and the size of the coefficient is very small as in the ECM specification, but here it is statistically not significant. As is discussed in this chapter further on, this could be explained by the fact that the Central Reserve Bank of El Salvador intervened in the official foreign exchange market to stabilize the black market. Thus, when official reserves increased, the Central Reserve Bank provided more of the demanded foreign exchange, which reduced the demand on the black market and therefore the black market exchange rate.

b. Blejer Model

Table V.4 reports the results for Blejer's model, suggesting that monetary factors were not very important in determining the movements of the black market exchange rate. The coefficient of the variable representing an excess supply of money – measured as the difference between the central bank domestic credit expansion (*CBDC*) and the increase in the demand for real cash balances (M_d)[12] – is only weakly significant when the dependent variable is the black market exchange rate. The coefficient of the world inflation rate variable (P^*) has the expected sign in most functional forms, but it is not statistically significant.

12 The equation of demand for real cash balances used in this model is presented in Appendix V.1.

TABLE V.2a

Parameter Estimates of the Error Correction Models

Method: OLS

Dependent Variable: Black Market Exchange Rate (d Log *be*)

Culbertson Model 1982:09 - 1990:05 Number of observations: 93		
Explanatory variables	Coefficients	t-statistics
constant	0.0178	0.267
Log (be_{t-1})	-0.123	-2.566*
Log (e_{t-1})	0.148	1.817
Log (P/P^*)	0.017	0.473
IR_{t-1}	-0.00006	-2.831
dLog (e)	0.274	1.795
dLog (P/P^*)	0.492	1.303
d (IR)	-0.0003	-1.032
R^2 = 0.161 Adj. R^2 = 0.092	Std. error of regression: 0.039 F-statistic: 2.331	D-W: 1.425
Blejer Model 1982:10 - 1989:07 Number of observations: 82		
Explanatory variables	Coefficients	t-statistics
constant	-1.470	-2.093
Log (be_{t-1})	-0.084	-2.197*
Log $(CBDC-M_d)_{t-1}$	0.108	1.809
Log (P^*_{t-1})	0.169	1.402
dLog ($CBDC - M_d$)	0.100	1.254
dLog (P^*)	-0.342	-0.482
R^2 = 0.090 Adj. R^2 = 0.030	Std. error of regression: 0.041 F-statistic: 1.498	D-W: 1.317

TABLE V.2a (continued)

Parameter Estimates of the Error Correction Model

Method: OLS

Dependent Variable: Black Market Exchange Rate (dLog *be*)

Gupta Model
1982:09 - 1989:07
Number of observations: 83

Explanatory variables	Coefficients	t-statistics
constant	1.120	0.931
Log be_{t-1}	-0.136	-2.633*
Log e_{t-1}	0.160	1.904
Log M_{St-1}	0.168	2.077
Log P^*_{t-1}	-0.289	-1.069
Log Y_{t-1}	-0.076	-0.626
i_{t-1}	-0.044	-3.629
dLog e	0.305	1.867
dLog M_S	0.008	0.0933
dLog P^*	-0.423	-0.606
dLog Y	-0.133	-0.933
d i	-0.050	-2.694

R^2 = 0.258 Std. error of regression: 0.038 D-W: 1.543
Adj. R^2 = 0.143 F-statistic: 2.244

Dornbusch Model
1982:09 - 1990:05
Number of observations: 93

Explanatory variables	Coefficients	t-statistics
constant	-0.083	-4.480
Log be_{t-1}	0.072	5.983*
Log (r_{t-1})	-0.041	-2.869
$(i^* + d - i)_{t-1}$	0.008	16.020
dlog r	-0.066	1.133
dLog $(i^* + d - i)$	-0.0007	-1.513
DUCR	-0.003	-0.611

R^2 = 0.845 Std. error of regression: 0.017 D-W: 0.409
Adj. R^2 = 0.834 F-statistic: 78.29

*t - test on ECM

Critical values of t-ratio ECM Test (in Banerjee, Dolado, and Mestre, 1992)

k	5 percent	10 percent
(2)	-3.03	-2.68
(3)	-3.36	-3.01
(4)	-3.63	-3.26
(5)	-3.87	-3.50

----

k denotes the number of exogenous regressors.

TABLE V.2b

Parameter Estimates of the Reduced Form of ECMs

Method: OLS

Dependent Variable: Black Market Exchange Rate (d Log *be*)

Culbertson Model

1982:09 - 1990:05

Number of observations: 93

Explanatory variables	Coefficients	t-statistics
constant	-0.003	-0.054
Log (be_{t-1})	-0.095	-2.009*
Log (e_{t-1})	0.136	1.742
Log (P/P^*)	0.017	0.479
IR_{t-1}	-0.00006	-2.994

$R^2 = 0.104$ Std. error of regression: 0.040 D-W: 1.371

Adj. $R^2 = 0.064$ F-statistic: 2.567

Blejer Model

1982:10 - 1989:07

Number of observations: 82

Explanatory variables	Coefficients	t-statistics
constant	-1.285	-1.954
Log (be_{t-1})	-0.084	-2.191*
Log $(CBDC-M_d)_{t-1}$	0.081	1.483
Log (P^*_{t-1})	0.174	1.481

$R^2 = 0.068$ Std. error of regression: 0.040 D-W: 1.352

Adj. $R^2 = 0.032$ F-statistic: 1.917

TABLE V.2b (continued)

Parameter Estimates of the Reduced Form of ECMs

Method: OLS

Dependent Variable: Black Market Exchange Rate (dLog *be*)

Gupta Model 1982:09 - 1989:07 Number of observations: 83		
Explanatory variables	Coefficients	t-statistics
constant	0.036	0.032
Log be_{t-1}	-0.118	-2.326*
Log e_{t-1}	0.093	1.114
Log M_{St-1}	0.110	1.595
Log P^*_{t-1}	-0.050	-1.099
Log Y_{t-1}	-0.025	-0.243
i_{t-1}	-0.031	-2.682
$R^2 = 0.137$ Adj. $R^2 = 0.070$	Std. error of regression: 0.0396 F-statistic: 2.035	D-W: 1.529
Dornbusch Model 1982:09 - 1990:05 Number of observations: 93		
Explanatory variables	Coefficients	t-statistics
constant	-0.090	-4.480
Log be_{t-1}	0.078	6.929*
Log (r_{t-1})	-0.038	-2.623
$(i^* + d - i)_{t-1}$	0.008	20.264
DUCR	-0.003	-0.561
$R^2 = 0.838$ Adj. $R^2 = 0.831$	Std. error of regression: 0.017 F-statistic: 114.20	D-W: 0.478

*t - tyåt on ECM

Critical values of t-ratio ECM Test (in Banerjee, Dolado, and Mestre, 1992)

k	5 percent	10 percent
(2)	-3.03	-2.68
(3)	-3.36	-3.01
(4)	-3.63	-3.26
(5)	-3.87	-3.50

----

k denotes the number of exogenous regressors.

TABLE V.3

Culbertson Model: OLS Estimates

1982:10 - 1990:05

Number of Observations 92

DEPENDENT VARIABLE	*be*	
EXPLANATORY VARIABLES	First diff. log	First diff.
Constant	0.004 (0.545)	0.0084 (0.237)
e	0.198 (1.426)	0.279 (1.520)
*P/P**	0.167 (0.476)	0.294 (0.303)
IR	-0.00001 (0.693)	-0.00003 (0.1724)
be_{t-1}	0.312 (3.067)	0.272 (2.602)
Statistics		
R^2	0.148	0.127
Adj. R^2	0.109	0.086
Std. error	0.039	0.242
Durbin-h	1.19	
DEPENDENT VARIABLE	*x: be/e*	
Constant	0.006 (0.751)	0.001 (0.137)
e	-0.749 (5.349)	-0.174 (3.849)
*P/P**	0.244 (0.686)	0.154 (0.634)
IR	-0.00001 (0.6782)	0.00001 (0.2427)
x_{t-1}	0.220 (2.401)	0.209 (2.111)
Statistics		
R^2	0.285	0.190
Adj. R^2	0.252	0.153
Std. error	0.039	0.061
Durbin-h	1.93	1.66

Numbers in parentheses are t-statistics.

c. Gupta Model

Tables V.5a and V.5b report the results for Gupta's model. Some estimated coefficients have the expected sign, but they are not statistically significant. Only the coefficient of the interest rate is statistically significant. The coefficient of the official exchange rate is only weakly statistically significant and is positively related to the black market rate. That is, a nominal devaluation of the official exchange rate will depreciate the black market rate. This is contrary to the Gupta conclusions, but confirms the result obtained in the estimation of the Culbertson model. This implies that a nominal devaluation of the official exchange rate will reduce the supply in the black market in a greater proportion than the reduction on demand for foreign exchange in that market. This can be explained by the fact that in El Salvador strict exchange controls existed, especially on capital account transactions, and some imports were also prohibited. This means that even if the Central Bank increased its ability to supply all the foreign exchange demanded, they did not provide foreign exchange for importing certain prohibited items and for international capital market transactions. In other words, certain foreign exchange had to be obtained in the black market. When the premium is the dependent variable, the coefficient is obviously negative, because an increase in the official exchange rate will reduce the premium but not necessarily the level of the black market rate.

The coefficient of the black market rate with respect to the interest rate is statistically significant but, contrary to Gupta's theoretical assumptions and empirical results, an increase in the domestic interest rate will cause the black market rate to appreciate.

d. The Dornbusch et al. Asset Price Model

Table V.6 presents the empirical results based on the model of Dornbusch et al. (1983). Most estimated coefficients have the expected sign and they are statistically significant. The exception is the official real exchange rate coefficient when the dependent variable is the black market exchange rate. But when the dependent variable is the black market premium, also this coefficient has the expected sign and is statistically significant. The negative sign of the coefficient of the real exchange rate implies that a real depreciation of the official rate or an increase in (*r*) leads to a decline in the black market premium.

TABLE V.4

Blejer Model: OLS Estimates

1982:10 - 1989:07

Number of observations: 92

DEPENDENT VARIABLE	*be*	
EXPLANATORY VARIABLES	First diff. log	First diff.
Constant	0.0071	0.0340
	(1.1235)	(0.8900)
$CBDC\text{-}M_d$	0.1009	0.0003
	(1.5158)	(1.6554)
P^*	0.5313	-0.0225
	(1.0492)	(0.7399)
Statistics		
R^2	0.160	0.134
Adj. R^2	0.128	0.101
Std. error	0.039	0.236
F-statistic	4.969	4.017
D-W	2.055	2.107
DEPENDENT VARIABLE	*x: be/e*	
EXPLANATORY VARIABLES	First diff. log	First diff.
Constant	-0.0034	0.0039
	(0.4980)	(0.3887)
$CBDC\text{-}M_d$	0.0466	0.0001
	(0.5584)	(0.7740)
P^*	-0.2598	-0.0044
	(0.3739)	(0.4518)
Statistics		
R^2	0.057	0.057
Adj. R^2	0.020	0.020
Std. error	0.047	0.068
F-statistic	1.559	1.558
D-W	1.904	1.980

Numbers in parentheses are t-statistics.

TABLE V.5a

Gupta Model: OLS Estimates

1982:10 - 1989:07

Number of observations: 82

DEPENDENT VARIABLE	*be*	
EXPLANATORY VARIABLES	First diff. log	First diff.
Constant	0.0928 (1.6728)	0.0273 (0.8868)
e	0.1943 (1.2246)	0.3409 (1.6039)
Ms	-0.0424 (0.5420)	-0.0002 (1.0420)
*P**	-0.2656 (0.3659)	0.0026 (0.0614)
i	-0.0073 (1.5882)	-0.2657 (1.9743)
Y	-0.1733 (1.2627)	-0.0016 (0.5024)
Statistics		
R^2	0.071	0.075
Adj. R^2	0.010	0.014
Std. error	0.041	0.247
F-statistic	1.157	1.226
D-W	1.439	1.530

Numbers in parentheses are t-statistics.

TABLE V.5b
Gupta Model: OLS Estimates
1982:10 - 1989:07
Number of observations: 82

DEPENDENT VARIABLE	*x: bele*	
EXPLANATORY VARIABLES	First diff. log	First diff.
Constant	0.1137 (3.1890)	0.0066 (0.7135)
e	-0.8782 (5.7854)	-0.1953 (3.7173)
Ms	0.0207 (0.3105)	-0.00002 (0.34917)
*P**	-0.5411 (1.0081)	-0.0049 (0.5278)
i	-0.0089 (2.9937)	-0.0647 (1.994)
Y	-0.1162 (0.8785)	-0.0006 (0.7387)
Statistics		
R^2	0.366	0.279
Adj. R^2	0.315	0.221
Std. error	0.039	0.061
F-statistic	7.210	4.839
D-W	2.066	1.893

Numbers in parentheses are t-statistics.

TABLE V.6
The Dornbusch et al. Asset Price Model
1982:10 - 1990:05
Number of observations: 92

DEPENDENT VARIABLE	*be*	
EXPLANATORY VARIABLES	First diff. log	First diff.
Constant	0.0221	0.1212
	(3.9060)	(3.5032)
r	0.1306	0.9554
	(0.9934)	(0.9953)
i + d - i*	0.0023	0.0116
	(2.7864)	(2.3192)
DUCR	-0.0244	-0.1462
	(2.2886)	(2.2013)
<u>Statistics</u>		
R^2	0.151	0.127
Adj. R^2	0.123	0.097
Std. error	0.038	0.240
F-statistic	5.234	4.300
D-W	1.740	1.745
DEPENDENT VARIABLE	*x: bele*	
EXPLANATORY VARIABLES		
Constant	0.0095	0.0140
	(1.7400)	(1.6878)
r	-0.7450	-1.1202
	(5.7363)	(4.8813)
i + d - i*	0.0024	0.0033
	(3.0666)	(2.7433)
DUCR	-0.0197	-0.0306
	(1.8758)	(1.9266)
<u>Statistics</u>		
R^2	0.322	0.262
Adj. R^2	0.299	0.237
Std. error	0.038	0.057
F-statistic	14.059	10.537
D-W	1.844	1.873

Numbers in parentheses are t-statistics.

The coefficient of depreciation-adjusted interest rate differential (i^*+d-i)[13] has the correct sign and is statistically significant at the 1 percent significance level in most functional forms. An increase in the U.S. interest rate relative to domestic rate will increase the premium in the black market.

The seasonal dummy variable (*DUCR*) attempts to capture the effect of high inflows of remittances on the premium during Christmas time. This variable takes the value of 1 in November-December and 0 during the rest of the year. The estimated coefficient is statistically significant in most functional forms and suggests that seasonal factors, which affect the supply of dollars in the black market, also influence the premium.

3. Some Concluding Remarks

Before concluding this section, it would be useful to summarize the main findings of the application of the models of black market exchange rate determination advanced in the literature to the case of El Salvador. They are the following:

1. Monetary factors are not significant in explaining the movements of the black market exchange rate. The fact that money supply and central bank credit expansion are not significant in explaining the black market exchange rate movements reflects the fact that the black market in El Salvador was not a free or "clean" float. As long as the Central Reserve Bank intervened in the official market and supplied more foreign exchange at the official rate for current ac-

---

13 The expected rate of depreciation of the black market exchange rate (d) is assumed to be equal to the next period black market exchange rate depreciation (leading values of the black market exchange rate depreciation), which is consistent with perfect foresight assumption. Note that Dornbusch et al. (1983) used in the calculation of the interest rate differential, the rate of depreciation of the official exchange rate (d_o). This is because in Brazil the volume of transactions in the black market is negligible with respect to the total financial market transactions. However, this is inadequate for the case of El Salvador due to the strict exchange controls on international capital market transactions which diverted the portfolio motive demand of foreign exchange from the official market to the black market. On the other hand, other measures of expected exchange rate depreciation were tried, for example, d was considered equal to the observed discrepancy between the PPP nominal exchange rate and the actual black market rate. This assumes that agents form their expectations about future black market exchange rate developments on the basis of information on the behavior of the real exchange rate and that they expect the black market exchange rate to follow the pattern of the PPP exchange rate. However, I found that, using that measure of expected depreciation, the signs of the coefficients and their t-values were very sensitive to the functional form and, in most cases, were not significant and had the wrong sign.

count transactions, importers did not need to buy foreign exchange in the black market, which stabilized the black market exchange rate. Incomplete market separation between markets permitted the intervention of the Central Reserve Bank in the official market to sustain stability in the black market.

2. The significance of portfolio decision variables such as the interest rate differential suggests that black market dollars were at least partly considered an asset.

3. The statistically significant negative relationship between the real official exchange rate and the premium suggests that the official exchange rate policy influences the black market premium and a real devaluation of the official exchange rate may reduce the premium, at least in the short-run.

D. A Model of Black Market Exchange Rate Determination

1. Specification of the Model

In this section an attempt is made to specify a model that explains the determinants of the black market exchange rate premium in El Salvador as well as the effects of changes of the black market exchange rate on prices and on the real exchange rate.

Our model is based mainly on the portfolio balance approach discussed in Chapter IV. This particular analytical framework is considered to be adequate to analyze the black market in El Salvador for the following reasons: First, the black market has existed in El Salvador since 1962 as a result of the implementation of exchange controls. However, the black market came into prominence only in the 1980's when the country faced a serious deficit in the balance-of-payments that resulted from a more basic macroeconomic imbalance and particularly from political and economic policy instability.[14] Under such circumstances, portfolio diversification can be expected to prevail and to represent a key determinant of the demand for foreign exchange in the black market. Second, the portfolio balance approach is particularly adequate for countries that impose restrictions on private capital outflows as has been the case in the 1980's in El Salvador. In these countries, the black market provides the possibility to circumvent regulations and carry out foreign capital market transactions. Third, the empirical evidence presented above suggests that factors related to portfolio decisions are an important determinant of the black market premium.

14 See Chapter III for details of the emergence of the black market in El Salvador.

The model developed here, however, integrates some important aspects of the various analytical approaches discussed in Chapter IV as well as the special features of the black market for foreign currency in El Salvador. The model incorporates expectations of political change and policy reforms and takes into account leakages between the official and the black markets, indirect central bank intervention in the black market, and seasonal inflows of remittances that were the major source of supply in the Salvadorean black market.

Consider a small open economy under a dual regime of official and black markets with two exchange rates: the official exchange rate (*e*),[15] which is fixed or depreciated through transferring transactions from the official to the legal parallel market during the period of the official dual exchange rate regime; and the exchange rate in the black market (*be*), which is determined by supply and demand conditions. Commercial transactions are settled mostly in the central bank and in the legal parallel markets at an average exchange rate of *e*. The rest of the commercial transactions and all private capital transactions are carried out in the black market at the rate *be*.

There are two financial assets available, domestic money that bears interest when it is held in savings account deposits, and black market foreign currency that bears no interest but could be used to buy interest-bearing foreign assets.

The main sources of flow supply of foreign currency are remittances, overinvoicing of imports, and underinvoicing of exports which, in turn, depend on the black market premium, seasonal factors, and official exchange rate policy. The supply function can be expressed as:

$$S_b = a_o + a_1 (be/e) + a_2 r + a_3 DUCR \qquad (1)$$

$$a_1 > 0,\ a_2 < 0,\ a_3 > 0.$$

Where:

S_b: the supply of foreign exchange in the black market.

be/e: the black market premium.

r: the real official exchange rate.

DUCR: dummy variable reflecting the seasonally high inflows of Christmas remittances which takes the value of 1 in November-December and 0 for the rest of the year.

---

15 As noted earlier, *e* is the volume-trade-weighted average of e_{CB}, which is a fixed rate, and of e_{LP}, which is gradually depreciated by the authorities during the period of the official dual exchange rate regime (August 1982 to January 1986 and July 1989 to May 1990); and *e* is equal to the Central Bank exchange rate during the period of the official pegged exchange rate regime (February 1986 to June 1989).

Foreign exchange was demanded in the black market for two purposes: (1) as a medium of exchange for current account transactions (smuggling and for imports which, in principle, were eligible to be imported on the official market(s), but for which no foreign exchange could be obtained at the official rate, or for which the corresponding amount of foreign exchange could only be obtained with a lag of two to three months) and (2) as an asset for hedging against inflation and political and economic instability as well as for buying foreign assets.

The transaction component of foreign currency demand in the black market should be mainly a function of overall economic activity, and the black market premium.

Based on the currency substitution hypothesis, the portfolio component of the demand for foreign currency in the black market is positively related to the expected rate of return of holding foreign assets and negatively related to the expected rate of return of holding domestic currency assets. Thus, the opportunity cost of buying foreign currency in the black market is given by the rate of return on domestic money (i). The demand for foreign exchange in the black market can be expected to be a function of the differential between the expected rates of return of holding domestic and foreign assets ($i - i^* + d$). When this differential is expected to be negative because foreign interest rates increase and/or the expected rate of the depreciation of the black market exchange rate increases, the expected return from holding foreign currency assets rises and agents tend to substitute domestic assets for foreign ones as the opportunity costs of holding domestic money increase. This leads to an increase in the demand for foreign currency in the black market. Expectations of policy reforms also play a key role in determining the demand for foreign currency in the black market.

Taking into account both components, the demand for foreign exchange is assumed, therefore, to be a function of the level of real income, portfolio decision variables such as interest rate differential, expected rate of depreciation of the black market exchange rate, and expectation of changes in economic policy or government reforms.

In addition, the demand for foreign currency in the black market would be influenced by the level of the central bank's international reserves and the rate of growth of the money supply. Since the money supply includes the central bank's international reserves, it is not necessary to include the latter variable in the equation.

$$D_b = d_o + d_1\, be/e + d_2\, Y + d_3\, M_s + d_4\, ird + d_5\, DUP \qquad (2)$$

$$d_1 < 0,\ d_2 > 0,\ d_3 > 0,\ d_4 < 0,\ d_5 > 0.$$

Where

D_b: the demand for foreign exchange in the black market.

Y: the real income.

M_s: money supply.

ird: the depreciation-adjusted interest rate differential, defined as $(i-i^*+d)$, where d in period t is assumed to be equal to black market exchange depreciation in period $t+1$ (leading depreciation of the black market exchange rate).

DUP: dummy variable reflecting the expectations of changes in economic policy or government reforms.

The *DUP* dummy variable is considered necessary in the light of the experience during July-October 1985, when the black market exchange rate rose at rates never observed before as a result of rumors of government policy changes (see Figure III.2 of Chapter III). *DUP* takes the value of 1 in July-October 1985 and of 0 for the rest of the sample period.

In equilibrium, S_b must equal D_b. Setting expression (1) equal to (2) and solving for *be/e*, the premium, yields

$$be/e = a + b_1 Y + b_2 M_s + b_3\, ird + b_4 r + b_5 DUP + b_6 DUCR\,. \qquad (3)$$

The expected signs of the coefficients are:

$b_1 = d_2/(a_1\text{-}d_1) > 0$
$b_2 = d_3/(a_1\text{-}d_1) > 0$
$b_3 = d_4/(a_1\text{-}d_1) < 0$
$b_4 = a_2/(a_1\text{-}d_1) > \text{or} < 0$
$b_5 = d_5/(a_1\text{-}d_1) > 0$
$b_6 = a_3/(a_1\text{-}d_1) < 0$.

Thus, the premium is determined by real income, the central bank indirect intervention, the money supply, portfolio decision variables, expectations, and seasonal factors. An increase in real income, in the foreign interest rate, and in expectations of exchange rate depreciation and changes in economic policy, as well an official exchange rate devaluation may increase the premium.[16] By contrast, the premium will fall with the central bank's selling of foreign exchange at the official rate (indirect official intervention), and with a high seasonal inflow of remittances.

16 The black market premium may also decline with an official devaluation, if the reduction in demand is higher than the reduction in supply in the black market.

The economy produces and consumes two goods: traded and nontraded goods. The domestic price level (P_D) is defined as a geometric average of the prices of the traded goods (P_T) and the nontraded goods (P_N):

$$P_D = P_T^{a} \; P_N^{1-a} . \tag{4a}$$

Equation (4) can be written in logarithmic form:

$$\text{Log } P_D = \text{a Log } P_T + (1\text{-a})\text{Log } P_N , \tag{4b}$$

where P_T is a function of the black market exchange rate (*be*), the official exchange rate (*e*), the price level of El Salvador's major trade partner (P^*), the international prices of coffee (*Pco*), and the international price of oil (*Poil*). Thus,

$$\text{Log } P_T = w_0 + w_1 \text{ Log } be + w_2 \text{ Log } e + w_3 \text{ Log } P^* + w_4 \text{ Log } Pco + w_5 \text{ Log } Poil. \tag{5}$$

The price of nontraded goods P_N is a function of traded goods prices and of variables representing excess demand in the economy (X):[17]

$$\text{Log } P_N = z_0 + z_1 \text{ Log } P_T + z_2 \text{ Log } X \tag{6}$$

This simple model can be written in error correction dynamic specification (Box V.2), which, as noted earlier, has the advantage of modeling both the long-run relationships between the variables and the short-run dynamics.

Box V.2. Error Correction Representation of a Model of Black Exchange Rate

Black Market Exchange Rate Equation

$$\Delta be_t = a + b_1\, be_{t-1} + b_2\, M_{st-1} + b_3\, \Delta M_{st} + b_4\, r_{t-1} + b_5\, \Delta r_t + b_6\, ird_{t-1} + b_7\, \Delta ird_t + b_8\, DUP + b_9\, DUCR + u_t$$

Traded Goods Price Equation

$$\Delta P_{Tt} = w_0 + w_1\, P_{Tt-1} + w_2\, be_{t-1} + w_3\, \Delta be_t + w_4\, e_{t-1} + w_5\, \Delta e_t + w_6\, P^*_{t-1} + w_7\, \Delta P^*_t + w_8\, Pco_{t-1} + w_9\, \Delta Pco_t + u_t$$

Nontraded Goods Price Equation

$$\Delta P_{Nt} = z_0 + z_1\, P_{Nt-1} + z_2\, P_{Tt-1} + z_3\, \Delta P_{Tt} + z_4\, X_{t-1} + z_5\, \Delta X_t + u_t$$

where the symbol Δ denotes a first difference of a variable.

17 At the estimation level, the central bank domestic credit is used as a proxy of X.

Since the black market premium is stationary (Table V.1), in the error correction specification, the black market exchange rate (*be*) is used as the dependent variable in equation (3), in order to use nonstationary variables on both sides of the equation.

2. *Econometric Methodology and Estimation Results*

All variables except the interest rates were transformed by taking natural logarithms, and after a preliminary analysis to establish the order of integration of the data series (see Table V.1), equations (3), (5), and (6) were specified at the estimation level in the following form:

$$dLog(be) = a + b_1 Log(be_{t-1}) + b_2 Log(M_{st-1}) + b_3 dLog(M_s) + b_4 Log(r_{t-1}) + b_5 dLog(r) + b_6 ird_{t-1} + b_7 d(ird) + b_8 DUP + b_9 DUCR + u_t \quad (3a)$$

$$dLog(P_T) = w_0 + w_1 Log(P_{Tt-1}) + w_2 Log(be_{t-1}) + w_3 dLog(be) + w_4 Log(e_{t-1}) + w_5 dLog(e) + w_6 Log(P^*_{t-1}) + w_7 dLog(P^*) + w_8 Log(Pco_{t-1}) + w_9 dLog(Pco) + u_t \quad (5a)$$

$$dLog(P_N) = z_0 + z_1 Log(P_{Nt-1}) + z_2 Log(P_{Tt-1}) + z_3 dLog(P_T) + z_4 Log(X_{t-1}) + z_5 dLog(X) + u_t\,. \quad (6a)$$

At the estimation level it was considered to be preferable to exclude the real income variable for two reasons: First, the coefficient of this variable was not statistically significant. Second, a lack of reliable data on real income was a warning about the dangers of drawing any worthwhile conclusions from these results. As is explained in Appendix V.1, the monthly income data used were interpolated from quarterly data provided by the Central Reserve Bank which they had also interpolated from annual observations.

Equations (3a), (5a), and (6a) were estimated using ordinary least squares (OLS).[18] Table V.7 reports the estimated parameters of the ECM for the period October 1982 to May 1990.

The black market exchange rate equation again appeared not to be a cointegrated relationship and in this case an error correction model may not be the correct specification.

18 Engle and Granger (1987) show that OLS provides consistent estimates of the parameters of ECMs.

TABLE V.7

Parameter Estimates of the Error Correction Model (Method: OLS)

Period 1982:10 - 1990:05

Numbers of observations: 92

Dependent Variable: Black Market Exchange Rate (dLog *be*)		
Explanatory variables	Coefficients	t-statistics
constant	-0.637	-10.243
$\text{Log}(be_{t-1})$	-0.016	-1.013
$\text{Log}(M_{st-1})$	0.084	9.005
$\text{Log}(r_{t-1})$	0.114	4.472
ird_{t-1}	-0.009	-20.583
dLog $M2$	0.096	1.509
dLog r	0.026	0.570
d(ird)	0.0002	0.664
$DUCR$	-0.003	-0.649
DUP	-0.001	-0.163
$R^2 = 0.919$	Std. error of regression: 0.012	D-W: 0.432
Adj. $R^2 = 0.911$	F-statistic: 103.869	

Dependent Variable: Traded Goods Prices (dLog P_T)		
Explanatory variables	Coefficients	t-statistics
constant	-0.998	-1.908
Log $(P_{T\,t-1})$	-0.181	-3.419
Log (be_{t-1})	0.037	1.593
Log (e_{t-1})	0.093	1.994
Log (Pco_{t-1})	0.033	2.856
Log (P^*_{t-1})	0.332	2.630
d Log (be)	0.028	0.509
d Log (e)	0.155	1.966
d Log (Pco)	0.030	0.935
d Log (P^*)	0.083	0.244
$R^2 = 0.311$	Std. error of regression: 0.019	D-W: 2.380
Adj. $R^2 = 0.236$	F-statistic: 4.160	

Dependent Variable: Nontraded Goods Prices (dLog P_N)		
Explanatory variables	Coefficients	t-statistics
constant	-0.458	-3.825
Log $(P_{N\,t-1})$	-0.057	-3.987
Log $(P_{T\,t-1})$	0.073	3.817
Log (X_{t-1})	0.0487	2.937
d Log (P_T)	0.053	1.007
d Log (X)	0.052	1.612
$R^2 = 0.223$	Std. error of regression: 0.010	D-W: 1.870
Adj. $R^2 = 0.177$	F-statistic: 4.869	

Concerning the price equations of traded and nontraded goods, the t-statistic of the lagged dependent variable in both equations provided enough support for being considered cointegrated relationships and therefore for the use of an ECM specification.[19] Although, the contemporaneous differences (the short-run coefficients) did not appear to be statistically significant for most variables.

Under these circumstances, equation (3) was reestimated in first differences logarithmic form,[20] and for those equations, equations (5) and (6), for which cointegration relationships were found, a reduced-form ECM where no contemporaneous differences appear in the model, was estimated (Table V.8).

The parameter estimates of the black market premium equation have, in most cases, the expected signs and are statistically significant. The empirical results show that a real depreciation of the official exchange rate by 1 percent leads to a proportional decline in the premium. This result confirms the theoretical expectations that the black market premium would probably rise in the period preceding the devaluation and then fall when the devaluation had actually taken place. Additionally, the negative sign of the real official exchange rate coefficient may be interpreted to indicate that a depreciation of the official exchange rate may increase official foreign exchange receipts, which in turn may lower the demand for foreign exchange in the black market, leading to a fall in the premium. This implies that the demand of foreign exchange in the black market was not independent of the supply of foreign exchange in the official market.[21]

An important finding is that portfolio decision variables seem to play a significant role in the determination of the black market premium. An increase in the U.S. interest rate relative to that in El Salvador, or an increase in the expected rate of depreciation, as well as an increase in expectations of changes in economic policy or government reforms leads to an increase in the premium.

The dummy variable reflecting the seasonally high inflows for Christmas remittances has the expected sign and is statistically significant. Inflows of remittances increase the supply of foreign exchange leading to an appreciation of the black market exchange rate.

Concerning the money supply, this variable, contrary to the earlier results, is statistically significant, but the coefficient is negative, which is contrary to the

---

19 According to the critical values in Banerjee, Dolado, and Mestre (1992).

20 This is due to the fact that the premium is a stationary variable and the explanatory variables are nonstationary. Since those variables are not cointegrated, the residual would be I(1) and this results in a low value of the Durbin-Watson statistic. Thus, the equation of the black market premium will be more adequately represented by first differences.

21 These empirical results support the intuitive discussion on the leakages between the official and the black markets of Chapter III.

theoretical expectations.[22] This result could have two possible explanations: (1) The hypothesis of indirect official intervention, mentioned above, can be confirmed. Thus, the negative sign could be interpreted to indicate that the monetary authorities reduced the money supply when the premium was high. This suggests a causal relationship going from the exchange rate to the money supply.[23] (2) The money supply (broad money) includes savings and time deposits in colones. Thus, the negative sign could be interpreted as the black market foreign exchange being viewed as a financial asset and considered substitute for domestic currency assets. For example, loss of confidence in domestic currency or fears about inflation led to a decrease in interest-rate bearing domestic currency deposits and to an increase in the demand for foreign currency and, therefore, in the premium in the black market.

Thus, the econometric results of this section confirm the significant role of the real official exchange rate, the adjusted-depreciation interest rate differential, and of the variable reflecting the expectation of changes in economic policy or government reforms in determining the black market premium.

The parameter estimates of the ECM for prices of traded and nontraded goods have the expected sign and they are statistically significant. In some cases, they are statistically significant only according to traditional t-tests, but not according to I(1) criteria. However, if the regressors of interest are weakly exogenous, then traditional t-tests can legitimately be used to test the significance of the ECM parameters. In the specific case of the black market exchange rate variable, the individual t-statistic on the coefficient of the error correction term gives a value of -1.013 and thus the black market exchange rate may be treated as weakly exogenous for the respective parameter within the traded goods price equation.

The long-run elasticities were estimated using the Bewley transform, which implied the reestimation of those equations for which cointegration status was found (5 and 6), by using the instrumental variables method. Instruments used for the estimation are the constant term, the lagged dependent variable, and all explanatory variables.[24]

---

22 There should be a positive relationship between the black market premium and the money stock, as postulated by simple monetarist models (e.g., Blejer, 1978a).

23 See the empirical results using the VAR procedure presented further on in this chapter.

24 For details of this procedure, see Bewley (1979). See also Hansen and Kim (1995) for an empirical application of the Bewley transform.

TABLE V.8

Parameter Estimates of the Black Market Model

Method: OLS

Period 1982:10 - 1990:05

Number of observations: 92

Black Market Premium Equation

dLog(x) =	0.016 -	1.074 dLog(r) -	0.667 dLog(Ms) -	0.003 $(i-i^* + d)$
	(2.937)	(11.812)	(4.856)	(4.672)
	-0.009 $DUCR$ + 0.044 DUP			
	(1.961) (3.199)			

R^2	0.648	Std. error	0.028	D-W	1.974
Adj. R^2	0.622	F-statistic	25.724	ρ	0.256

Traded Goods Prices Equation

dLog P_T =	-1.334 +	0.199 Log(P_{Tt-1})	+0.051 Log(be_{t-1}) +	
	(-2.711)	(-3.974)	(2.394)	
	0.420 Log(P^*_{t-1}) +	0.083 Log(e_{t-1})	+ 0.034 Log(Pco_{t-1})	
	(3.565)	(1.848)	(3.092)	

R^2	0.270	Std. error	0.019	D-W	2.239
Adj. R^2	0.229	F-statistic	6.452		

Nontraded Goods Prices Equation

dLog P_N =	-0.449 +	-0.054 Log(P_{Nt-1}) +	0.069 Log(P_{Tt-1}) +	0.048 Log X
	(-3.863)	(3.841)	(3.599)	(3.045)

R^2	0.192	Std. error	0.010	D-W	1.826
Adj. R^2	0.164	F-statistic	6.876		

Domestic Price Level Equation

$$P_D = 0.587\ P_N + 0.413\ P_T$$

VARIABLES

Dependent Variables

be = Black market rate or

x = Black market premium (*be/e*)

Explanatory Variables

e = Official exchange rate

P_D = Domestic prices

P^* = Foreign prices

P_T = Price of traded goods

Pco = International price of coffee

r = Real official exchange rate

ird = Depreciation-adjusted interest rate differential, defined as $(i-i^*+d)$

X = Central bank domestic credit

DUCR = Dummy variable reflecting the seasonally high inflows for Christmas remittances

DUP = Dummy variable reflecting changes in economic policy or government reforms

P_N = Price of nontraded goods

Ms = Money supply (M2)

Log = Natural logarithms

dLog = First differences logarithms

The estimated long-run elasticities of prices using the Bewley transform are reported in Table V.9. The elasticity of the traded goods prices with respect to black market exchange rate is positive and statistically significant, suggesting that an increase in the black market rate will increase the internal price of traded goods, which in turn increases the price of nontraded goods. The long-run elasticity is 0.254. The black market exchange rate elasticity of traded goods prices is rather small, suggesting that the dual official-black market system provides some insulation, at least in the short run. However, this interpretation could be misleading for two reasons: first, exchange rates typically adjust faster than prices; thus, even if the effect were large, this might take several months to be fully reflected in domestic prices;[25] and second, the coefficient may underestimate the true coefficient owing to the price controls implemented in El Salvador during the black market period.

The official exchange rate coefficient is also statistically significant and its effect on prices is higher than the black market exchange rate effect. The long-run official exchange rate elasticity of traded goods prices is 0.418.

TABLE V.9

Estimated Long-Run Elasticities of Prices of Traded and Nontraded Goods

Method: Bewley Transform Using Instrumental Variables

Traded Goods Prices		
Variables	Elasticities	t-statistics
constant	-6.684	-2.438
be	0.254	1.860
e	0.418	2.804
Pco	0.172	2.853
P^*	2.104	3.712
Nontraded Goods Prices		
Variables	Elasticities	t-statistics
constant	-8.367	-7.170
P_T	1.285	7.423
X	0.901	4.067

The elasticity of nontraded goods prices to the price of traded goods is higher than 1, which could be taken as an indication that anything that increases the prices of traded goods will increase the prices of nontraded goods more than

25 The evidence of section E indicates that the response of domestic prices to shocks in the black market exchange is increasingly higher over time.

proportionally. An official exchange rate devaluation, for example, would lead to a real exchange rate appreciation over time because the price of nontraded goods increases more than proportionally with an increase in the price of traded goods.

The long-run elasticity of the price of nontraded goods with respect to the central bank domestic credit suggests that an increase in domestic credit leads to an increase in the price of nontraded goods. A 1 percent increase in the central bank domestic credit leads to a 0.901 percent increase in nontraded goods prices in the long run.

To conclude, the black market premium was mainly determined by the Central Bank (indirect intervention) and official exchange rate policy as well as by portfolio decision variables such as interest rate differentials and expectations concerning exchange rate depreciation and economic policy developments.

The empirical evidence also indicates that the dual official-black market exchange rate regime provides only partial insulation of domestic prices from exchange rate movements.

E. Additional Empirical Evidence: Time-Series Analysis

In this section, evidence is provided on the black market exchange rate dynamic interrelationships with other Salvadorean and foreign macroeconomic variables, using an alternative method of empirical analysis not based on explicit economic theory. This method is the so-called vector autoregressive analysis (VAR), which allows the data to interrelate without imposing prior restrictions. In this way, the method permits to learn more about the historical dynamics of the relationships among the variables under study.[26]

The empirical results are based on the dynamic relationships of seven variables, five domestic macroeconomic variables and two foreign variables. The domestic variables explained by the model are the black market exchange rate (*be*), the official exchange rate (*e*), the El Salvador consumer price index (*P*), the money supply (measured as *M1* or as *M2*) and the domestic time deposit interest rate (*i*). The corresponding foreign variables are the U.S. wholesale price index (*Pus*) and U.S. Treasury bill rate (*i**). These two variables are considered as exogenously determined and not influenced by the Salvadorean variables. The domestic variables chosen characterize the foreign exchange market and mone-

26 For details on VAR methodology, see, for instance, Sims (1980), Sargent (1979), Hamilton (1994). See also Genberg and Swoboda (1985) for an empirical application of VAR procedure.

tary conditions of the Salvadorean economy. The foreign variables were chosen to represent external shocks facing the El Salvador economy.

If these variables are cointegrated, then a VAR model in vector autoregressive error correction form (VEC) can be used. The vector error correction model is a restricted VAR designed for use with nonstationary series that are known to be cointegrated. The difference is that the VEC specification restricts the long-run behavior of the endogenous variables to converge to their cointegrating relationship(s) while allowing a wide range of short-run dynamics.[27] By contrast, an unrestricted VAR does not impose cointegration on its variables.

1. Testing for Cointegration

Tests for unit roots are performed on univariate time series. In contrast, cointegration deals with the relationships within a group of variables, where each has a unit root.

To test for cointegration among endogenous variables the Johansen procedure (Johansen, 1991) was run, which is available in the *Econometric Views* program. The Johansen tests can determine the number of cointegrating equations. This number is called the *cointegrating rank.* The Johansen test depends on the trend characteristics of the data and on the number of lags. Concerning the trend characteristics of the data, the *Econometric Views* program has five possibilities available, but only two possibilities are considered here: (a) The data have means and linear deterministic trends and the cointegrating equations have intercepts but no trend. (b) The data have means but no deterministic trend and there are no intercepts or trends in the cointegrating equations. These choices were based on the proposition that long-run equilibrium relationships probably do not have trends. The tests indicate two cointegrating equations at the 5 percent significance level under assumption (a): Table V.10a. By contrast, under a more restrictive assumption (b), the test reports only one cointegrating equation (Table V.10b).

In the present case, when the cointegrating rank is neither zero nor *n*, a cointegration method, specifically a VEC in level rather than a VAR, is the appropriate estimation strategy. Although an unrestricted VAR in levels of the variables does not imply misspecification but involves a loss of efficiency because some important constraints are omitted, namely, the long-run relationship(s).[28]

---

27 *Econometric Views* manual, p. 136.

28 See, for example, Engle and Granger (1987) and Campbell and Perron (1991).

TABLE V.10a

Johansen Cointegration Test

Eigenvalue	Likelihood Ratio	5 Percent Critical Value	1 Percent Critical Value
0.4189	100.02	68.52	76.07
0.2590	52.80	47.21	54.46
0.1855	26.72	29.68	35.65
0.0839	8.87	15.41	20.04
0.0142	1.24	3.76	6.65

Test assumption: The data have a linear deterministic trend and there are intercepts but no trend in the cointegrating equations.
Test indicates two cointegrating equations at the 5 percent significance level.

TABLE V.10b

Johansen Cointegration Test

Eigenvalue	Likelihood Ratio	5 Percent Critical Value	1 Percent Critical Value
0.3188	69.49	59.46	66.52
0.2197	36.09	39.89	45.58
0.0844	14.51	24.31	29.75
0.0756	6.84	12.53	16.31

Test assumption: The data have no deterministic trend and there are no intercepts or trend in the cointegrating equations.
Test indicates one cointegrating equation at the 1 percent significance level.

2. Estimation Results

In order to impose cointegration on the endogenous variables, a Vector Error Correction (VEC) model was set up for the Salvadorean variables and the foreign variables which are assumed exogenous were excluded.[29] The estimates of the vector error correction model are based on the same assumptions that (a) and (b) used in the Johansen's test.

The VEC equations were estimated using monthly data from August 1982 to May 1990 which provide 87 observations for each series. Each equation included four lagged values of each variable (lags one through three and a single lag at six). The lag selection was made using the Akaike information criterion (AIC) and Schwartz criterion as a guide. All variables except the interest rate variable were transformed by taking natural logarithms.

---

29 Exogenous variables, other than an intercept or trend, are not allowed in the VEC procedure of the *Econometric Views* program (see manual, p. 136).

If there is more than one cointegrating equation, the results are difficult to interpret because this means that there is not a unique long-run relationship. In Appendix V.2 the error correction estimates are reported.

Instead, this section concentrates on the analysis of the impulse response functions and variance decomposition of the VEC system.

As VAR models, VEC representation models can provide answers to two broad questions. First, how do the variables respond dynamically to specific exogenous shocks? Does the black market exchange rate respond to an exogenous change in the official exchange rate (e.g., a devaluation)? Do prices respond to exchange rate changes? Do money supply changes influence the behavior of prices and the exchange rate? Or rather, are money supply changes the response to price and exchange rate movements? Second, what are the important sources of fluctuations in the variables under study? Are fluctuations in prices largely the result of exchange rates shocks? Or do their own shocks play a dominant role?

The first question – the dynamic response of the variables to exogenous shocks – is answered by the moving average representation of a VEC model and its associated impulse response functions. The second question – concerning the relative importance of different sources of fluctuations in the variables – can be answered using the decomposition of forecast error variance.[30]

Tables V.11 and V.12 present the impulse response functions and the decomposition of forecast error variance for each of the five variables. For a given forecast horizon (say, 12 months) and for a given variable (say, *be*), the coefficients in Tables V.11a and V.11b measure the response of the black market exchange rate to exogenous changes in *be*, *e*, *P*, *M2*, and *i*; while Tables V.12a and V.12b present the percentage of the expected squared prediction error of a variable (say, *be*) produced by a shock in other variables.

The dynamic interrelationships between variables confirm some of the findings obtained in Section D by estimating a structural econometric model.

The black market rate responds positively to its own shocks, and negatively to shocks in the official exchange rate in the third and fourth months and becomes positive from the fifth month on. A nominal devaluation of the official exchange rate would lead first to an appreciation and then to a depreciation of the black market exchange rate. This is, partly, consistent with the findings of Kamin (1993), who examined more than 40 devaluation episodes in developing countries, concluding that the black market rate will depreciate in response to an official devaluation.

30 See, for example, Watson (1993) and Hamilton (1994).

TABLE V.11a

Impulse Response Functions

Dependent Variable: Black Market Exchange Rate (*be*)

Shocks in: Horizon	*be*	*e*	*P*	*M2*	*i*
3 months	0.037	-0.002	0.002	0.0001	0.013
6 months	0.033	0.005	0.013	0.011	0.020
12 months	0.019	0.028	0.021	-0.003	0.008
18 months	0.016	0.033	0.011	-0.006	0.004

Dependent Variable: Official Exchange Rate (*e*)

Shocks in: Horizon	*be*	*e*	*P*	*M2*	*i*
3 months	0.012	0.018	0.006	0.002	0.0031
6 months	0.015	0.021	0.009	0.004	-0.001
12 months	0.029	0.032	0.015	0.003	0.003
18 months	0.026	0.045	0.019	-0.002	-0.00006

Dependent Variable: Domestic Prices (*P*)

Shocks in: Horizon	*be*	*e*	*P*	*M2*	*i*
3 months	0.004	-0.003	0.009	0.002	0.0007
6 months	0.006	-0.003	0.013	0.003	0.0001
12 months	0.010	-0.001	0.017	0.002	0.0007
18 months	0.012	0.002	0.019	0.002	0.0007

Dependent Variable: Money Supply (*M2*)

Shocks in: Horizon	*be*	*e*	*P*	*M2*	*i*
3 months	0.007	-0.0009	0.008	0.012	-0.005
6 months	0.006	0.012	0.010	0.002	-0.012
12 months	0.016	0.017	0.014	0.003	-0.008
18 months	0.017	0.025	0.017	0.0005	-0.009

Dependent Variable: Domestic Time Deposit Interest Rate (*i*)

Shocks in: Horizon	*be*	*e*	*P*	*M2*	*i*
3 months	-0.058	0.132	0.065	-0.100	0.221
6 months	0.080	0.094	0.030	-0.036	0.198
12 months	0.273	0.083	0.093	0.021	0.254
18 months	0.247	0.193	0.192	-0.010	0.242

TABLE V.12a

Forecast Error Variance Decomposition

Contribution of Various Shocks to Domestic Macroeconomic Variables Fluctuations

Dependent Variable: Black Market Exchange Rate (*be*)

Shocks in: Horizon	*be*	*e*	*P*	*M2*	*i*
3 months	92.274	0.111	0.066	0.401	7.148
6 months	79.414	0.378	4.221	4.154	11.832
12 months	56.435	12.037	17.841	2.747	10.940
18 months	43.618	29.042	16.841	2.464	8.036

Dependent Variable: Official Exchange Rate (*e*)

Shocks in: Horizon	*be*	*e*	*P*	*M2*	*i*
3 months	16.488	77.439	3.346	0.326	2.400
6 months	20.677	67.884	6.904	3.248	1.287
12 months	37.238	54.214	7.006	1.031	0.511
18 months	31.967	57.293	9.956	0.498	0.285

Dependent Variable: Domestic Prices (*P*)

Shocks in: Horizon	*be*	*e*	*P*	*M2*	*i*
3 months	9.311	5.357	83.394	0.326	0.175
6 months	12.174	6.285	77.380	3.248	0.224
12 months	20.580	3.274	73.202	1.031	0.153
18 months	24.368	1.819	71.731	0.498	0.154

Dependent Variable: Money Supply (*M2*)

Shocks in: Horizon	*be*	*e*	*P*	*M2*	*i*
3 months	9.520	14.429	18.963	67.257	2.818
6 months	12.417	13.620	22.849	31.500	19.614
12 months	25.018	23.722	22.279	13.899	15.082
18 months	24.962	33.760	23.664	6.764	10.850

Dependent Variable: Domestic Interest Rate (*i*)

Shocks in: Horizon	*be*	*e*	*P*	*M2*	*i*
3 months	3.110	17.573	1.667	4.895	72.755
6 months	4.823	17.906	1.923	3.916	71.433
12 months	29.590	11.223	2.240	2.258	54.689
18 months	33.471	11.815	8.672	1.114	44.927

Note: Tables V.11a and V.12a are based on a 5-variable VEC system including the black market exchange rate, the official exchange rate, the consumer price index, the money supply and 180-day time deposit interest rate. All variables except interest rates were transformed by taking natural logarithms. The VEC model assumes series have means and linear trends but the cointegrating equations have only intercepts.

On the other hand, using a more restrictive assumption (i.e., series have means but the cointegrating equations do not have intercepts) in Johansen's test and in the VEC model, the results support the view that an official devaluation will appreciate the black market exchange rate (Table V.11b), which is also consistent with the findings of Section D, which used a structural model.

The results also show that the black market responds to changes in interest rates and after 6 months the response starts to be decreasing and until 18 months the response is still not negative, as it should be according to the theoretical expectations.[31]

Concerning the black market exchange rate fluctuations, about forty percent are attributed to its own shocks for a horizon of 18 months, and shocks in the official exchange rate and in domestic prices also play an important role in the black market exchange rate fluctuations.

In the second set of results (Tables 11b and 12b) the role of the official exchange rate in black market exchange fluctuations is substantially reduced; instead, the money supply shocks seem to contribute substantially to fluctuations in this rate. This is not a contradiction between the two sets of results; rather, it confirms the close relationship between the exchange rate and monetary policies and the indirect policy intervention in the black market of the Central Reserve Bank.

These empirical results confirm, partly, the findings of the structural models of Section D, i.e., portfolio decision variables such as interest rate as well as official exchange rate policy play an important role in determining the black market exchange rate.

The black market exchange rate has a relatively strong influence on the official exchange rate. After one year, the official exchange rate response to exogenous changes in the black market exchange rate is similar (Table V.11a) or even stronger (Table V.11b) than its response to its own shocks.

In addition, the results of Tables V.12 show that over thirty percent of official exchange rate fluctuations can be attributed to shocks in the black market exchange rate. This evidence supports the assumption that there was no complete market separation between the foreign exchange markets in El Salvador.

---

31 In the VAR representation (Appendix V.3), after nine months the response is negative, suggesting that an increase in the domestic interest rate would induce a decline in the black market exchange rate. This behavior also appears in a VEC model which assumes that series and the cointegrating equations have intercepts (see Appendix V.4).

TABLE V.11b

Impulse Response Functions

Dependent Variable: Black Market Exchange Rate (*be*)

Shocks in: Horizon	*be*	*e*	*P*	*M2*	*i*
3 months	0.038	-0.003	0.006	-0.0006	0.011
6 months	0.036	0.002	0.021	0.023	0.018
12 months	0.025	-0.003	0.036	0.033	0.017
18 months	0.026	-0.007	0.032	0.028	0.015

Dependent Variable: Official Exchange Rate (*e*)

Shocks in: Horizon	*be*	*e*	*P*	*M2*	*i*
3 months	0.012	0.018	0.006	0.005	0.004
6 months	0.015	0.017	0.009	0.017	0.003
12 months	0.031	0.014	0.021	0.025	0.009
18 months	0.032	0.009	0.034	0.035	0.012

Dependent Variable: Domestic Prices (*P*)

Shocks in: Horizon	*be*	*e*	*P*	*M2*	*i*
3 months	0.006	-0.004	0.011	0.003	0.0005
6 months	0.009	-0.006	0.017	0.008	0.0006
12 months	0.018	-0.013	0.029	0.017	0.004
18 months	0.026	-0.018	0.042	0.026	0.007

Dependent Variable: Money Supply (*M2*)

Shocks in: Horizon	*be*	*e*	*P*	*M2*	*i*
3 months	0.007	-0.003	0.008	0.026	-0.002
6 months	0.005	-0.005	0.009	0.028	-0.003
12 months	0.018	-0.012	0.018	0.031	0.002
18 months	0.021	-0.016	0.030	0.040	0.005

Dependent Variable: Domestic Interest Rate (*i*)

Shocks in: Horizon	*be*	*e*	*P*	*M2*	*i*
3 months	-0.078	0.140	0.031	-0.104	0.235
6 months	0.043	0.115	-0.021	-0.030	0.217
12 months	0.235	0.125	0.063	0.031	0.258
18 months	0.226	0.092	0.208	0.155	0.287

TABLE V.12b

Forecast Error Variance Decomposition

Contribution of Various Shocks to Domestic Macroeconomic Variables Fluctuations

Dependent Variable: Black Market Exchange Rate (*be*)

Shocks in: Horizon	*be*	*e*	*P*	*M2*	*i*
3 months	92.804	0.172	0.980	0.512	5.532
6 months	72.527	0.180	9.589	9.862	7.842
12 months	41.047	0.183	27.316	22.599	8.856
18 months	33.916	0.606	31.469	25.273	8.736

Dependent Variable: Official Exchange Rate (*e*)

Shocks in: Horizon	*be*	*e*	*P*	*M2*	*i*
3 months	15.493	76.820	3.063	1.642	2.982
6 months	18.315	54.308	6.971	18.802	1.605
12 months	38.024	25.774	12.280	21.459	2.464
18 months	34.456	13.259	21.831	27.087	3.367

Dependent Variable: Domestic Prices (*P*)

Shocks in: Horizon	*be*	*e*	*P*	*M2*	*i*
3 months	11.412	5.472	80.256	2.798	0.063
6 months	13.618	7.093	70.117	9.071	0.102
12 months	18.173	9.085	57.675	14.577	0.491
18 months	19.622	9.430	53.018	16.989	0.941

Dependent Variable: Money Supply (*M2*)

Shocks in: Horizon	*be*	*e*	*P*	*M2*	*i*
3 months	4.370	1.142	7.593	86.560	0.335
6 months	2.668	1.727	8.575	86.476	0.554
12 months	10.807	6.116	13.099	69.694	0.285
18 months	13.035	7.002	20.245	59.267	0.451

Dependent Variable: Domestic Interest Rate (*i*)

Shocks in: Horizon	*be*	*e*	*P*	*M2*	*i*
3 months	4.213	18.357	0.655	4.478	72.297
6 months	4.907	20.202	0.492	3.640	70.759
12 months	19.901	17.276	1.042	3.242	58.539
18 months	24.412	11.772	7.838	5.289	50.689

Note: Tables V.11b and V.12b are based on the same variables and number of lags included in the VEC system for Tables V.11a and V.12a, but in this case the VEC model assumes that series have only means and the cointegrating equations do not have intercepts.

It seems to be that domestic prices respond primarily to their own shocks and to unexpected changes in the black market exchange rate, and to a lesser extent to changes in the official exchange rate. The last interrelationship is negative, suggesting that a devaluation of the official exchange rate would be deflationary. Such influence is probably indirectly transmitted through the effect of devaluation on the black market exchange rate. The black market appreciation after an official devaluation would induce an offsetting effect on the increase in domestic prices normally associated with devaluation. Domestic prices also respond to shocks in the money supply. This response appears to be more important in the results of Table V.11b.

The corresponding decomposition of the forecast error variance in Tables V.12, shows that black market exchange rate shocks play an important role in domestic prices fluctuations. Apart from its own shocks, black market exchange rate shocks are the major source of fluctuations in this variable.

For the remaining two variables, the money supply and domestic interest rate, the money supply seems to be an endogenous variable that responds to shocks in the official exchange rate, the black market rate, and the domestic price level, suggesting that money supply changes were associated with movements in the exchange rate and prices. As has been mentioned before, the Central Reserve Bank intervened in the foreign exchange market to control the exchange rate and inflation.

Somewhat surprising is the endogeneity of the domestic interest rate and the important role played by the black market exchange rate as a source of fluctuations in this variable. After one year about thirty percent of the domestic interest rate fluctuations can be attributed to shocks in the black market exchange rate. It might have been thought that the interest rate is an exogenous variable, since it was controlled and for most of the sample period the nominal interest rate did not change over long periods of time, say 3 or 4 years.

To conclude, the black market exchange rate responds primarily to its own and official exchange innovations and secondly to domestic prices shocks. On the other hand, black market exchange rate shocks have had a dominant influence on all other variables under study (i.e., on the official exchange rate, on domestic prices, on the money supply and on interest rates).

F. Concluding Remarks

The empirical evidence of this chapter confirms many of the theoretical hypotheses of Chapter IV. First, black markets have effects on the determination of a number of macroeconomic variables. Second, the findings presented above permit a discussion not only of the determinants of the black market exchange rate in El Salvador, but also of the macroeconomic effects of various economic policies when there exists a black market.

Concerning the effects of the black market on others macroeconomic variables, the empirical evidence shows that: First, the dual system of official-black market exchange rate does not insulate domestic prices from the black market exchange rate movements. Particularly, the evidence of section E suggests that the black market exchange rates play an important role in the determination of the price level. Second, the money supply responds to shocks in the black market exchange rate, confirming the hypothesis of indirect official intervention in the black market. Third, the interest rate responds to shocks in the black market exchange rate, suggesting that an increase in the black market exchange rate will lead to an increase in the domestic interest rate.

With respect to the macroeconomic effects to policy changes under the presence of a black market, the empirical evidence suggests the following effects:

1. A devaluation of the official exchange rate reduces the black market premium, thereby reducing the domestic rate of inflation and increasing competitiveness. A devaluation of the official exchange rate leads to an appreciation of the black market exchange rate, which in turn would lead to a reduction in domestic prices. This result is the opposite of that found in Section D using a structural model, which suggests that a devaluation of the official exchange rate would increase the domestic price of traded goods. The different results confirm the limitations of the data used in the econometric work, noted earlier in this chapter (i.e., the short time period of the data used). Moreover, this result is also the opposite of those derived from the standard models of dual exchange rate systems. In a dual exchange rate system with a reserve adjustment mechanism in the official market, unification of the exchange markets through devaluation of the official exchange rate would have adverse repercussions on the rate of inflation.

2. A restrictive monetary policy that raises domestic interest rates reduces the black market premium by inducing the substitution of foreign for domestic assets. Since El Salvador, like many developing countries, does not have a well-developed capital market and savings must be channeled through the money market; financial reforms aimed at increasing the availability of a wide array of financial instruments, with a view to increasing alternatives for portfolio diversification, would also lead to a decline in the black market exchange rate.

3. The credibility and transparency of government policy would stabilize the black market exchange rate. This is inferred from the fact that the last dummy variable coefficient is positive and statistically significant. Such a variable was introduced in the light of the experience during July-October 1985, when the

black market exchange rate rose at rates never observed before as a result of rumors of government policy changes.

4. A reduction of the central bank's domestic credit expansion rate leads to a decline in prices of nontraded goods, which in turn increases the real exchange rate (defined as the relative prices of traded to nontraded goods), increasing external competitiveness and reducing the black market premium.

Appendix V.1

Definitions and Sources of Data

In this appendix is provided the specific data definitions and sources of data used in the empirical analysis of Chapter V.

Exchange Rates and Prices

Data for exchange rates for El Salvador were defined in term of domestic currency units per unit of U.S. dollar and were provided by the Exchange Department of the Central Reserve Bank of El Salvador. Data on exchange rate for other countries (i.e., the United States, Germany, and Japan) were defined in term of dollars per domestic currency and were taken from the International Monetary Fund's International Financial Statistics (IFS), lines rf (monthly average rate).

Domestic prices of traded goods were proxied by Wholesale Price Index (WPI), and for nontraded goods by Consumer Price Index (CPI).

The foreign price level was proxied as a weighted average of the CPI of El Salvador's major trade partner:

$$P^* = \Sigma\, w_i\, CPI_i$$

where w_i is the bilateral trade weight of El Salvador vis-à-vis the *i*th trading partner, $\Sigma w_i = 1$. The subscript *i* refers to El Salvador's major trade partners outside the CACM, namely, United States, Germany, and Japan. Data on CPI and WPI were taken from *IFS*, lines 64 and 63, respectively.

Data on international prices of coffee were taken from *IFS*, Commodity Prices pages, line 386.

The trade-weighted real exchange rate index (r) was estimated using the same methodology as Rhomberg (1976) and it is defined as:

$$r = ee\, P^*/P$$

ee is the effective exchange rate index, defined as the colones price of a trade weighted average of the currencies of El Salvador's major trade partners.

$$ee = \Sigma w_i(e)(e^*)$$

e is the official exchange rate: volume-trade-weighted average of the Central Reserve Bank exchange rate (e_{CB}) and the legal parallel market rate (e_{LP}) in colones per U.S. dollar.

e^* is the exchange rate of the ith trading partner (dollar units per unit of currency of ith El Salvador's trade partner).

P is El Salvador CPI.

P^* is El Salvador's trading partners CPI.

The base period was August 1982.

Monetary Aggregates

Both narrow money (*M1*) – currency plus demand deposit – and broad money (*M2*) – narrow money (*M1*) plus time and saving deposits (quasi-money) – were used as explanatory variables of the black market exchange rate.

Data for narrow and quasi-money were taken from lines 34 and 35, respectively, of the *IFS*.

Data for central bank domestic credit were taken from *Quarterly Review*, Central Reserve Bank of El Salvador.

Equation of Demand for Real Cash Balances used for the estimation of Blejer's Model

$$\underset{}{Log(M_d/P)} = \underset{(0.67)}{0.427} + \underset{(7.77)}{0.614}\ Log(M_d/P)_{t-1} + \underset{(3.06)}{0.391}\ Log\ (Y) - \underset{(4.94)}{0.166}\ Log(P_{t-1})$$

R^2 : 0.89
R^2 Adj: 0.89
Durbin-h : 0.20
Std. error of the regression : 0.05.

Interest Rates

Data on domestic interest rates, 180-day deposit rates were taken from *IFS* line 60l and data for U.S. Treasury bill rate were taken from line 60c.

Real Income

Monthly data on real GDP were interpolated from quarterly data estimates. The latter estimates were provided by the Department of Macroeconomic Accounts of the Central Reserve Bank of El Salvador and they were also interpolated from annual obervations.

Appendix V.2
Error Correction Estimates

Table 1
Long-Run Relationships between the Black Market Exchange Rate, the Official Exchange Rate, Domestic Prices, the Money Supply (*M2*) and Domestic Interest Rates

Dependent variables	dLog(*be*)	dLog(*e*)	dLog(*P*)	dLog(*M2*)	dLog(*i*)
Cointegrating Equation 1					
Log (be_{t-1})	-0.245 (4.104)	0.0247 (0.537)	0.026 (1.529)	-0.049 (1.257)	1.110 (2.012)
Log (e_{t-1})	----	----	----	----	----
Log (P_{t-1})	0.292 (1.187)	0.292 (1.187)	0.292 (1.187)	0.292 (1.187)	0.292 (1.187)
Log ($M2_{t-1}$)	-0.456 (1.687)	-0.456 (1.687)	-0.456 (1.687)	-0.456 (1.687)	-0.456 (1.687)
i_{t-1}	-0.054 (2.538)	-0.054 (2.538)	-0.054 (2.538)	-0.054 (2.538)	-0.054 (2.538)
Cointegrating Equation 2					
Log (be_{t-1})	----	----	----	----	----
Log (e_{t-1})	0.0115 (0.0827)	0.071 (0.659)	-0.018 (-0.451)	0.476 (5.229)	-0.1673 (-0.130)
Log (P_{t-1})	0.712 (8.185)	0.712 (8.185)	0.712 (8.185)	0.712 (8.185)	0.712 (8.185)
Log ($M2_{t-1}$)	-1.315 (-13.766)	-1.315 (-13.766)	-1.315 (-13.766)	-1.315 (-13.766)	-1.315 (-13.766)
i_{t-1}	-0.056 (-7.557)	-0.056 (-7.557)	-0.056 (-7.557)	-0.056 (-7.557)	-0.056 (-7.557)

The numbers in parentheses are t-statistics.

Appendix V.2
Table 2
Vector Error Correction Estimates

Dependent Variables	dLog(*be*)	dLog(*e*)	dLog(*P*)	dLog(*M2*)	dLog(*i*)
Error Correction Term	-0.245	0.0247	0.026	-0.0489	1.110
	(-4.104)	(0.537)	(1.529)	(-1.257)	(2.012)
Error Correction Term	0.012	0.071	-0.018	0.476	-0.167
	(-0.083)	(0.659)	(-0.451)	(5.229)	(-0.130)
dLog(be_{t-1})	0.710	0.211	0.024	0.057	0.459
dLog(be_{t-2})	(5.617)	(2.164)	(0.681)	(0.693)	(0.392)
	-0.199	-0.138	0.0316	0.106	-5.505
dLog(be_{t-3})	(-1.660)	(-1.499)	(0.925)	(1.353)	(-4.970)
	0.598	-0.015	-0.047	-0.187	0.173
dLog(be_{t-6})	(4.446)	(-0.144)	(-1.231)	-(2.127)	(0.139)
	0.412	0.237	0.0088	0.183	-0.012
dLog(e_{t-1})	(2.651)	(1.986)	(0.199)	(1.802)	(-0.009)
	0.026	-0.121	-0.030	-0.596	7.129
dLog(e_{t-2})	(0.127)	(-0.776)	(-0.509)	(-4.495)	(3.791)
	-0.465	-0.350	-0.046	-0.368	-0.271
dLog(e_{t-3})	(-2.319)	(-2.265)	(-0.810)	(-2.818)	(-0.146)
	0.248	0.069	0.004	-0.202	1.717
dLog(e_{t-6})	(1.191)	(0.428)	(0.065)	(-1.490)	(0.891)
	-0.050	0.121	-0.018	-0.205	1.001
dLog(P_{t-1})	(-0.321)	(1.010)	(-0.415)	(-2.013)	(0.694)
	0.183	0.478	0.056	0.159	-1.257
dLog(P_{t-2})	(0.435)	(1.472)	(0.466)	(0.578)	(-0.322)
	0.087	-0.045	-0.068	-0.099	6.876
dLog(P_{t-3})	(0.201)	(-0.136)	(-0.552)	(-0.351)	(1.727)
	0.225	-0.228	0.191	-0.018	-3.085
dLog(P_{t-6})	(0.497)	(-0.654)	(1.478)	(-0.063)	(-0.736)
	0.672	-0.245	0.001	0.076	-2.246
dLog($M2_{t-1}$)	(1.603)	(-0.760)	(0.012)	(0.277)	(-0.579)
	-0.228	0.133	0.073	0.341	0.955
dLog($M2_{t-2}$)	(-1.161)	(0.883)	(1.301)	(2.658)	(0.525)
	0.139	0.211	0.031	0.382	-3.773
dLog($M2_{t-3}$)	(0.737)	(1.452)	(0.579)	(3.098)	(-2.157)
	0.537	0.359	0.097	0.355	-0.136
dLog($M2_{t-6}$)	(2.908)	(2.524)	(1.830)	(2.943)	(-0.079)
	0.009	-0.080	0.044	0.103	-0.672
dLog(i_{t-1})	(0.052)	(-0.637)	(0.944)	(0.959)	(-0.443)
	0.031	0.026	0.0011	0.024	-0.008
dLog(i_{t-2})	(2.159)	(2.342)	(0.273)	(2.557)	(-0.059)
	-0.026	-0.012	0.001	0.007	-0.283
dLog(i_{t-3})	(-1.789)	(-1.084)	(0.253)	(0.731)	(-2.131)
	0.014	0.002	0.002	0.003	0.011
dLog(i_{t-6})	(1.328)	(0.228)	(0.531)	(0.387)	(0.108)
	0.013	-0.002	0.002	0.006	-0.055
Constant	(1.314)	(-0.216)	(0.683)	(0.962)	(-0.602)
	-0.0266	0.004	0.011	0.006	0.056
	(-2.131)	(0.453)	(0.683)	(0.842)	(0.487)

Appendix V.3

Vector Autoregression (VAR)

Table 1

Impulse Response Functions

Dependent Variable: Black Market Exchange Rate (*be*)

Shocks in: Horizon	*be*	*e*	*P*	*M2*	*i*
3 months	0.029	-0.002	-0.006	0.003	0.006
6 months	0.021	-0.003	-0.008	0.012	0.010
12 months	0.002	0.002	-0.006	-0.005	-0.004
18 months	-0.005	0.003	-0.001	-0.002	-0.0008

Dependent Variable: Official Exchange Rate (*e*)

Shocks in: Horizon	*be*	*e*	*P*	*M2*	*i*
3 months	0.003	0.010	0.0005	0.003	0.006
6 months	0.005	0.004	-0.003	0.003	0.002
12 months	0.011	0.006	-0.007	0.002	0.005
18 months	0.008	0.009	-0.008	0.001	0.003

Dependent Variable: Domestic Prices (*P*)

Shocks in: Horizon	*be*	*e*	*P*	*M2*	*i*
3 months	0.002	-0.002	0.003	0.001	0.002
6 months	0.001	-0.002	0.001	0.003	0.002
12 months	0.002	-0.002	0.0006	0.0007	0.001
18 months	0.0004	-0.002	0.0008	0.0008	0.001

Dependent Variable: Money Supply (M2)

Shocks in: Horizon	*be*	*e*	*P*	*M2*	*i*
3 months	0.006	-0.003	-0.0008	0.010	-0.003
6 months	0.004	0.0006	-0.0018	0.002	-0.003
12 months	0.0003	0.0007	-0.00001	-0.001	0.005
18 months	0.0005	0.0001	-0.0006	0.001	-0.003

Dependent Variable: Domestic Interest Rate (*i*)

Shocks in: Horizon	*be*	*e*	*P*	*M2*	*i*
3 months	-0.137	0.173	0.086	-0.059	0.157
6 months	0.022	0.089	-0.022	0.016	0.053
12 months	0.175	0.037	-0.055	0.070	0.062
18 months	0.116	0.075	-0.090	0.012	0.048

Appendix V.3

Table 2

Forecast Error Variance Decomposition

Contribution of Various Shocks to Domestic Macroeconomic Variables Fluctuations

Dependent Variable: Black Market Exchange Rate *(be)*

Shocks in: Horizon	*be*	*e*	*P*	*M2*	*i*
3 months	96.700	0.083	1.372	0.209	1.635
6 months	81.443	1.141	3.332	7.363	6.721
12 months	72.841	1.680	9.404	9.191	6.883
18 months	70.442	2.205	9.390	11.080	6.883

Dependent Variable: Official Exchange Rate *(e)*

Shocks in: Horizon	*be*	*e*	*P*	*M2*	*i*
3 months	3.397	86.499	1.061	1.550	7.492
6 months	5.394	80.095	1.852	4.098	8.562
12 months	28.305	50.515	8.509	2.286	10.385
18 months	31.856	42.387	14.873	1.880	9.004

Dependent Variable: Domestic Prices *(P)*

Shocks in: Horizon	*be*	*e*	*P*	*M2*	*i*
3 months	4.512	6.959	83.040	1.931	3.557
6 months	5.966	12.827	58.623	13.385	9.198
12 months	17.086	16.776	39.315	16.114	10.708
18 months	18.598	23.423	33.468	14.187	10.324

Dependent Variable: Money Supply *M2*

Shocks in: Horizon	*be*	*e*	*P*	*M2*	*i*
3 months	6.556	2.406	2.925	86.395	1.719
6 months	8.823	2.356	3.438	76.697	8.685
12 months	10.728	2.198	3.121	71.081	12.871
18 months	10.434	2.477	3.175	68.572	15.342

Dependent Variable: Domestic Interest Rate *(i)*

Shocks in: Horizon	*be*	*e*	*P*	*M2*	*i*
3 months	10.858	32.244	3.572	2.001	51.325
6 months	14.491	34.347	3.447	1.649	46.069
12 months	35.965	24.689	3.406	4.924	31.016
18 months	43.072	19.541	8.386	5.190	23.810

Note: Tables 1 and 2 of Appendix V.3 are based on a 7-variable VAR system including the black market exchange rate, the official exchange rate, the consumer price index, the money supply (M2) and 180-day time deposit interest rate as domestic variables, and the U.S. wholesale price index and the U.S. Treasury bill rate as foreign variables. Each equation also includes a time trend. All variables except interest rate were transformed by taking natural logarithms.

Appendix V.4
Vector Error Correction (VEC)

Table 1
Impulse Response Functions

Dependent Variable: Black Market Exchange Rate *(be)*

Shocks in: Horizon	*be*	*e*	*P*	*M2*	*i*
3 months	0.0361	-0.0034	0.0047	0.0008	0.0093
6 months	0.0314	-0.00002	0.0178	0.0119	0.0123
12 months	0.0146	0.0177	0.0238	-0.0015	-0.0002
18 months	0.0051	0.0181	0.0107	-0.0046	-0.0045

Dependent Variable: Official Exchange Rate *(e)*

Shocks in: Horizon	*be*	*e*	*P*	*M2*	*i*
3 months	0.0116	0.0168	0.0078	0.0027	0.0007
6 months	0.0151	0.0188	0.0094	0.0040	-0.0036
12 months	0.0258	0.0257	0.0173	0.0038	-0.0029
18 months	0.0194	0.0336	0.0199	-0.0014	-0.0079

Dependent Variable: Domestic Prices *(P)*

Shocks in: Horizon	*be*	*e*	*P*	*M2*	*i*
3 months	0.0047	-0.0030	0.0086	0.0017	0.0012
6 months	0.0065	-0.0022	0.0116	0.0029	0.0015
12 months	0.0113	0.0015	0.0158	0.0022	0.0025
18 months	0.0143	0.0059	0.0192	0.0017	0.0023

Dependent Variable: Money Supply *M2*

Shocks in: Horizon	*be*	*e*	*P*	*M2*	*i*
3 months	0.0073	0.0003	0.0071	0.0116	-0.0038
6 months	0.0072	0.0152	0.0066	0.0008	-0.0081
12 months	0.0175	0.0220	0.0126	0.0029	-0.0047
18 months	0.0215	0.0300	0.0176	-0.0000	-0.0068

Dependent Variable: Domestic Interest Rate *(i)*

Shocks in: Horizon	*be*	*e*	*P*	*M2*	*i*
3 months	-0.0756	0.1009	0.1229	-0.0859	0.153
6 months	0.0630	0.0123	0.0759	-0.0251	0.0988
12 months	0.2011	-0.0719	0.1530	0.0503	0.1145
18 months	0.0813	-0.0569	0.2029	0.01309	0.0724

Appendix V.4

Table 2

Forecast Error Variance Decomposition

Contribution of Various Shocks to Domestic Macroeconomic Variables Fluctuations

Dependent Variable: Black Market Exchange Rate *(be)*

Shocks in: Horizon	*be*	*e*	*P*	*M2*	*i*
3 months	94.105	0.283	0.599	0.363	4.651
6 months	79.793	0.335	8.374	5.500	5.998
12 months	57.927	4.9122	29.031	3.996	4.134
18 months	48.423	13.727	30.495	3.735	3.619

Dependent Variable: Official Exchange Rate *(e)*

Shocks in: Horizon	*be*	*e*	*P*	*M2*	*i*
3 months	15.465	76.975	6.0276	0.460	1.073
6 months	19.826	63.685	10.749	4.091	1.649
12 months	37.684	48.235	11.471	1.452	1.158
18 months	32.049	49.398	16.318	0.772	1.463

Dependent Variable: Domestic Prices *(P)*

Shocks in: Horizon	*be*	*e*	*P*	*M2*	*i*
3 months	11.042	4.348	82.213	1.774	0.063
6 months	15.108	4.394	75.500	3.902	1.096
12 months	25.287	1.706	68.882	2.563	1.566
18 months	29.825	2.665	64.510	1.609	1.393

Dependent Variable: Money Supply *M2*

Shocks in: Horizon	*be*	*e*	*P*	*M2*	*i*
3 months	11.276	1.049	16.278	69.746	1.650
6 months	9.841	19.718	17.124	42.541	10.775
12 months	27.993	38.772	14.737	12.773	5.725
18 months	27.991	45.542	17.330	5.356	3.780

Dependent Variable: Domestic Time Deposit Interest Rate *(i)*

Shocks in: Horizon	*be*	*e*	*P*	*M2*	*i*
3 months	5.702	15.619	8.323	4.532	65.824
6 months	8.671	13.429	14.989	3.916	58.996
12 months	35.220	8.664	17.805	2.965	35.347
18 months	31.963	7.274	33.028	2.158	25.577

Note: Tables 1 and 2 are based on a VEC system using the same assumptions as in Tables V.11b and V.12b, except that here the cointegrating equations have intercepts.

Chapter VI

Unification of Foreign Exchange Markets

A. Introduction

The existence of black markets for foreign exchange has important implications for the functioning of an economy, as compared with a uniform exchange rate system. In particular, black markets have an impact on the determination of a number of macroeconomic variables, especially on the inflation rate, the fiscal deficit, the real exchange rate, the balance-of-payments, and economic welfare.[1] These effects may have some potential gains,[2] but also entail a variety of costs.[3] First, the black market premium may be seen as an implicit tax on exports (Pinto 1990 and 1991), creating distortions in the allocation of resources. Second, black markets may cause high exchange rate and price volatility, and the exchange rate in the black market would be higher than under a uniform exchange rate regime. Third, the black market creates inefficiencies and market fragmentation associated with quasi-illegal activities.

In addition, from the point of view of the authorities, black markets have some undesirable effects. First, there is a loss of tariff and export tax revenues as a result of smuggling and underinvoicing. Second, black markets induce rent-seeking activities (e.g., corruption of government officials). Third, the existence of black markets facilitates currency substitution and may reduce the government revenues from the inflation tax.[4] Fourth, the expansion of a black market weakens the effectiveness of exchange controls, and may lead to a loss in official

1 For details of the macroeconomic effects of the black markets, see Chapter IV.

2 The major gains that have been mentioned in the literature are the following: first, the black market makes imports available which would otherwise not have been possible, due to the rationing and restrictions in the official market(s); second, it increases employment by raising the availability of imported inputs; third, it actually raises the flow of foreign currency to the Central Bank (see Chapter IV for details).

3 Black markets for foreign exchange typically emerge with the imposition of exchange controls which have been regarded as nonoptimal from the resource allocation point of view (Krueger, 1983). Although the black market mitigates these costs, it would be suboptimal in comparison to the case under a uniform exchange rate regime.

4 The real demand for domestic money is the base for the inflation tax. Thus, a reduction in the real demand for money will reduce the revenues from inflationary finances (see Friedman, 1971, Tanzi, 1978, and Tanzi and Blejer, 1982).

reserves. The unification of foreign exchange markets is thus an important objective of macroeconomic policy in countries with sizable black market transactions. One way of approaching the unification process used recently in some developing countries is by adopting a dual exchange rate regime, setting up a legal parallel market with the aim of absorbing and legalizing an existing black market for foreign exchange.[5]

El Salvador, after nearly a decade of operating either under an exchange rate pegged to the U.S. dollar[6] or a dual exchange rate system, and, under both of them, with a black market for foreign exchange operating illegally, adopted a uniform flexible exchange rate system in June 1990. The process of unification started in July 1989 with the adoption of a dual exchange rate regime where the legal parallel market, at least during the first six months emulated price developments on the black market. The process concluded with unification of the foreign exchange markets and the removal of most exchange controls on current account transactions.[7]

The unification of the foreign exchange markets was accompanied by a trade and financial liberalization.

The main purpose of this chapter is to discuss the theoretical and policy aspects of exchange rate unification, illustrated by the recent experience of El Salvador.[8] First, the general principles of the unification of foreign exchange markets are duly underlined to provide a framework for analyzing El Salvador's recent experience. The chapter concludes with some lessons in the light of the experience with exchange rate unification in El Salvador in 1990.

---

5 The country under study is an example of such a case. Other examples include the Dominican Republic, Guyana, and Guatemala (see Country Pages, IMF, *Annual Report on Exchange Arrangements and Exchange Restrictions,* several issues, and also *World Currency Year Book,* 1988-1989).

6 Clearly, in the present international environment with most major currencies floating independently, fixed exchange rate regimes are not strictly fixed; the exchange rate floats vis-à-vis third currencies.

7 The capital account was later liberalized in August 1991. For details, see Chapter II and III.

8 The analysis will be limited to the experience of exchange rate unification of June 1990. However, in January 1986, El Salvador also attempted to adopt a unified fixed exchange rate regime, but the unification of the exchange rate markets did not materialize because the devaluation of the official exchange rate was not accompanied by the abolition of exchange controls. As a consequence, the black market did not vanish (see Chapter III for details).

B. Analytical Considerations and the Experience of El Salvador

Generally speaking, in considering unification of the foreign exchange markets, the authorities face four types of issues. The first issue concerns the speed of unification of the exchange markets, the second the choice of the appropriate uniform system, the third the macroeconomic effects of exchange rate unification, and the fourth the role of macroeconomic policy under exchange rate unification.[9]

1. Pace of Exchange Rate Unification[10]

Following Lizondo (1990), the unification of the exchange rate can be sudden or gradual. In a sudden unification, the new uniform exchange rate system is adopted at once, while in a gradual unification it is adopted after a series of measures in preparation of the unification of markets.

a. Advantages and Disadvantages of a Gradual as Opposed to a Rapid Approach

The first and most broad argument in favor of a gradual approach rests on the prudence and the fine tuning and mid-course corrections that are possible under this approach.

The second argument for a gradual approach, particularly important in developing countries, is that it lowers the cost of adjustment in terms of inflation and income distribution.[11] The necessary change in prices due to exchange rate adjustment will be distributed over time, and also gives more time for some other complementary policies (e.g., fiscal and monetary restraint) and compensatory policies (e.g., poverty alleviation programs) to produce effects. However, this argument may not be completely valid in countries with a sizable black market where at least part of the price adjustment will already have taken place before the unification of foreign exchange markets. The empirical evidence of Chapter V shows that a dual official-black market regime does not completely insulate prices from movements in the black market exchange rate.

---

9 The last issue will be limited to monetary policy and is the topic of Chapter VII.

10 This discussion is based upon the analysis of Lizondo (1990).

11 The term "income distribution effect" refers here to the different effects that the most vulnerable groups in society experience with a uniform measure, rather than differentiated measures that favor some groups at the expense of other groups.

The third argument for a gradual approach is that when reforms are simultaneously applied in several areas (e.g., exchange rate reform applied simultaneously with trade reforms, public sector reforms, and financial liberalization), gradualism is preferable on credibility grounds. When the scope of reforms is broad, the chances of contagion from failures in any one area and the potential for policy conflict are higher.[12] For example, if unification through an overnight float leads to a very high inflation and exchange rate volatility, these may hamper the whole adjustment process, when other reforms are still in an early stage. For example, liberalization of the trade and capital account might require stable prices and exchange rates, but stable exchange rates might require the central bank's intervention in the foreign market to such an extreme as to turn a flexible exchange rate system into a *de facto* fixed rate. This solution would generate credibility problems for two reasons: first, the time-inconsistency problem: the ex-post-strategy (*de facto* pegged exchange rate regime) may differ from its optimal ex-ante-strategy (flexible rate regime);[13] second, the solution to exchange rate volatility (the *de facto* pegged exchange rate regime) may be inconsistent with other policies being pursued simultaneously (e.g., trade reform would call for exchange rate depreciation). Under these circumstances, it is, of course, perfectly rational for private agents to doubt the continuation of the package of reforms.

Among the disadvantages of gradualism, the following can be mentioned: First, slowing the pace of the reform increases costs in terms of efficiency losses. From the efficiency point of view, the economy should move rapidly to the new long-run equilibrium position consistent with its optimal long-run exchange rate policy. However, it has been pointed out (Froot, 1988) that when reforms lack credibility, this acts as a distortion which is intensified under the typical first-best policy of rapid approach and ultimately leads to a reverse in the policy. Using an optimizing two-period model, Froot (1988) shows that in the presence of a lack of credibility, a second-best gradual approach leads to higher welfare and greater probability that the program will succeed because it tends to lessen the distortion generated by the lack of perfect credibility. He found that imperfect credibility tends to undermine an important motivation for liberalization

12 Rodrik (1989), p.12.

13 The problem known as "time-inconsistency" was initially formalized by Kydland and Prescott (1977), and can be summarized in the following way: A policy is dynamically inconsistent when a future policy decision that forms part of an optimal plan formulated at the initial date is no longer optimal at a later date, even though no relevant new information has appeared in the meantime (see Blanchard and Fischer, 1989, p. 592).

attempts: to shift productive resources out of the protected import sector and into the efficient export sector.[14]

Second, it has been pointed out (Rodrik, 1989) that a rapid approach rather than a gradual one may enhance credibility when government commitment to the reform is doubted. Radical actions, or in Rodrik's (1989) terms, a "cold-turkey" strategy may be used to convince the public about the commitment of policy-makers to reform.

Third, gradualism may not, in practice, reduce the impact on prices, thus resulting only in a painfully slow transition that lasts several years.

In the case of El Salvador, there were economic and noneconomic reasons to pursue a gradual exchange rate reform as opposed to a rapid one. First, when the new government, led by President Cristiani, assumed office in June 1989, it was already clear that a uniform exchange rate regime would be in the country's long-run best interest. However, it was not yet clear which of the two recommended exchange rate systems was the most appropriate one for El Salvador.[15] Under these circumstances, the authorities adopted a middle-ground position, temporarily instituting a dual exchange rate regime.

Second, the exchange rate policy was part of a comprehensive economic program that included reforms in several areas (trade policy, monetary policy, tax and public sector administration, financial sector, agricultural sector, and social sector and poverty alleviation programs) in which gradualism was adopted as a general rule. Concerning the disadvantage mentioned above, namely, that a gradual approach may give signals indicating a lack of the government's commitment to reform, this is not applicable in the case of El Salvador, since neither the private sector nor the international community could have doubted the ideological and economic preferences of President Cristiani.[16]

Third, the argument of reducing the cost of adjustment in terms of inflation and income distribution mentioned above was particularly important in the case

---

14 See Froot (1988) for details of these findings. Although Froot's analysis concentrates on trade liberalization, specifically on the removal of tariffs, his conclusions can be applied to the case of unification of foreign exchange markets. The latter policy is usually accompanied by the removal of trade restrictions, and both policies share similar motivations.

15 In a policy study for El Salvador that served as a guideline for the Salvadorean policymakers, Harberger and Wisecarver (1989) recommended two different exchange rate systems as capable of meeting the specific adjustment needs of El Salvador: a pegged exchange rate system with occasional devaluations, or a flexible exchange rate system of a managed type.

16 President Cristiani's commitment to undertake a comprehensive economic program designed to create a more market-oriented and private-sector-led economy were beyond doubt. He has been a strong believer in free trade and the market economy.

of El Salvador in view of the critical economic and political situation of the country at that time. A sharp increase in the exchange rate and prices could have aggravated the distributional effects and encountered considerable political opposition.[17]

Fourth, a legal institutional basis for a floating system had to be developed prior to the adoption of a uniform flexible system (e.g., authorizing exchange houses and providing them with a legal standing to act as intermediaries in the foreign exchange market).

b. Process of Gradual Exchange Rate Unification

There are essentially two types of processes of gradual exchange rate unification. One of them is to adopt a dual exchange rate regime and gradually transfer transactions from the official to the parallel market.[18] For example, a dual system with a fixed exchange rate for the public sector and some private commercial transactions, and a floating exchange rate for the remaining commercial transactions and for financial transactions. If the newly chosen uniform regime is a floating exchange rate system, commercial transactions will be gradually transferred from the fixed exchange rate market to the floating exchange rate market. In this case, the unification of the exchange rate markets is expected and the temporary nature of the dual exchange rate regime has important effects on the exchange rate behavior before unification takes place. If the unification is anticipated as in most cases, economic agents react before the unification takes place. Most probably, the parallel market rate moves towards the level the uniform floating rate is expected to have at the time of unification. If the new floating rate is expected to be above the parallel market, the parallel rate jumps upwards at the moment the reform announcement is made.

The transition from one regime to the other has been analyzed by Flood and Marion (1983), who examined the Italian experience in 1974, namely, the period from February 1973 to March 1974 during which Italy had a two-tier float regime. The authors assumed that forward-looking agents believed the Italian two-tier float to be temporary, and they knew with certainty the reform date, but they

17 Note that in the case of El Salvador the exchange rate in the black market at the beginning of the unification process was lower than the uniform exchange rate (see Figure VI.2). This was because of the Central Reserve Bank's indirect intervention in the black market. Thus, some positive impact on the uniform exchange rate and prices was expected.

18 As noted earlier, in many cases this system has been adopted to set up a legal parallel market emulating price developments of an existing black market for foreign exchange.

were uncertain about the type of exchange rate regime the authorities would adopt next. Accordingly, Flood and Marion developed a model general enough to examine the transition from a dual exchange regime in which both exchange rates are floating to the two feasible alternatives for Italy: (i) a unified floating system, and (ii) a dual system in which one of the exchange rates is fixed and the other is floating.[19] Their model shows that expectations of a transition in regime which are generated by the *perceived temporariness* of an exchange rate regime combined with uncertainty about the nature of the post-transition regime can cause a jump in the exchange rate at the moment of the announcement and could be volatile in the transition period between the reform announcement and the implementation date.[20] Flood and Marion's model suggests that this exchange rate behavior under a dual exchange rate regime cannot be explained by standard market fundamentals; rather, it can be explained by expectations, and that the *perceived temporariness* of the exchange rate regime should be treated as a market fundamental.[21]

Expectations dominate the behavior of the exchange rate in the transition period and they could have some undesirable effects. Specifically, the changes in the black market rate before unification takes place could have important wealth effects (e.g., foreign exchange losses), and therefore influence the effects of unification.[22]

The second way of gradual unification is through the adoption of policies that result in a reduction of the spread(s). Official indirect intervention in the black market by selling foreign exchange at the official exchange rate(s), reduces the spread between the black market rate and the official rate(s).[23] A restrictive

---

19 The authors considered that the uniform fixed exchange rate regime was not a viable option for Italy during that period because of turmoil in the foreign exchange markets, including the pressures of massive interest-sensitive and speculative capital flows.

20 This behavior has recently been experienced in El Salvador. The black market exchange had a discrete jump after the modification of the dual exchange rate regime on March 19, 1990 and showed some volatility during the transition period until June 1, 1990 (see Figure VI.1).

21 Flood and Marion (1983), p. 293.

22 This was the case in El Salvador before the January 1986 devaluation, where the black market jumped at rates never before observed as a result of expectations of exchange rate unification. In anticipation of devaluation, agents demanded foreign exchange in the black market, driving up the black market exchange rate well above the future uniform exchange rate. In fact, the official exchange rate was devalued at a rate substantially below the expected devaluation, resulting in important capital losses.

23 Clearly, this assumes the most common case, where the parallel or black market rate is higher than the official rate.

monetary or fiscal policy also reduces the spread. It has also been suggested (Nowak, 1984) that a devaluation of the official exchange rate produces a permanent decline of the spread between the black market rate and official rate.[24]

In El Salvador, as noted above, the process of unification was gradual. It was initiated on July 11, 1989, with the adoption of a legal dual-exchange-rate system on a temporary basis, setting up a legal parallel market in which the exchange rate was managed by the authorities according to black market exchange rate developments. But this objective was only partly achieved. In the first semester of the dual regime, from July to December 1989, the spread between the black market and the legal parallel market narrowed (see Figure VI.1). However, political events in late 1989, as well as the easing up of monetary policy and the adjustment of certain public services prices, led to acceleration of the inflation rate and depreciation of the black market exchange rate in the first quarter of 1990; the parallel market rate, established by the authorities, sluggishly followed the black market rate, increasing the spread between the two rates during that period. Consequently, by mid-March, the authorities devalued the official exchange rate and modified the dual exchange rate system, which afterwards consisted of three exchange rates.[25] Subsequently, in preparation for unification of the foreign exchange markets, regulations on the establishment of exchange houses were announced (on April 10, 1990) and exchange houses were effectively permitted to operate by the end of May 1990. This implied the legalization of the black market. The process concluded with the unification of the foreign exchange markets on June 1, 1990.[26]

In this way, the unification of the foreign exchange markets was widely expected by private agents, and the rational behavior would be that the black market rate would experience an initial jump and would keep depreciating steadily toward the expected post-unification exchange rate level.

Figure VI.1 illustrates the behavior of the black market and legal parallel market exchange rates with daily data during the transition period from a dual regime of official-black market to a uniform flexible exchange rate regime, namely, the period from July 1989 to May 1990. In fact, during the first six months of the transition period the black market exchange rate showed some short-run volatility, but in general had the expected behavior described above. The legal parallel rate, jointly determined by the Central Reserve Bank and the commercial banks, followed the black market's pattern, maintaining a very nar-

24 For details of various policy effects on the black market premium, see section E of Chapter IV.
25 See Chapter III.
26 See Chapter III.

row spread of less than 1 percent for most of the period, until mid-November. In December the spread increased to around 3-4 percent and then declined in early January 1990 to less than 1 percent. In the second part of the transition period (from January to May 1990), the behavior of the black market exchange rate was different. The black market rate was rather volatile during that period. Figure VI.1 also shows that the rate of depreciation in the black market accelerated and the premium grew from around 1 percent at the beginning of 1990 to 18 percent on March 16, 1990. On March 19, 1990, the multiple exchange rate regime was modified, allowing the legal parallel market rate (the banking rate) to have greater flexibility. The premium, then started to narrow and by mid-April, after the announcement of the authorization of the foreign exchange houses, both rates moved together during the rest of the transition period, and in May 1990, the last month of the multiple regime, the premium was not higher than 2 percent.[27]

Some items may explain the differences in the black market exchange rate behavior between the first half and the second half of the transition period. First, in the first part of the period, agents probably believed that the post-transition regime to be adopted would be a fixed exchange rate regime.[28] Thus, the black market exchange rate moved to the expected level. By contrast, during the second half of the period, agents may have realized that a fixed exchange regime was no longer a viable option for El Salvador[29] and uncertainty, at least in the beginning, about the nature of the exchange regime may have caused some volatility in the exchange rate. Second, the legalization of the black market for foreign exchange with the announcement of the regulation on the establishment of the exchange houses could have generated expectations that the possible post-transition regime would be a flexible exchange rate regime.

27 Figure VI.1a plots the exchange rates during the last five months of the transition period to show their movements more clearly.

28 Agents experienced in 1986, after over three years of a multiple exchange regime, that the official rate was devalued to the level of the legal parallel market rate, and, with that, the return to a fixed exchange rate system.

29 The modification of the legal multiple exchange rate regime could have been taken as a signal of the unsustainability of the fixed exchange rate regime.

Figure VI.1
EXCHANGE RATE IN THE TRANSITION PERIOD
July 1989 - May 1990

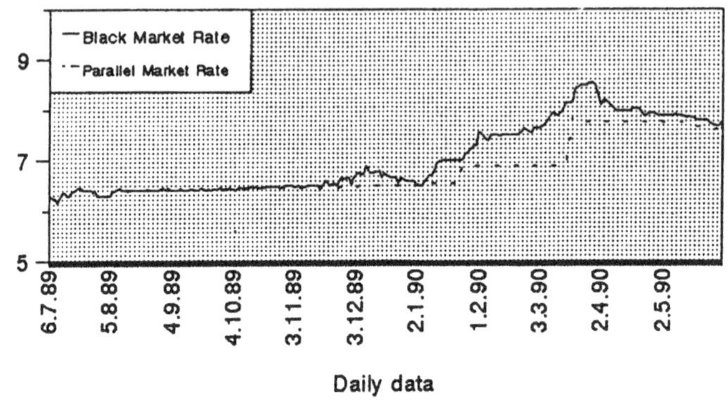

Source: Data provided by the Exchange Department, Central Reserve Bank of El Salvador.

Figure VI.1a
EXCHANGE RATE IN THE TRANSITION PERIOD
January 1990 - May 1990

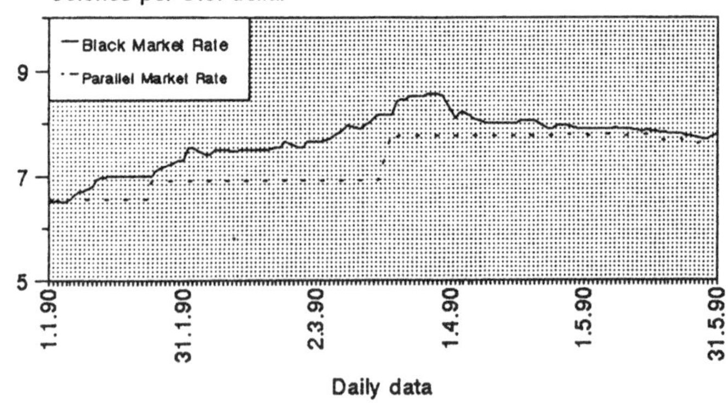

Source: Data provided by the Exchange Department, Central Reserve Bank of El Salvador.

2. *The Choice of the Uniform Exchange Rate Regime*

a. Pegged vs. Floating Rates

A second issue that policymakers have to face in adopting unification of the foreign exchange markets is the choice of the optimal exchange rate regime.

In the literature, the capacity of developing countries to operate under flexible exchange rates has been questioned. The discussion has been based on the characteristics of exchange and money markets in developing countries. In these countries, exchange markets are thin, forward exchange markets are absent, and financial markets are underdeveloped, increasing the potential volatility of the exchange rate and the cost of hedging or of risk in foreign exchange transactions.[30]

Despite these shortcomings, in recent years many developing countries have adopted more flexible exchange rate arrangements.[31] The more widespread use of unified floating by developing countries has motivated analytical discussions of the choice of the appropriate exchange rate regime for developing countries.[32] The discussion has been based on the large theoretical literature of the choice between fixed and flexible exchange rate regimes, which has been developed mainly in the context of industrial countries engaged in seeking macroeconomic stability,[33] but could serve as a guide for developing countries.[34]

---

30 See, for example, Black (1976), and Branson and Katseli-Papaefstratiou (1978). See also Wickham (1985) for a survey of the literature on the choice of exchange rate regimes in developing countries.

31 An analysis of the recent experience of developing countries with floating exchange rates is provided by Quirk and others (1987). A more recent study is by Galbis (1993). The latter concludes that the recent experiences of five developing countries with a floating interbank exchange rate system show that this system can operate with a minimum banking infrastructure, as is the case in Gambia and Guyana, where Gambia only had three commercial banks and Guyana five.

32 See Aghevli, Khan, and Montiel (1991).

33 Representative references on the debate on fixed and flexible regime are Johnson (1970) and Kindleberger (1970). Genberg (1989) provides a very useful analysis of the main issues of the long-standing debate on fixed versus flexible exchange rates.

34 The literature refers to the choice between fixed and flexible regimes; however, these broad arrangements include various categories. According to the IMF classification (*Annual Report on Exchange Arrangements and Exchange Restrictions*, 1993), pegged exchange rate arrangements include: (a) pegged to a single currency (e.g., the U.S. dollar) and (b) pegged to composite (SDR or currency basket); flexible arrangements include the following categories: (a) limited flexibility vis-à-vis single currency, (b) cooperative arrangements (e.g., EMS), (c) adjusted according to a set of indicators, (d) managed floating, and (e) independent floating.

Although the first contributions of this literature in the late 1960's and the early 1970's had as a reference an international monetary system of the Bretton-Woods type, this literature has evolved since the debate over the relative merits of fixed and flexible exchange rates of that time and has extended this theoretical framework in several respects, such as modeling the labor market (Aizenman and Frenkel, 1985) and developing of a multicountry world framework under different assumptions about exchange rate arrangements between the major countries and wage setting (Argy, McKibbin, and Sieggloff, 1989), and complex intervention rules (Turnovsky, 1985)). The objective in this section, however, is not to survey all the developments in this literature, but rather to outline the general principles for choosing an exchange rate regime which are general enough to accommodate different particular cases.[35,36]

The choice of the optimal exchange rate regime should ideally be based on a criterion along the lines of standard welfare economics. It should compare regimes in terms of costs and benefits and derive net welfare gains for every country under different types of regimes.[37] However, this type of analysis is hardly available. Instead, the literature has focused on a proxy-welfare criterion of macroeconomic stability, which is defined in terms of minimizing the variance of real output, the price level, and the like.[38]

This literature, which focused on the choice between a completely fixed and a completely flexible exchange rate regime, centered the discussion of the effectiveness of fixed and flexible exchange rate regimes in insulating the economy from external and domestic shocks. The main question in the analysis was: What is the optimal exchange rate regime for a small country in the face of random shocks arising from diverse external and domestic sources? Thus, the criterion of optimality refers to which exchange rate regime minimizes the variance of real output or the price level with respect to its desired level in the face of random transitory shocks.

Previous analyses of this literature emphasized the geographical location of the shocks as the main criterion for the choice of the exchange rate regime, concluding that when external shocks are more frequent, flexible exchange rates are desirable.[39] Subsequent papers following the framework proposed by

---

35 Genberg (1989) covers many of the relevant issues of the development of this literature.

36 The general prescriptions of this literature have been shown by those authors to be rather robust under the various alternative assumptions and model specifications.

37 See Helpman and Leiderman (1991).

38 See Aghevli, Khan, and Montiel (1991).

39 Representative writings in this line of analysis are Johnson (1970) and several other contributions edited by Halm (1970).

Poole (1970) in the context of a closed economy model have shifted the focus of analysis to the nature of the domestic shocks, whether they are monetary (i.e., originating in the money market) or real (i.e., originating in the goods market). When domestic shocks are monetary (e.g., unstable money demand), a fixed exchange rate regime would be more effective in stabilizing output. Given that the money supply is endogenous under a fixed exchange rate, disturbances in the domestic money market would be absorbed by changes in international reserves without affecting the supply-demand conditions in the goods market that determine the level of economic activity. In contrast, if domestic shocks are real, then a floating exchange rate is preferable since the exchange rate should be adjusted to stabilize output through changes in aggregate demand.[40,41]

An important result of the latter literature is that, in general, neither of the extremes (permanently fixed or completely floating) would be optimal to stabilize output. Instead, intermediate exchange rate regimes have been proposed as more efficient arrangements in stabilizing the economy.

These arrangements involve, in general, either a variant of a crawling peg or managed flexible exchange rate. In this case, the main question is the optimal degree of exchange rate flexibility or exchange rate management that should be adopted under specific shocks to the economy in question. Thus, when shocks originate more frequently in the domestic goods markets or abroad, flexibility in exchange rate management has been perceived as desirable, but more fixed arrangements are more efficient when shocks originate more frequently in the domestic money market.

These propositions are usually made within a framework of a one- or two-country model, but also they have been theoretically and empirically examined in a multicountry world framework, in which one country is small relative to the other two countries.[42] Argy, McKibbin, and Siegloff's analysis was carried out under alternative assumptions of exchange rate arrangements between the major countries and different forms of wage setting within the small open economy and abroad. Such an abundance of possibilities makes it very difficult to draw any definitive conclusions. However, their results generally support the standard

40 See Boyer (1978), Turnovsky (1976), Parkin (1978), and Genberg (1989). Also see the papers collected in Bhandari (1985).

41 These prescriptions assume that the trade balance responds normally to exchange rate changes (contrary to what a J-curve model would predict).

42 See Argy, McKibbin, and Siegloff (1989). These authors assume that the small country has no macroeconomic impact on the two large countries, but the small open economy is strongly affected by what happens in the two large economies.

conclusion that, for domestic real shocks, a floating exchange rate regime performs well, but a fixed rate regime exactly offsets a monetary shock.[43]

The choice of the exchange rate regime also depends on the country's specific situation in terms of structural characteristics, the degree of capital mobility, and conditions in the labor market.[44]

Moreover, the choice of the exchange rate regime depends fundamentally on the macroeconomic policy adopted and on specific policymakers' objectives. The macroeconomic policy must be consistent with the chosen exchange rate regime. A pegged exchange rate regime requires the financial discipline to sustain the exchange rate parity; specifically, it requires that monetary and fiscal policies be oriented toward maintaining the level of domestic credit consistent with keeping the pegged exchange value of the currency without exhausting the central bank's foreign reserves and borrowing capacity.

The price of inconsistency is either a retreat from convertibility, the reemergence of a black market, and a reversal of the unification of the foreign exchange markets, or a balance-of-payments crisis and abandonment of the fixed exchange rate regime (Krugman, 1979).

In practice, however, it is very difficult to apply some of these criteria to selecting the appropriate exchange rate regime, not only because it is very difficult to discern the source of the shocks and identify the relevant structural characteristics, but also because some other reasons may exist that make it difficult to follow these prescriptions. They may enter into conflict with the country's specific situation and policy objectives. For example, for an economy that is exposed more often to monetary shocks but whose level of international reserves is already below the desired level and has as a main policy objective achieving a balance-of-payments equilibrium, choosing a fixed exchange rate regime to channel a positive monetary shock abroad will not be possible if foreign reserves are exhausted and the borrowing capacity is approaching a limit. Similarly, fixing the exchange rate to channel a positive monetary shock abroad will further deteriorate the balance-of-payments, which might be incompatible with others policy objectives.

Thus, in practice, the most relevant criteria for choosing the appropriate uniform exchange rate regime are the consistency of domestic policies and the specific policy objectives adopted by the authorities. This is consistent with the experience of El Salvador.

---

43 Their results are less clear for foreign shocks; for details see Argy, McKibbin, and Siegloff (1989).

44 For a general discussion of these criteria, see Aghevli, Khan, and Montiel (1991).

El Salvador's major reasons for choosing a flexible exchange rate regime were as follows: First, the exchange rate policy was part of a more outward-oriented trade strategy aimed at improving external competitiveness in order to achieve a sustainable balance-of-payments position. The move towards a more outward-oriented trade strategy required a more flexible exchange rate arrangement.

Second, a fixed exchange rate regime requires a degree of financial discipline that El Salvador was not in a condition to maintain, given the civil war environment and the resulting high level of fiscal expenditures.

Third, when international capital movements and transfers are important, as they are in El Salvador, macroeconomic stability may require a more flexible exchange rate regime. For example, an inflow of capital would increase aggregate demand, and an appreciation of the exchange rate would be required to stabilize output by reducing external demand.

Fourth, the domestic rate of inflation has accelerated sharply in comparison with the U.S. inflation rate in the 1980's (see Figure III.1 of Chapter III).

Fifth, in the case of El Salvador, the experience for nearly a decade with an active black market, in which the exchange rate varied freely, paved the way for the adoption of a unified flexible exchange rate regime. In fact, it has been recognized that in developing countries with parallel or black markets, where the exchange rate normally floats, a unified floating regime may work fairly well.[45]

Sixth, a floating exchange rate regime does not incur the political costs that would have been caused by the devaluation that would have been unavoidable if El Salvador had adopted a pegged exchange rate regime. In fact, in the policy study for El Salvador cited above (Harberger and Wisecarver, 1989), the authors alerted the authorities to the likely need for possibly two or three significant upward adjustments of the nominal exchange rate over the next several years in case El Salvador opted for a pegged exchange rate regime.[46] With a flexible exchange rate system, by contrast, the Central Reserve Bank withdrew as a major direct player in the foreign exchange markets and surrendered the power to alter the exchange rate to the market.

The question of exchange rate policy is not solved by the choice between pegged and flexible regimes; it is also necessary, if the country chooses to peg, to decide to what to peg, and if the country chooses to float, to decide the type of flexible exchange arrangement. Since the issues discussed in this chapter are

45 See Wickham (1985).

46 See Harberger and Wisecarver (1989), p. 23.

based on the Salvadorean experience with exchange rate unification, the following concentrates on the choice of the floating arrangement.[47]

b. Interbank vs. Auction Systems for Floating Rates

Once the policymakers have decided on the type of uniform system to adopt, they have to select the specific exchange rate arrangement. In the case of a flexible system, there are basically two forms of floating arrangements, the interbank and the auction systems.[48] The basic differences between the two arrangements are the following: an *interbank arrangement* operates within the private sector and involves commercial banks and licensed foreign exchange dealers. Under this arrangement, the exchange rate is determined in negotiations between banks and their clients and in transactions between banks. The exchange rate is free to vary from hour to hour and day to day. In contrast, in an *auction market arrangement,* the central bank conducts the market and serves as a channel for the auction process. Foreign exchange is surrendered to the central bank and these foreign exchange resources are sold to those who value them most. The auction-determined exchange rate applies until the next auction date to all exchange transactions, including surrenders for the next auction.[49]

The choice between the two forms of arrangement must take into account the institutional and economic structure of the country concerned.

The system instituted by El Salvador is an interbank system under which commercial banks and exchange houses are free to purchase and sell foreign exchange at rates determined by supply and demand conditions. The exchange rate is free to vary from day to day. The Central Reserve Bank establishes the exchange rate daily to be applicable to its transactions. This exchange rate is the arithmetic average of the exchange rate set by banks and exchange houses for the previous working day. The system is basically a market-determined exchange rate with central bank intervention limited to smoothing out cyclical fluctuations.[50]

In El Salvador, the major considerations in the choice of an interbank arrangement were: First, the existence of a sufficient number of capable commer-

47 A good survey of the literature on the choice of the optimal peg is provided by Williamson (1982).

48 For an overview of these arrangements and the experience of developing countries that have adopted them, see Quirk, et al. (1987). See also Galbis (1993).

49 See Quirk et al. (1987), pp. 4-12.

50 For details of the structure and performance of the foreign exchange market in El Salvador, see Chapter III.

cial banks,[51] together with a pre-existing network of operators dealing in the black market for foreign exchange,[52] which made the interbank arrangement likely to be successful. Second, this system requires less manpower resources at the official level. In fact, the Central Reserve Bank of El Salvador does not have sufficient manpower and expertise to conduct auctions. Third, the interbank system was considered a simpler arrangement and more similar to that of the previous black market. By contrast, the auction system may involve some technical requirements that inhibit entry to the market to some participants who might not be eligible to participate or may complicate the system. For example, bids from recipient families of workers' remittances, which are very small transactions, would have required the commercial banks to accumulate and present them on behalf of their clients. This could complicate the mechanism and may lead to a continuing existence of the black market. Fourth, the operation of the interbank system was envisaged by the authorities as being more efficient and in agreement with the philosophy of the whole economic reform initiated in mid-1989.

3. Macroeconomic Effects of Exchange Rate Unification

The macroeconomic effect of exchange rate unification depends on the uniform exchange rate regime to be adopted. Since the interest here is to analyze the Salvadorean experience, this section extensively discusses the macroeconomic effects of adopting a uniform floating exchange rate system and make some references to the alternative uniform exchange rate systems, namely, pegging to single currency.

Usually, in considering the policy of unification of the exchange markets, the authorities are concerned with two types of effects; first, whether the adoption of a unified floating system will lead to a sharp depreciation of the exchange rate in the short run, and second, what the macroeconomic effects of such a system are, particularly the effects on prices, the balance-of-payments, and the real exchange rate.

To analyze the macroeconomic effects of exchange rate unification, it is useful to compare two alternative dual regimes, discussed in Chapter IV, from which unification of exchange markets would take place. As was pointed out in

51 A fact that was expected to be enhanced by the financial reform already initiated at the time of the exchange market unification. For a description of the banking system in El Salvador, see Chapter II.

52 Before the adoption of a unified floating exchange rate regime, foreign exchange dealers were legalized and authorized to operate as exchange rate houses.

Chapter IV, under one regime, the official market clears through changes in international reserves. Under the alternative regime, the central bank implements a rationing scheme to allocate all the surrendered foreign exchange among public and private sector importers, so as to keep official international reserves constant and, in this case, the balance-of-payment is necessarily zero.[53] In the following sections, the macroeconomic effects of exchange rate unification under both cases will be discussed separately at the theoretical level.

a. From a Dual Exchange Market Regime with Reserve Adjustment

As noted in Chapter IV, under this system the domestic currency price of traded goods will reflect the weighted average exchange rate in the two foreign exchange markets. The domestic price level is thus defined as:

$$P = P_N^{\,1-a}\, e^{a(1-v)}\, be^{av}.$$

All variables are defined as in Chapter IV.

The fiscal deficit is financed by revenues from an implicit exchange tax,[54] through a decline in international reserves, and by printing money (inflation tax).[55] The implicit exchange rate tax depends on the exchange rate spread (which is endogenous) and the specific allocations of transactions between the two markets, which are determined by the authorities.[56] Clearly, this assumes that the government is a net buyer of foreign exchange. For the net seller case, this would imply an implicit subsidy on foreign exchange to the private sector.

The second source of finance may be central bank's disaccumulation of reserves (the central bank is a net seller at a price lower than in the free market)

53 In practice, some developing countries, including El Salvador, have implemented a combination of both regimes which involved some rationing scheme in the official market to avoid losses of reserve but also intervention in the official market to keep the black market premium low (indirect official intervention in the black market). Thus, the foreign exchange market clears through reserve movements and a depreciation of the black market exchange rate. In the case of El Salvador, the Central Bank actually accumulated reserves during the period of dual official-black market exchange rate regime. This was possible because of the large inflows of balance-of-payments support and foreign aid received by the country and because of the accumulation of external arrears of the Central Reserve Bank during that period.

54 Multiple rates become an important source of hidden fiscal revenues. See Chapter IV for a discussion on the multiple exchange rate systems as a method of taxation.

55 This refers to internal sources of financing a fiscal deficit. Internal borrowing from the private sector by selling government bonds can be an additional internal source. However, this source is not commonly used in developing countries.

56 The higher the premium and the proportion of exports exchanged in the official market at the lower rate, the higher the revenue from the implicit tax on export.

and, in this case, the central bank provides the necessary foreign exchange to finance part of the fiscal deficit from its own reserves. By contrast, it could also be the case that the central bank may profit from the dual exchange rate regime, buying more foreign exchange from the private sector than needed to finance public sector imports and official market private imports, and accumulating reserves (the central bank is a net buyer at a price that is lower than the market price). Thus, in the latter case, the second source of financing can be interpreted as an additional exchange tax and not as the central bank's disaccumulation of reserves. The third source of finance, printing money, is exogenously determined by the official exchange rate depreciation rule. Under this system, it is ambiguous whether the fiscal deficit leads to monetary expansion because printing money is partly offset by a monetary contraction produced by the central bank's loss of international reserves.

The distribution of deficit financing among these three sources depends on the government's specific objectives, particularly between exchange rate stabilization and inflation rate objectives.

At the time of unification and the adoption of a flexible exchange rate regime, the international reserves and the implicit exchange rate tax sources of financing will vanish. Therefore, unless real government spending is simultaneously lowered or other compensating sources of tax revenues are raised, the fiscal deficit will increase, thus requiring a higher inflation tax revenue.[57] As Pinto (1991a) points out, "Given the time consuming nature of fiscal reforms and the limited choice of tax instruments available, the most likely outcome is that this additional deficit will be monetized, which may raise inflation." Whether this produces an increase in inflation would depend on the elasticity of the demand for money with respect to the inflation rate. If this elasticity is lower than one, the inflation rate will rise with exchange rate unification, as will the exchange rate depreciation. By contrast, if this elasticity exceeds one, the rate of inflation would fall, as will the rate of exchange rate depreciation.[58]

Moreover, the adoption of a uniform floating exchange rate has some additional short- and long-run effects on the exchange rate, the rate of inflation, and the balance-of-payments.

The short-run effects would depend on expectations concerning the unification of the foreign exchange markets. Assuming the improbable case that unification is unanticipated, at the time of unification the uniform floating rate de-

57 The fiscal effect of exchange rate unification and the tradeoff between the implicit exchange tax and the inflation tax have been extensively examined by Pinto (1990, 1991a, and 1991b).

58 See Pinto (1990, 1991a, and 1991b). Lizondo (1990 and 1991) has also provided the same conclusion.

preciates with respect to the official rate of the dual system, but it can depreciate or appreciate with respect to the parallel rate of the dual system.[59]

If the unification of the exchange rate is fully anticipated, then the economic agents will react before exchange rate unification takes place. Probably, the central bank would have a loss of reserves and the parallel market rate would move to the level that the uniform floating rate is expected to have at the time of unification. The loss of official reserves would be similar to that described in the literature on balance-of-payments crises.[60, 61]

The long-run effect on the balance-of-payments will be a balance-of-payments equilibrium; under the new regime the balance-of-payments will be zero, and the mechanism of adjustment will be a depreciation or appreciation of the exchange rate.

b. From a Dual Exchange Market Regime with Reserve Rationing

Under the reserve-rationing regime there are only two sources of financing the fiscal deficit, namely, the implicit tax on exports and the inflation tax. Under such a regime, there are no movements of international reserves to clear the official market and, in this way, official international reserves remain constant.[62] Thus, under this regime the part of the fiscal deficit that would be financed by the inflation tax would lead to a monetary expansion. Additionally, under this type of regime, in the models advanced in the literature it is assumed that the domestic prices adjust fully to the free market (black market) rate while the economy is still under the dual regime.[63] Taking both facts into account, the inflation rate under this type of dual regime would probably be higher than under the reserve adjustment dual exchange markets.

With the unification of the exchange rate markets, the spread disappears and with it the implicit tax on exports. If public sector expenditure is not reduced and this source of revenue is not replaced by alternative taxes, the inflation tax must increase and, again, if the elasticity of the demand for money is less than unity,

59 See Lizondo (1990), p. 65.
60 See, for example, Krugman (1979) and Obstfeld (1984).
61 However, under a dual regime of the type assumed here, capital transactions at the official market are not allowed, and agents can only deplete official reserve by illegally diverting exports to the parallel market and overinvoicing eligible imports.
62 See Chapter IV.
63 This Assumption is made in Nowak (1984), Pinto (1990, and 1991), Kharas and Pinto (1989), and Lizondo (1991). See the discussion in Chapter IV.

the rate of inflation must increase.[64] The reason is straightforward. The more inelastic the demand for money with respect to inflation, the less the erosion in the base of the tax (demand for money) produced by raising the inflation rate and, hence, the higher the inflation rate required to yield the desired tax revenue.[65]

In summary, the "fiscal view" of unification (Pinto 1991a and 1991b) emphasizes that the fiscal deficit resulting from unification of foreign exchange markets is likely to be monetized, leading to higher inflation.

Using this framework, the El Salvador experiences with exchange rate unification will be analyzed below.

c. *Macroeconomic Effects of Unification of the Foreign Exchange Markets: El Salvador's Empirical Evidence*

As noted earlier, the dual regime from which unification took place in El Salvador was a combination of both of the regimes discussed above.

This section examines the effects of the unification of foreign exchange markets in El Salvador on a number of macroeconomic variables, namely, on the exchange rate, inflation, the fiscal deficit, and the balance-of-payments.

i. Effects on the Exchange Rate and Inflation

To examine the effects on the exchange rate and inflation, let us recall the empirical results of the model of Chapter V. First, the black market premium was determined by central bank indirect intervention, portfolio decision variables, the money supply, and seasonal factors.

The econometric estimates of Chapter V show that an increase in the foreign interest rate and in expectations on exchange rate depreciation will increase the premium. By contrast, the premium will fall with the central bank's selling of foreign exchange at the official rate (indirect official intervention), with an official exchange rate depreciation, and with an increase of any of the black market supply sources. Second, it was found that the official-black market dual system

64 This is the conclusion provided by Pinto (1990, 1991a, and 1991b) and by Lizondo (1987, 1990, and 1991). In contrast, Nowak (1984) argued that a devaluation of the official exchange rate would appreciate the parallel exchange rate and might lead to a deflationary effect. The reason for the different conclusions is that Nowak has not considered the hidden fiscal revenue from the dual regime and that, at the time of unification, this source of revenue vanishes and the fiscal deficit may increase.

65 For technical issues of the revenue from inflation, see Bailey (1956) and Friedman (1971).

only partly insulated domestic prices from black market exchange rate movements. Thus, domestic prices reflected both the official and black market exchange rates.

What can we learn from the model of the black market premium that could be applicable under the new regime of uniform flexible exchange rate? Three main results are of relevance under the new regime. First, anything that disturbed the premium would influence the uniform flexible exchange rate. Second, with unification and the adoption of a flexible exchange rate regime, central bank intervention in the foreign exchange market should vanish or at least be substantially reduced. In this way, any expansionary monetary or fiscal policy would have its full effect on the exchange rate and its subsequent effect on prices. In other words, under the uniform flexible regime an expansionary monetary policy would not be partly offset by monetary contraction produced by the Central Reserve Bank's selling of foreign exchange, as was the case under the dual regime of official-black market. Thus, an expansionary monetary or fiscal policy would depreciate the exchange rate and increase inflation. Third, under the new regime of a uniform flexible rate, a depreciation of the exchange rate would have its full effect on prices of traded goods, by contrast to a dual system of official-black market where domestic prices were partly insulated from movements in the black market exchange rate. Thus, a depreciation of the exchange rate will be fully reflected in the domestic prices of traded goods, which in turn will influence the prices of nontraded goods as demonstrated in Chapter V.

How, in fact, did exchange rate and prices behave? Table VII.2 of Chapter VII presents a summary of the recent behavior of prices and exchange rates in El Salvador. After some real depreciation in 1990,[66] the colon has appreciated by about 13 percent with respect to the level of 1990, but it has appreciated by about 50 percent with respect to the level of 1980.

The exchange rates and price behavior can be more clearly examined using monthly data. In the post-reform period from June 1990 to December 1993, the colon remained rather stable in nominal terms relative to the U.S. dollar (see Figure VI.2). Figure VI.3 depicts the index for relative prices (El Salvador's main trade partner consumer price index to El Salvador´s consumer price index), the nominal effective exchange rate, and the real effective exchange rate for the period 1980-1993.[67] During the 1990's the nominal effective exchange rate has kept depreciating smoothly, but this has not been enough to maintain the exchange rate depreciating in real terms, due to a faster decline in relative prices,

---

66 Actually, a decline in the rate of appreciation.

67 The methodology used to calculate these variables is described in Appendix VII.2.

reflecting the higher inflation rate of El Salvador relative to its main trade partners.

Using monthly data, Figure VI.4 shows that the inflation rate accelerated from August 1989 up until April 1990, and started to decelerate slightly in May 1990 and continued more rapidly during the month that the exchange unification of the foreign exchange markets was implemented (June 1990). This behavior is consistent with the fact that the reform was widely expected by private agents and that the effect on the exchange rate and on prices had already occurred when the reform was actually implemented. Moreover, the deceleration of the inflation rate is also consistent with the fact that the currency appreciated after unification. In fact, the behavior of prices following unification fits the theoretical expectations rather well.

Before concluding this section, it is important to note that the acceleration on the rate of inflation in the transition period cannot be attributed entirely to the exchange reform, but also to the impact of price liberalization, adjustment in certain public services prices, the easing up of monetary policy in early 1990, and uncertainty caused by the outbreak of political conflicts in late 1989. Thus, it is practically impossible to separate the effects of exchange rate unification from other macroeconomic and structural policies that were part of the economic program initiated in mid-1989 as well as from political events.

Figure VI.2
NOMINAL EXCHANGE RATE

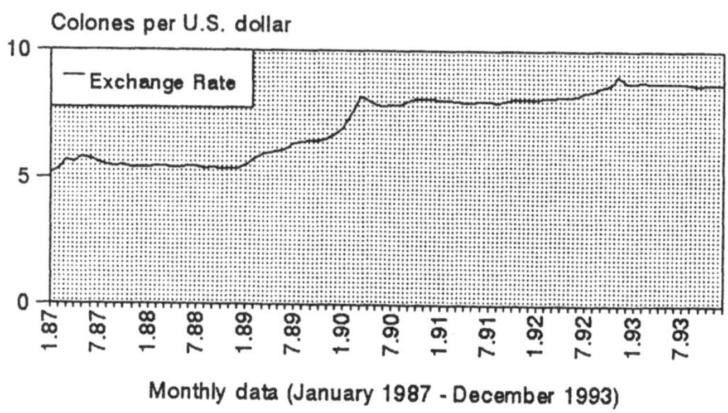

Source: Department of Exchange, Central Reserve Bank of El Salvador.
The exchange rate is the black market rate from January 1987 to May 1990, and the exchange houses rate from June 1990 to December 1993.

Figure VI.3
EL SALVADOR: REAL EXCHANGE RATES
(base year 1980)

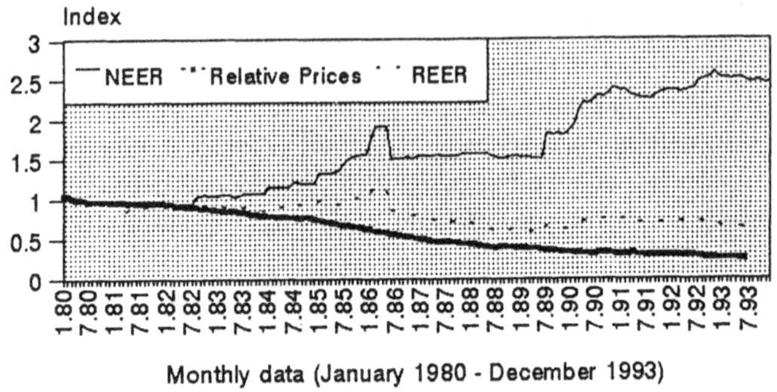

Source: International Monetary Fund, *International Financial Statistics*, and author's calculations (see Appendix VII.2).
An increase (decrease) indicates depreciation (appreciation).

Figure VI.4
INFLATION RATES
El Salvador and its main trade partners

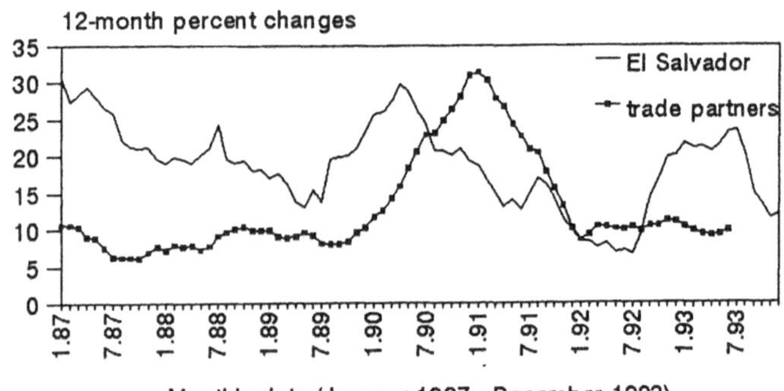

Source: International Monetary Fund, *International Financial Statistics*.
Inflation rates are 12-month percent change in consumer prices (line 64) from the corresponding month in the previous year.

ii. Fiscal Effects

In the case of El Salvador, the fiscal effects of exchange rate unification are expected to be positive or not negative to a significant degree (see Table VI.1). The government was a net seller of foreign exchange to the private sector, since all official external aid and borrowing were exchanged at the official exchange rate. Thus, unification eliminated the subsidy to the private sector, increasing government revenues. Additionally, beginning from the last quarter of 1989, the government implemented a medium-term plan of fiscal reforms that increased revenues from 7.62 percent of GDP in 1989 to 8.11 percent of GDP in 1990 (the year that unification of foreign exchange markets took place) and held current expenditure somewhat below the level reached in 1989 in relation to the GDP (see Table VI.2). In the following years, revenues and expenditures increased, resulting in a higher fiscal deficit, which was partly financed with the Central Reserve Bank's credit. However, this fiscal deterioration cannot be attributed to exchange rate unification, but rather can be related to an increase in the interest payments and capital expenditures associated with political and economic reforms implemented recently.

Table VI.1
Government's Foreign Exchange Proceeds and Payments
(millions of U.S. dollars)

	1987	1988	1989
Proceeds	456.2	392.8	468.6
Proceeds from external loans	110.8	119.7	186.2
Official grants	345.4	273.1	282.4
Payments		424.1	402.4
Payments for imports	n.a.	318.4	326.8
Payments for debt service	105.2	105.7	75.6
Net proceeds	n.a.	-31.3	66.2

Source: Data provided by the Fiscal department, Central Reserve Bank of El Salvador, January 1995.

Therefore, from the fiscal point of view of exchange rate unification, the rise in the average annual inflation rate in 1990 was not a consequence of the unification and the adoption of a flexible exchange rate system. There are three main reasons for this: First, exchange rate unification was gradual and the short-run impact on prices and exchange rate depreciation took place before June 1990,

Table VI.2

El Salvador: Government Finances 1987 - 1993
(in million of colones and as a percent of GDP)

	1987	1988	1989	1990	1991	1992	1993
Total Revenues	3306.2	3385.8	3182.6	4437.0	5246.7	6440.6	7924.0
(as % of GDP)	14.3	12.4	9.9	10.8	11.0	11.7	11.9
Tax Revenues	2588.2	2531.9	2457.4	3330.1	4061.0	4805.0	6246.0
(as % of GDP)	11.2	9.3	7.6	8.1	8.5	8.8	9.4
Non-tax Revenues*	147.2	166.0	160.0	205.0	303.0	574.0	288.0
(as % of GDP)	0.6	0.6	0.5	0.5	0.6	1.0	0.4
Capital Revenues	0.0	0.0	0.0	2.0	0.0	0.0	1.0
(as % of GDP)	0.0	0.0	0.0	0.0	0.0	0.0	0.0
External Aid	545.7	542.0	522.6	869.0	851.0	962.0	1223.0
(as % of GDP)	2.4	2.0	1.6	2.1	1.8	1.8	1.8
Total Expenditures	3592.8	3690.2	4233.0	4882.0	6603.0	8081.0	8680.0
(as % of GDP)	15.5	13.5	13.1	11.9	13.8	14.7	13.1
Current Expenditures	2761.8	3042.2	3398.4	4148.0	5158.0	5783.0	6670.0
(as % of GDP)	11.9	11.1	10.5	10.1	10.8	10.5	10.0
Capital Expenditures	703.4	588.0	745.9	753.0	1113.0	2049.0	1906.0
(as % of GDP)	3.0	2.1	2.3	1.8	2.3	3.7	2.9
Government Deficit or Surplus	-286.6	-304.4	-1050.0	-445.0	-1356.0	-1641.0	-756.0
(as % of GDP)	-1.2	-1.1	-3.3	-1.1	-2.8	-3.0	-1.1
Government Deficit or Surplus Excluding External Aid	-832.3	-846.4	-1572.6	-1314.0	-2207.0	-2603.0	-1979.0
(as % of GDP)	-3.6	-3.1	-4.9	-3.2	-4.6	-4.7	-3.0
External Financing	279.5	278.0	200.0	484.0	699.0	1320.0	1007.0
(as % of GDP)	1.2	1.0	0.6	1.2	1.5	2.4	1.5
Internal Financing	7.1	26.4	850.1	-38.6	657.0	321.0	-251.0
(as % of GDP)	0.0	0.1	2.6	-0.1	1.4	0.6	-0.4
of Which Central Bank Financing**	84.4	-69.6	888.1	280.0	849.0	817.0	-124.0
(as % of GDP)	0.4	-0.3	2.8	0.7	1.8	1.5	-0.2

Sources: Central Reserve Bank and Ministry of Finance of El Salvador, *Monetary and Financial Program*, various issues.

* Includes dividends, rent on real assets, sales of products, material and services, profits from government enterprises, etc.

** Central Bank financing higher than total internal financing, which means that the government used the central bank credit to pay back overdue debts to other internal financing sources.

followed by a decrease in the rate of inflation (see Figure VI.4). The fiscal view (Pinto 1991a) focuses on the long-run impact on prices, namely, the effect on prices in the post-reform period, which depends on the fiscal impact of the exchange rate reform. Second, exchange rate unification eliminated the fiscal burden of rents implicit in the black market premium, which may therefore entail a decrease in the rate of inflation rather than an increase; and third, exchange rate unification was part of a fully integrated medium-term plan which includes fiscal reforms, monetary restrictions, and other financial reforms (see Chapter II), which contributed to bringing the inflation rate down in the post-reform period. In fact, the inflation rate during the twenty-five months following the float decreased.

iii. Effects on the Balance-of-Payments

The balance-of-payments data (Tables V.3a and V.3b) show an increase in the trade balance deficit since 1989, as imports increased more than exports. By contrast, the current account and especially the overall balance-of-payments improved because of substantial increases in transfers and capital inflows. Probably, the unification of the foreign exchange markets and the introduction of a liberalized exchange rate regime, together with the introduction of financial reforms, contributed to these positive effects on private transfers and capital inflows, which probably represent past black market sources of foreign exchange that are now exchanged in the legal financial system, that represent the repatriation of previous capital flight as well as borrowing by the private sector from foreign private banks.

The observed increase in transfers and capital inflows has been partly matched by an increase in the trade account deficit and by an increase in the central bank's official reserves.

The observed increase in inflows of transfers and foreign capital may be one factor explaining the appreciation of the colon noted above (see Table VII.2) for two reasons:

(a) The increased supply of foreign exchange causes an appreciation of the nominal exchange rate (or a slower rate of depreciation).[68] (b) Transfers and capital inflows allow a higher level of absorption than would occur under normal circumstances, resulting in a greater consumption of both traded and nontraded goods. The increase in demand for nontraded goods puts upward pressure on the price of nontraded goods, causing, *ceteris paribus*, a further appreciation of the real exchange rate.

---

68 From January 1991 to December 1993 the average annual depreciation was 3.6 percent.

Table VI.3a

El Salvador: Balance of Payments

(millions of U.S. dollars)

	1987	1988	1989	1990	1991	1992	1993
Export of Goods	590.9	608.8	497.5	580.2	588.0	597.5	732.0
i. Traditional	386.4	393.6	252.7	294.8	271.6	217.2	272.9
Coffee	351.5	358.1	228.5	258.9	219.0	151.2	221.1
Others	34.9	35.5	24.2	35.9	52.6	66.0	51.8
ii. Nontraditional	204.5	215.3	244.1	285.4	315.9	380.3	450.0
CACM	119.6	139.8	160.0	173.0	193.7	257.3	315.0
Rest of the World	84.9	75.5	84.1	112.4	122.2	123.0	135.0
Imports	994.1	1006.9	1161.3	1262.4	1406.0	1698.5	1912.0
Trade Balance	-403.2	-398.1	-663.8	-682.2	-818.0	-1101.0	-1180.0
Net Services Account	-30.3	-58.1	-39.2	-23.0	-21.1	15.1	32.0
Net Transfer	573.2	508.6	519.8	569.2	722.0	935.0	1043.0
i. Official Transfers	371.6	282.8	282.4	223.2	178.5	227.0	220.0
ii. Private Transfers	201.6	225.8	237.4	346.0	543.5	708.0	823.0
Current Account	139.6	52.4	-183.8	-136.6	-117.8	-151.5	-100.0
Capital Account	-72.6	-145.1	139.0	396.4	137.8	138.7	248.0
i. Official Capital	57.6	62.0	150.2	89.0	116.9	89.4	141.0
ii. Banking Capital	-96.2	-46.4	55.2	41.0	-78.7	-36.7	-45.0
iii. Private Capital and Errors Omissions	-34.0	-160.7	-66.4	266.4	99.6	86.0	152.0
Overall Balance	67.0	-92.7	-44.8	259.8	20.0	-12.8	148.0
Others Financing	-16.1	28.8	69.5	-104.5	0.0	78.0	-10.0
Change in Net International Reserves (decrease -)	50.9	-63.9	24.7	155.3	20.0	65.2	138.0
Change in Official Reserves of the Central Bank	50.9	-63.9	36.6	117.1	42.0	59.8	144.0
Change in International Reserves of Commercial Banks	0.0	-0.0	-11.9	38.2	-22.0	5.4	-6.0

Source: Central Reserve Bank of El Salvador, *Quarterly Review*, various issues

Table VI.3b

El Salvador: Balance of Payments

(as a percent of GDP)

	1987	1988	1989	1990	1991	1992	1993
Export of Goods	12.8	11.1	8.6	10.8	9.9	9.2	9.6
i. Traditional	8.3	7.2	4.4	5.5	4.6	3.3	3.6
Coffee	7.6	6.5	4.0	4.8	3.7	2.3	2.9
Others	0.8	0.6	0.4	0.7	0.9	1.0	0.7
ii. Nontraditional	4.4	3.9	4.2	5.3	5.3	5.8	5.9
CACM	2.6	2.6	2.8	3.2	3.3	3.9	4.1
Rest of the World	1.8	1.4	1.5	2.1	2.1	1.9	1.8
Imports	21.5	18.4	20.2	23.5	23.7	26.0	25.2
Trade Balance	-8.7	-7.3	-11.5	-12.7	-13.8	-16.9	-15.5
Net Services Account	-0.7	-1.1	-0.7	-0.4	-0.4	0.2	0.4
Net Transfer	12.4	9.3	9.0	10.6	12.2	14.3	13.7
i. Official Transfers	8.0	5.2	4.9	4.2	3.0	3.5	2.9
ii. Private Transfers	4.4	4.1	4.1	6.4	9.2	10.9	10.8
Current Account	3.0	1.0	-3.2	-2.5	-2.0	-2.3	-1.3
Capital Account	-1.6	-2.7	2.4	7.4	2.3	2.1	3.3
i. Official Capital	1.2	1.1	2.6	1.7	2.0	1.4	1.9
ii. Banking Capital	-2.1	-0.8	1.0	0.8	-1.3	-0.6	-0.6
iii. Private Capital and Errors Omissions	-0.7	-2.9	-1.2	5.0	1.7	1.3	2.0
Overall Balance	1.4	-1.7	-0.8	4.8	0.3	-0.2	1.9
Others Financing	-0.3	0.5	1.2	-1.9	0.0	1.2	-0.1
Change in Net International Reserves (decrease -)	1.1	-1.2	0.4	2.9	0.3	1.0	1.8
Change in Official Reserves of the Central Bank	1.1	-1.2	0.6	2.2	0.7	0.9	1.9
Change in International Reserves of Commercial Banks	0.0	-0.0	-0.2	0.7	-0.4	0.1	-0.1

Source: Central Reserve Bank of El Salvador, *Quarterly Review*, various issues.

Concerning the trade balance, it seems to be that the unification of the foreign exchange markets and the adoption of a liberalized exchange and trade system has been helpful in producing a positive impact on export performance, particularly nontraditional exports, but it is not enough to restrain imports; and it seems that a financial tightening to avoid excess demand pressures is probably required.

Finally, it should be noted that although El Salvador maintains a floating rate regime, the balance-of-payments is determined by the intervention behavior of the Central Reserve Bank. This implies that the Salvadorean floating exchange rate regime is of a managed type,[69] which is consistent with the general view that a small open developing economy lacking a developed capital market is unlikely to be able to adopt a pure floating exchange rate regime.

C. Lessons from El Salvador's Experiences with Exchange Rate Unification

The main lessons that can be derived from the experiences with unification of the foreign exchange markets in El Salvador are as follows:

1. In countries with a black market for foreign exchange, the unification of the exchange markets can be approached through the adoption of a legal dual exchange rate regime setting up a legal parallel market emulating price developments of the existing black market for foreign exchange.[70] In the transition period, both rates (black and legal parallel market) keep depreciating. Thus, no jump occurs when unification is actually implemented and the spread between the two rates approaches zero. This behavior was observed in the Salvadorean exchange rates during the last month of the transition period.

2. The dual exchange rate regime in general is perceived as temporary and the unification of the foreign exchange markets is widely expected. Under these circumstances, there are two possible behaviors of the exchange rate during the transition period:

---

69 Under a pure floating exchange rate regime, the balance-of-payments result is equal to zero, so that the exchange rate is the clearing variable in the foreign exchange market.

70 This gradual approach was adopted in El Salvador to unify the foreign exchange markets into a uniform flexible exchange rate on June 1, 1990. The parallel market rate followed the black market exchange rate very closely during the first five months of the dual exchange rate regime. As mentioned earlier, political events at the end of 1989 accelerated the depreciation of the black market rate and then the parallel market rate only sluggishly followed the black market exchange rate developments.

a. If economic agents are certain about the nature of the post-transition regime, the black market exchange rate and the legal parallel rate move together to the expected level. This is especially true if the expected post-transition regime is a uniform fixed exchange rate regime. This fits exactly the behavior of the Salvadorean exchange rates during the first six months of the transition period. As noted above, both exchange rates move together, with there being practically no spread between the two rates (less than 2 percent), to the expected uniform rate.

b. If there is uncertainty about the nature of the exchange rate regime the authorities may adopt next, the black market exchange rate can show some volatility and the spread between the black market rate and the legal parallel rate may not narrow steadily during the transition period. The gap between the two rates will narrow shortly before market unification takes place. In the case of El Salvador, not only the uncertainty about the nature of the post-reform regime, but also political events may have contributed to the volatile exchange rate behavior observed, particularly during the first quarter of 1990.

3. The choice of the uniform exchange rate regime may be guided by criteria somewhat different from those more often proposed in the literature on the choice of exchange rate regime on developing countries (e.g., characteristic of exchange and financial markets). The experience of El Salvador shows that other criteria, such as policymakers' objectives and the type of macroeconomic policy and development strategy the authorities have decided to follow for one reason or another, are more important criteria.

4. The experience of El Salvador confirms one of the most important principles of the unification of foreign exchange markets and the choice of the appropriate exchange rate regime: *consistency of policies*. In particular, fiscal and monetary policies as well as the trade regime must be supportive of the unification policy and of the chosen exchange rate regime.

In this respect, someone who knows the recent economic history of El Salvador can ask: Why was the unification attempt in 1986 not successful, whereas the unification attempt in 1990 was? There were many aspects that were different in both events,[71] but the key issue to explaining the different outcomes may be *inconsistency of policies* in 1986.

Policy inconsistency in the 1986 unification attempt included:

a. The new official exchange rate was set at approximately the level of controlled parallel market (5 colones per U.S. dollar), which was below the black market exchange rate. By the end of 1985, the black market exchange rate was about 6.60 colones per U.S. dollar.

71 For details of both processes, see Chapter III.

b. New trade restrictions were imposed along with the devaluation, and exchange controls were not removed.

c. Fiscal and monetary policies in 1986 were not supportive of the unification attempt.[72]

5. A floating interbank exchange rate system can operate fairly well even in countries where the financial markets are underdeveloped and forward exchange markets are absent.[73] In El Salvador it was only necessary to allow commercial banks to act as intermediaries in the foreign exchange markets and to license the pre-existing network of operators dealing in the black market.

6. The experience of El Salvador also confirms the theoretical expectations that when the premium in the black market is not an important source of hidden fiscal revenues, the unification of the foreign markets will have an impact on prices in the short run, but the long-run rate of inflation will decrease.

7. Finally, to improve the balance of trade, exchange rate and trade liberalization may not be enough in the face of capital inflows. The appreciation of the exchange rate resulting from capital inflows may lead to an increase in imports and prevent exports from increasing. In El Salvador, that was especially true of imports because exports have grown, but not enough to offset the increase on imports.

---

72 In 1986, the unification of the foreign exchange markets took the form of the adoption of a fixed exchange rate regime. This was accompanied by expansionary domestic financial policies which were inconsistent with the financial discipline required to sustain a pegged exchange rate regime.

73 An early study leading to this conclusion is by Galbis (1993).

Chapter VII

Monetary Policy under a Uniform Flexible Exchange Rate Regime in the Wake of Financial Liberalization: The Case of El Salvador

A. Introduction

The unification of the foreign exchange markets in El Salvador was accompanied by a trade and financial liberalization process.[1] These developments have altered the environment under which monetary policy is conducted. The purpose of this chapter is to examine the monetary effects and the implications in the conduct of monetary policy with the resulting changes in exchange rate policy and financial and trade structure in El Salvador. Specifically, the chapter investigates the problems and issues that the Central Reserve Bank of El Salvador is facing in the wake of exchange and financial reforms. Because the experience under these reforms is very recent, the inferences that may be drawn must be regarded as tentative, both because the full effects of the reforms take time to work in an economy and because the sample period of the data is very short.

Following this short introduction, this chapter is divided into four sections. Section B presents a theoretical framework to analyze El Salvador's monetary policy in the following sections. Section C examines the Central Reserve Bank's objectives of monetary policy and their compatibility. This section also describes the Central Reserve Bank's operating procedure of monetary policy, namely, policy formulation, targets, and instruments. Section D discusses the recent economic experience, particularly the performance of the exchange rate, inflation, interest rate and monetary aggregates, and capital flows. Section E examines the links of these developments to the adoption of a uniform flexible exchange rate regime and to the financial liberalization process. Specifically, this section tries to answer the following questions: Do unification and exchange rate flexibility create any problems? What are the monetary policy implications of the exchange rate and financial liberalization? Has exchange rate unification and/or financial liberalization made monetary control difficult? Section E will also make some policy recommendations on the basis of the discussion in the above sections. Specifically, recommendations will be made with regard to the new role of

1 The latter has not yet been totally completed. For details of economic reforms and policies adopted in El Salvador since mid-1989, see Chapters II and III.

monetary policy, the objectives of the Central Reserve Bank, new strategy for monetary policy.

B. General Principles

This section discusses the theoretical aspects of the design and implementation of monetary policy within the framework of a uniform flexible exchange rate. However, to make the analysis clear, some references will be made to the case of pegged exchange rate regime (pegged to a single currency).

In conducting monetary policy, the central bank has to define the objectives to be pursued; in so doing, it must evaluate the feasibility of the objectives for monetary policy. The insistence upon unrealistic or contradictory goals may lead to a poor functioning of policy. Once the objectives of monetary policy have been defined, it remains for the central bank to formulate and implement the optimal strategy to obtain the objectives.

1. Strategies of Monetary Policy

A strategy presupposes the definition of ultimate objectives, intermediate targets and policy instruments. Generally speaking, there are two types of strategies that the central bank can choose: single-stage or multistage procedures. The essential difference between the two strategies is that the latter requires the designation of a key intermediate variable to serve as a pivot for the two-stage decision process, in addition to the selection of actual instruments.[2] In other words, the central bank has another problem in addition to the choice-of-instruments problem, that is, the selection of an appropriate intermediate target variable.

The strategy for implementing monetary policy most popular in the 1970's and early 1980's is of the second type, which distinguishes between instruments (e.g., open market operations or discount rate), intermediate targets (e.g., rate of growth of monetary aggregates), and ultimate objectives or goals (e.g., low inflation rate).

The essence of the intermediate target approach is that the central bank acts to influence the intermediate target (which in turn affects the final objective) as if it were itself the final objective. Thus, the central bank attempts, for example, to reach an optimal value of the money stock which is consistent with the desired level of inflation, or any other ultimate target variable. In this context, the central

---

2 See Bryant (1980), p. 240.

bank can continuously monitor the money growth, and this can provide an early warning of random shocks. Then, policy can be adjusted accordingly before the disturbance affects the final objective.

The choice of the intermediate target should be guided by three important criteria.[3] First, the intermediate target should be close and stable, related to the ultimate objective. An intermediate target that has no effect on the final objective has no role at all in the monetary policy process. Moreover, there should be a causal relationship between the intermediate target and the ultimate objective. Specifically, the causality should go from the intermediate target variable to the final objective variable. Thus, it is not enough that the selected intermediate target variable moves in step with the variable that represents the final objective, but should also affect the subsequent movements of an ultimate objective variable. The intermediate target should contain information about the future movements of the final objectives of monetary policy.

Second, the intermediate target should be controlled by the instruments at the disposal of the monetary authorities. There is no point in selecting as an intermediate target a variable that the central bank could not closely control, because, consequently, it would be difficult to achieve a target level.

Third, information about the behavior of the intermediate objective must be available more quickly and readily than data on the final objective.

However, several authors have criticized the logical validity of the two-stage process of monetary policy, arguing that it is a suboptimal strategy for conducting monetary policy.[4] Particularly, the recursiveness condition required for a two-stage strategy and the waste and inefficient use of information have been criticized.

In a two-stage strategy, the model representative of the structure of an economy must be decomposable into a lower-stage submodel and an upper-stage submodel. The endogenous variables of the lower-stage submodel (i.e., intermediate target variable) must be exogenous from the perspective of the upper-stage submodel, in which the endogenous variables are the ultimate-objective variable. This approach implies, for example, that if the money stock is the selected intermediate target, changes in the money stock should influence, but not be influenced by, the endogenous variables in the upper-stage level (e.g., inflation rate). Thus, it has been argued that this type of strategy fails to take into account the interdependence of elements of macroeconomic behavior.[5]

---

3 See Friedman (1983b), pp. 90-91.

4 See, for example, Bryant (1980), Friedman (1977) and Kareken, Muench, and Wallace (1973).

5 For details, see Bryant (1980).

The second important argument against the two-stage approach is the waste of valuable information or inefficiency in the use of information because, mainly, of the different periodicities corresponding to the two-stage decision process.[6] For example, during the recalculation of the intermediate target path, the two-stage approach ignores all new data for variables appearing in the upper-stage submodel.

The formulation and implementation of a strategy of monetary policy is influenced by the exchange rate system and the degree of capital mobility, as well as by the financial structure of an economy. Particularly, the instruments, targets, and channels of transmission of monetary policy are different under various assumptions of those elements.

2. *Instruments and Targets of Monetary Policy in an Open Economy*

The instrument problem is the choice of the variable(s) over which the central bank will exert direct control and that are judged most likely to obtain the ultimate target of monetary policy. In a closed economy the central bank can peg or stabilize the price of money (interest rate) and let the market determine the quantity, or it can peg or stabilize the quantity and let the interest rate be determined by the market. In reality, the money stock is not an exogenous variable in the strict sense required for the control problem. The central bank cannot set the money stock directly, but rather the central bank must use its open market operations and other policy tools (e.g., reserve requirements, discount credit, discount rate, credit ceiling) to control certain instruments which, in turn, influence the money stock and the interest rate. Then, the money stock and interest rate are targets of monetary policy rather than instruments. The problem of determining which of the potential instruments will allow the best control of the target variables and the problem of choosing the target variables themselves are the central bank's instrument and target choice problem, and this choice is significantly influenced by the exchange rate regime.

In an open economy with an exchange rate pegged to single currency, the monetary authority cannot control the money supply because changes in money supply can occur through changes in international reserves (balance-of-payments deficit or surplus). Monetary authorities would have control only over the domestic component of the money stock (domestic credit) and, therefore, can only affect the composition of the money stock sources (international reserve and

6 See Friedman (1977) and Bryant (1980) for a discussion of the most important elements of this argument.

domestic credit), but not the total volume of the money supply. For example, a restrictive monetary policy, through reduction of domestic credit, reduces the money supply relative to demand, which in turn improves the balance-of-payments (balance-of-payments surplus), increasing the money supply and reversing the initial reduction in the money supply.

The difficulty of controlling the money supply under a fixed exchange rate regime is exacerbated by international capital mobility, which prevents the domestic interest rate from being different from international levels. For example, a restrictive monetary policy will increase the domestic interest rate and attract capital inflows. This increase in capital inflows will reverse both the reduction in the money supply and the increase in the domestic interest rate.

Thus, for an open economy with a pegged exchange rate regime and capital mobility, the controllability of the money stock and interest rate is difficult and, as a consequence, the domestic inflation is not different from international levels. In other words, under a fixed exchange rate regime the central bank's choice of instruments is eliminated or at least significantly constrained.

By contrast, under a flexible exchange rate regime, the monetary authority has more autonomy in the conduct of monetary policy and the exchange rate becomes an important channel for the transmission of monetary policy. The effectiveness of monetary policy under a floating exchange rate is well known from the writings of Fleming and Mundell[7] and can be summarized briefly as follows.

The effect of monetary policy will always be greater if the country has a flexible exchange rate regime than if it has a fixed exchange rate, particularly if capital is mobile. The effect of monetary policy under the floating system will be greater, the greater the responsiveness of international capital flows to movements in the rate of interest. A restrictive monetary policy, for example, puts upward pressure on domestic interest rates and induces capital inflows and thus an appreciation of the exchange rate in response to the excess supply of foreign exchange. The appreciation of the exchange rate reinforces the effects of monetary contraction by reducing demand for domestically produced tradable goods and reduces inflationary pressures provided that the trade balance responds normally.

The choice of monetary policy instruments in the context of an open economy has been analyzed in the literature using the framework developed by Wil-

---

7 See Mundell (1968), Mundell (1963), and Fleming (1962). For more recent expositions of the Mundell-Fleming model, see Frenkel and Razin (1987) and Dornbusch (1980), Chps. 10 and 11.

liam Poole (1970).[8] The criteria for instrument choice in response to specific domestic shocks, as in the case of choosing an exchange rate regime (discussed in Chapter VI), is guided by the ability of each instrument to minimize deviations of the ultimate target variables (e.g., output and prices) from their objective levels. Thus, the concrete prescription in the case of monetary policy is that pegging or stabilizing rates (interest and exchange rates)[9] are likely to be the preferred instrument of monetary policy when the dominant sources of instability emanate from the financial sector. By contrast, pegging or stabilizing the monetary aggregates would be a preferable instrument where real sector disturbances (e.g., spending disturbances) are more important.[10]

While it is generally accepted that the monetary authority has better control over domestic monetary conditions in an open economy with flexible exchange rates,[11] it may also create conflicts between economic policy objectives, and the need to coordinate monetary with exchange rate policy is greater. This is particularly important for the case of a managed flexible exchange rate regime, where the central bank intervenes in the foreign exchange market to stabilize the exchange rate. It has been argued that there may often be a conflict between control of the money stock and control of the exchange rate.[12] For example, intervention in the foreign exchange market to prevent an appreciation of the exchange rate involves the purchase of foreign for domestic currency and thus an increase in the domestic money supply. This may not be consistent with the target of monetary growth, although, at least in the short run, the central bank may have some margin of operation. For example, the central bank might sterilize the effect of the foreign exchange market intervention on the money supply by selling domestic assets of the central bank or by increasing the reserve requirement, but this might enhance the conditions that appreciate the exchange rate. Hence, the central bank must be willing to accept some tradeoff between those two targets (i.e., exchange rate stability and monetary stability).

Genberg and Roth (1979) analyzed the possibility and advisability of interventions in the foreign exchange market in countries that let the exchange rate

8 See, for example, Gardner (1983), Benavie (1983), and Bryant (1980).

9 Stabilizing the exchange rate in the case of a flexible but managed exchange rate.

10 A very clear exposition of Poole's analysis is by Sellon and Teigen (1981).

11 However, the effectiveness of monetary policy under flexible exchange rates has been questioned. Niehans (1975) argues that this proposition is based on two assumptions. First, it assumes that the price elasticities of the demand for exports and imports are not affected by the transition to flexible rates. Second, capital flows are assumed to be independent of the exchange rate. He shows that if these assumptions do not hold, monetary policy could be less effective under the flexible exchange rate regime than has been suggested in the literature.

12 See Gardner (1983) and Genberg and Roth (1979).

float and establish annual targets for the rate of growth of their money supplies. They analyzed this issue under two different scenarios: (a) Under the assumption that the monetary target is known by the public, and when expectations are formed rationally, interventions in the foreign exchange market are counterproductive. (b) Under the assumption that if the target is not known and expectations are adaptive, although there is some scope for intervention, the amount of intervention must be kept small in order to prevent destabilization. Thus, the case for exchange market intervention in the presence of a money supply rule is, then, a fairly weak one. The central bank may want to keep one of the two policies, but should be cautious in attempting both.[13]

The degree of financial development also has implications for monetary policy. It has been argued that financial liberalization significantly changes the environment in which monetary policy is conducted. In particular, it has been pointed out that financial liberalization may affect (a) the money supply process, (b) the behavior of money demand, and (c) the channel of transmission of monetary policy.[14] The main theoretical arguments will be briefly summarized:

Concerning the money supply process, financial liberalization adds instability to this process. It has been pointed out that financial liberalization implies, *ceteris paribus*, upward pressure on the size of the money multiplier[15] for the following reasons: First, the increase in interest rates and the increasing availability of financial opportunities would tend to reduce the public's currency holdings. Second, a higher level of interest rates may induce a shift from demand deposits with higher reserve requirements to higher yielding deposits, which normally have lower reserve requirements. This lowers the banks' effective reserve-to-deposits ratio. These movements are, by their nature, uneven and unpredictable and so are the resulting changes in the money multiplier and in the money supply.[16]

Moreover, the composition of the monetary base may change as a result of financial liberalization, since this implies a change in the implementation of monetary and exchange rate policies. The "nonpolicy factors" or "autonomous factors" of the base may play a greater role in the determination of the base than

---

13 Genberg and Roth (1979), p. 543.

14 See Tseng and Corker (1991), Akhtar (1983b), Blundell-Wignall, Browne, and Manasse (1990), and Sijben (1988).

15 In any textbook of monetary theory, the money multiplier is expressed as $m=(c+1)/(c+r)$, where c denotes the currency-to-deposit ratio and r denotes the banks' reserve-to-deposit ratio (see, for example, Dornbusch and Fischer, 1990, Chapter 11). The money multiplier can also be broadly defined as the ratio of the stock of money to the stock of high-powered money.

16 See Akhtar (1983b), p. 15. See also Sijben (1988).

the policy factor[17] and even some policy factors have to be managed with caution. For example, interventions in the foreign exchange market under a flexible exchange rate are a policy factor, but the central bank should be cautious not to enter into potential contradictions (e.g., when the central bank carries its intervention to such an extreme as to turn a flexible exchange rate regime into a *de facto* fixed rate). Thus, the central bank could have a conflict of tasks between the control of money and exchange rate control. Both changes, i.e., the unpredictable movements in the money multiplier and the increased role of the nonpolicy factors in the determination of the base, might create potential monetary control difficulties for the authorities.

With regard to the impact of financial liberalization on the demand for money, it has been pointed out that financial liberalization that improves the quality of economic signals, alters the institutional environment, and expands the array of financial opportunities, creates a potential for instability in money demand.[18] Financial liberalization might upset the conventional relationships underlying the demand for the various monetary aggregates (i.e., the long-run relationship between monetary aggregates, economic activity, prices, and interest rates). First, if, for example, interest rates increase after financial liberalization, the demand for broad money (defined as currency plus demand, saving, and time deposits in the banking system) might rise at any level of income, but the demand for narrow money (currency plus demand deposits) might decline, increasing the velocity of money (M1). These portfolio shifts vary in size and are uneven and unpredictable, which make the demand for money unstable over time. In the case of M2 not only is the size unpredictable, but also the direction of the change because it is subject to opposing influences. Financial liberalization entails a proliferation of new financial instruments that are a close substitute for time deposits or other monetary aggregates included in M2. Thus, the demand for those instruments puts downward pressures on the demand for M2. Both influences are uneven, creating instability in money demand. Second, the interest rate before financial liberalization might not have varied sufficiently and the role of the interest rate in determining money demand might not be clear. However, with financial liberalization, the interest rate becomes more flexible and the role of interest in determining money demand could, therefore, become more trans-

17 The main factors affecting the monetary base can be grouped into "policy factors," those that are significantly influenced by the central bank's decisions and are used as tools of monetary policy (e.g., open market operations), and "nonpolicy factors," those that are outside the control of the central bank (e.g., credit to the government or foreign assets).

18 See, for example, Tseng and Corker (1991), Akhtar (1983a), Akhtar (1983b), and Sijben (1988).

parent.[19] Third, financial liberalization that increases competition between financial institutions could lower transaction costs in financial markets and cause money demand to respond more rapidly than before to interest rate changes. Thus, financial liberalization may alter the income and the interest rate elasticity of money demand.[20] Fourth, returns on alternative financial assets may become important determinants of money demand. Such assets include foreign assets if capital flows are also liberalized.

In summary, financial liberalization may lead to portfolio shifts in the level of money holdings and changes of the coefficient of the money demand functions, creating a potential for instability in money demand during the period of liberalization and in some cases over a longer period. Moreover, financial liberalization also enhances the role of the interest rate in transmitting monetary policy effects to the economy. More specifically, monetary policy impulses are transmitted to the ultimate objectives of economic policy (e.g., prices and economic growth) through interest rate fluctuations. In addition, if a more flexible exchange rate arrangement is adopted and capital controls are relaxed, the exchange rate also becomes an important channel of transmission of monetary policy in the liberalized environment. All these changes imply that financial liberalization may modify the environment in which monetary policy operates, which in turn may require a change of monetary policy strategy.

C. Monetary Policy Implementation in El Salvador

Prior to mid-1989, the implementation of monetary policy in El Salvador was based on credit restrictions, quantitative allocation, and administered interest rates. The Central Reserve Bank rediscount credit was the main instrument of monetary policy and, clearly, this was the main channel to transmit impulses from financial markets to the real economy.[21] The financial reform that was undertaken in mid-1989 had as a main objective the replacement of direct controls with more market-oriented instruments and gave a greater role to interest rates as a channel of transmission of monetary policy to the economy. The new operating procedures in conducting monetary policy will be analyzed next.

19 Tseng and Corker (1991), p. 11.
20 See Tseng and Corker (1991), p. 11.
21 See Chapter II.

1. Objectives of Monetary Policy

The new Organic Law of the Central Reserve Bank (Ley Orgánica del Banco Central de Reserva de El Salvador) has assigned to the bank the primary responsibilities of (a) maintaining the stability of the internal and external value of the colon and its convertibility, and (b) preventing or moderating inflationary and deflationary tendencies.[22] These objectives are very wide and they can be interpreted in several ways. In practice, the way these objectives have been interpreted is the following: "In the mid-term economic program 1989-1994, two main responsibilities have been assigned to the Central Reserve Bank: (a) to reduce and stabilize the inflation rate and (b) to avoid appreciation of the colon and, thus, to contribute to the reduction of the trade balance deficit."[23]

The Central Reserve Bank may have serious difficulties in achieving both objectives simultaneously because a Central Reserve Bank intervention to prevent an appreciation of the domestic currency involves purchases of foreign currency for domestic money that imply an increase in the domestic money supply that may be inflationary. By contrast, a restrictive monetary policy would increase the domestic interest rate and induce capital inflows, which, in turn, would appreciate the domestic currency in response to the excess supply of foreign exchange.

Monetary policy can control inflation. In the empirical evidence presented in Chapter V, it was found that a reduction of the Central Reserve Bank domestic credit rate would lead to a decline in prices of nontraded goods, which, in turn, would increase external competitiveness, and in this way the Central Reserve Bank could achieve the second objective.

Regarding the second objective, the Central Reserve Bank may influence the nominal exchange rate, but in so doing affects the money supply, which can reverse or may be incompatible with the monetary aggregate's targets consistent with the objective level of inflation rate.

Moreover, the Central Reserve Bank cannot control the real exchange rate. The real exchange rate is an endogenous variable that responds to both exogenous and policy-induced shocks. Policy changes that are not the sole responsi-

---

22 Articles 3b and 3c of the Ley Orgánica del Banco Central de Reserva de El Salvador.

23 International Monetary Fund (1992), p. v. On the second objective, it has been pointed out that the mid-term objectives of the exchange rate policy are (a) to maintain the stability of the real exchange rate, as a mechanism of export promotion, and (b) contribute to maintaining international competitiveness (Monetary Board meeting, JM-27/90, p. 4; and also in Central Reserve Bank of El Salvador, 1993, p. 3).

bility of the monetary authority, for example fiscal and trade policies, affect the real exchange rate as does monetary and exchange rate policy.

In adopting the real exchange rate as an objective of monetary policy,[24] the Central Reserve Bank faces another problem: namely, to establish the equilibrium real exchange rate. The determination of the equilibrium real exchange rate is not an easy task in practice, and estimating it at the wrong level could have serious consequences.

Appendix VII.1 reviews the various theories for determining the equilibrium real exchange rate. Here, we concentrate only on the problems associated with setting the real exchange rate as an objective of monetary policy.

Generally speaking, movements in real exchange rate indices based on either PPP or relative prices of tradeables and nontradables[25] have been commonly taken as an indication that the real exchange rate has diverged from its equilibrium value, and, therefore, as a change in external competitiveness. However, recent literature on the real exchange rate has shown that an observed change in the real exchange rate index may represent a change in the equilibrium real exchange rate.[26] These studies have emphasized that different types of external and domestic real shocks (such as differential rate of productivity growth, changes in the terms of trade, tariff reform, fiscal measures, and changes in international interest rate) would change the equilibrium real exchange rate.

El Salvador has undertaken a series of economic reforms that certainly affected the equilibrium real exchange rate, and the observed real appreciation should be associated with an appreciation of the equilibrium real exchange rate. For example, economic reforms – such as the removal of exchange controls, the introduction into the legal financial system of a large black market for foreign exchange in which a considerable amount of worker remittances was exchanged, and the financial liberalization, as well as other factors, such as the end of the civil conflict and implementation of a National Reconstruction Plan (NRP) to be financed with foreign financial assistance from multilateral organization and bilateral donors – have induced substantial capital inflows (particularly private transfers). These capital inflows would induce two effects. The first effect, which may contribute to the appreciation of the real exchange rate in the short run but does not induce a change in relative prices, namely, the increased supply of the foreign exchange, holds down the nominal exchange rate. The second effect is that capital inflows would induce a higher level of absorption, which would put

24 Usually, the Central Reserve Bank uses as a guide the real effective exchange rate based on PPP theory, but also takes into consideration others measures (i.e., relative prices of traded to nontraded goods.

25 See Appendix VII.1.

26 See, for example, Khan (1986), Khan and Montiel (1987), and Edwards (1989).

upward pressure on the price of nontraded goods, causing a real appreciation of the equilibrium exchange rate. The change in relative prices indicates that there are incentives to reallocate resources away from the traded goods sector toward the nontraded goods sector.[27]

Under these circumstances, the Central Reserve Bank should take into account the possibility that the equilibrium real exchange rate will vary owing to external or domestic shocks when it intervenes in the foreign exchange market. Therefore, it would be incorrect to measure changes in external competitiveness and the need for intervention based on the divergence of the observed real exchange rate from some constant base value which is considered the equilibrium real exchange rate for given values of other relevant variables – such as taxes, terms of trade, technology, and the financial environment – but these basic values may have changed with time and, therefore, the equilibrium value of the real exchange rate as well.

All the above reasons suggest that the Central Reserve Bank should not try to target the real exchange rate because the target level, the "equilibrium" level for some base period, may be chosen incorrectly, even if it was correct during certain periods, but it could have been rendered inconsistent with recent events of economic reforms.

Moreover, the Central Reserve Bank, in trying to influence the real exchange through nominal depreciation,[28] may fail to attain both of its objectives and it is likely to create price and exchange rate instability.[29] The reasons for this are discussed below.

The Central Reserve Bank has essentially used two types of instruments to depreciate the nominal exchange rate.[30] The first is purchases of foreign currency (dollars). A purchase of foreign currency, as it was pointed out above, will increase the money supply, raising domestic prices. Moreover, if the Central Bank sterilizes the monetary growth resulting from intervention in the foreign exchange market (sterilized intervention), it may intensify the conditions that attract inflows of capital. Sterilization would increase the interest rate, inducing capital inflows and further appreciating the exchange rate.

The second instrument used to achieve a nominal depreciation involves the sales of Monetary Stabilization Bonds (Certificados de Estabilización Monetaria,

---

27 The effect of inflows of official and private transfers received by El Salvador during the last few years have been analyzed in terms of Dutch disease economics, see Saca (1990b).

28 Buying dollars in the foreign exchange market.

29 By prices and exchange rate being unstable, I mean that their values would not converge to a long-run equilibrium value.

30 See Subsection C.3.

CEM) denominated in dollars, which has the advantage of avoiding the liquidity effect resulting from the purchase of foreign exchange described above. However, in the long run this policy could have some macroeconomic consequences. Proliferation of assets denominated in foreign currency may stimulate the currency substitution process, which in turn could create monetary instability that makes it more difficult to control inflation. The reasons for the possible stimulation of currency substitution process and the subsequent loss of control over inflation are straightforward: forward-looking agents may anticipate the Central Reserve Bank's policy and increase their expected exchange rate depreciation, and so the expected rate of return of holding foreign assets, which may reduce the demand for domestic money.[31] As the real demand for domestic money declines, the velocity grows rapidly, pushing up inflation and making the conduct of monetary policy more difficult. In addition, this policy would be ineffective in terms of preventing losses in international competitiveness, since the gain in competitiveness obtained with the initial nominal depreciation would be eroded within a short period of time.

2. Policy Formulation and Targets of Monetary Policy

In conducting monetary policy the Central Reserve Bank elaborates a monetary program on an annual basis which is presented to the rest of the government in December of the preceding year. Quarterly short-run projections are constructed using a simple method of interpolation of the annual data.

The annually based monetary program, which is designed by the Central Reserve Bank to orient economic policy, includes the usual basic goals of economic policy: objective levels of inflation rate, real growth, and international reserve accumulation. The monetary program contains the projections of the Central Reserve Bank and the commercial banks' balance accounts. These projections are integrated with the balance-of-payments and nonfinancial public sector projections.

The monetary program also contains a target level of money growth of M1 and M2 which, together with the monetary base, are the Central Bank's intermediate monetary targets and the operating target, respectively.[32] The targets for

31 Saca (1990a) found that the demand for money in El Salvador depends inversely on the expected rate of depreciation of the exchange rate.

32 An operating target is a variable that is closely linked to the intermediate target and over which the central bank can exercise quite close control. For example, the central bank might establish short-run targets for the high-power money and to main-

monetary growth are set according to the objective levels of inflation and real growth, and to the demand for money projections.

The monetary program also contains a projection of *net domestic assets* which serve as a tool of monetary policy and which are defined as the sum of high-power money (reserve money) minus the stock of net international reserves of the central bank. The net domestic assets variable contains all instruments of monetary policy available to the Central Reserve Bank: reserve requirements, net credit to the nonfinancial public sector and to the financial sector and Central Bank Stabilization Bonds (Certificados de Estabilización Monetaria).

The task of monitoring the short-run targets is delegated to the Committee of Monetary Operations (COMA),[33] which analyzes the weekly information on the liquidity and monetary situation of the economy and proposes procedures for open market operations and other types of interventions to the Directive Council accordingly.

3. Instruments of Monetary Policy

The Central Reserve Bank uses three types of instruments: reserve requirements, rediscount, and open market operations. The minimum reserve requirements are applicable to both banks' and savings associations' deposits. The minimum requirement rate is differentiated according to the type of deposits: 30 percent on demand deposits and 20 percent on saving and time deposits.[34] As of December 1993 the effective reserve requirements rate was 25 percent.

Substantial reforms were introduced in the area of credit policy in the context of financial liberalization. Direct controls on bank lending were eliminated, direct lending through discount credit to the commercial banks was reduced and this task was delegated to the Multisector Investment Bank.[35]

The third instrument of the Central Reserve Bank is open market operations. The Economic Stabilization Certificates (CEM) issued by the Central Reserve Bank are the principal vehicle for intervening in the domestic money market to control liquidity. Moreover, in 1992-1993 the Central Reserve Bank sought to

---

tain this variable near to its targeted value so as to control the intermediate variable (e.g., M2).

33 The COMA is composed of staff members of the Department of Monetary Operations and the Department of Economic Policy of the Central Reserve Bank.

34 The Law of Banks and Financial Institutions (Ley de Bancos y Financieras) authorizes the Central Reserve Bank to establish differentiated minimum reserve requirements by type of deposits and liabilities (Article 43).

35 See Chapter II.

absorb the excess supply of dollars stemming from remittances and capital inflows by issuing CEM in dollars.

Finally, the Central Bank usually intervenes in the foreign exchange market, buying and selling foreign exchange to smooth short-run fluctuations of the exchange rate. In 1992 and 1993, the Central Bank intervention in the foreign exchange market was oriented to avoid an appreciation of the nominal exchange rate resulting in a net purchase of dollars (Table VII.1).

Table VII.1

Central Reserve Bank's Foreign Exchange Market Intervention
(millions of U.S. dollars)

Months	1992			1993		
	Purchases	Sales	Net	Purchases	Sales	Net
January	7.60	2.00	5.60	0.00	24.90	-24.90
February	0.00	6.70	-6.70	8.00	0.00	8.00
March	0.00	0.00	0.00	22.40	0.00	22.40
April	13.10	0.00	13.10	23.80	0.00	23.80
May	15.56	0.00	15.56	40.50	0.00	40.50
June	0.55	5.00	-4.45	3.65	6.30	-2.65
July	0.00	10.00	-10.00	0.00	0.00	0.00
August	0.00	10.00	-10.00	0.00	0.00	0.00
September	0.00	19.80	-19.80	9.00	2.00	7.00
October	0.00	0.00	0.00	0.00	0.00	0.00
November	0.00	7.00	-7.00	0.00	3.00	-3.00
December	43.30	1.60	41.70	21.40	15.40	6.00
Total	80.11	62.10	18.01	128.75	51.60	77.15

Source: Department of Monetary Operations, Central Reserve Bank of El Salvador.

D. Recent Economic Experience

The main concerns of this chapter are, to examine first the effectiveness of the Salvadorean monetary policy and, second, the influence of the exchange rate regime and financial liberalization on monetary policy.

In this section, some key figures will be presented to highlight the current monetary problems in El Salvador and relate them to underlying macroeconomic developments. Most aspects are documented with annual data, but to provide greater detail monthly data on exchange rates and prices are used. The focus is on a few macroeconomic variables: the rate of inflation and output growth as objectives of policy, transfers and net capital inflows as a key exogenous variable, the nominal and real exchange rate and the interest rate as variables that play a key role in the transmission process; monetary aggregates such as rate of growth of money stock and credit as monetary targets, the monetary base as an operating target, and the net domestic assets of the Central Reserve Bank as an instrument of policy.

The period under review is 1987-1993:[36] 1987-1988 as a period previous to the exchange rate and financial reforms, 1989-1992 as a period of transition where most reforms took place, 1993 as a more "normal" year, but during which some more structural financial reforms were implemented.[37]

Figure VII.1
INFLATION RATES
El Salvador and Its Main Trading Partners

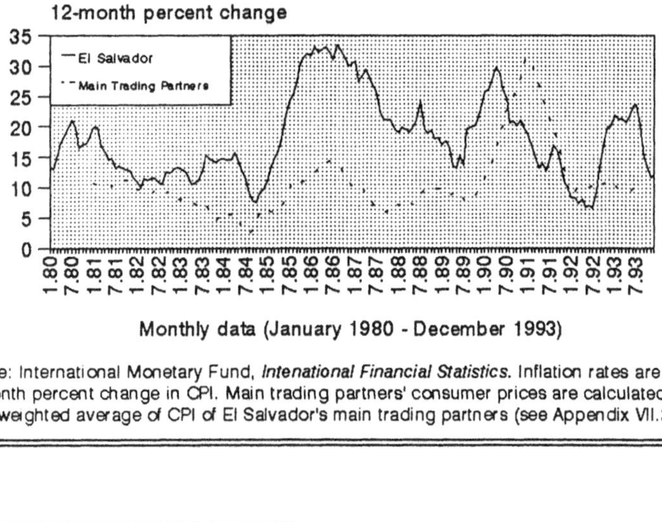

Source: International Monetary Fund, *Intenational Financial Statistics.* Inflation rates are 12-month percent change in CPI. Main trading partners' consumer prices are calculated as a trade-weighted average of CPI of El Salvador's main trading partners (see Appendix VII.2).

36 Unless otherwise indicated in text.

37 For example, some remaining structural reforms like the privatization of the two remaining state-owned commercial banks and other financial institutions took place in 1993. Also, as from July 1993 the prohibition on the establishment of financial institutions was lifted. There are still some other institutional financial reforms that are currently taking place. Briefly, they include an increase in the remunerated portion of mandatory bank reserves on saving and time deposits, from 5 to 10 percentage points, completion of the privatization process of the saving and loans associations, creation of an official development bank (Banco Multisectorial de Inversiones), and closure of the rediscount window of the Central Reserve Bank (IMF, 1994a, p. 40).

1. Inflation and the Real Exchange Rate

Figure VII.1 illustrates the evolution of the inflation rates using monthly data of El Salvador and of its major trading partners' consumer price index (CPI) from January 1980 to December 1993.[38]

The inflation rate in El Salvador for most of the 1980's was well above the inflation rate of its main trading partners as a consequence of macroeconomic disequilibrium caused mainly by the fiscal deficit existing during the war period, which was partly financed by the Central Reserve Bank's credit.

In the 1990's, El Salvador has experienced a lower level of inflation than in the 1980's, around 15 percent, on average, with short-run upward fluctuations owing to policy adjustments. From August 1990 to August 1992, inflation in El Salvador was lower than in its main trading partners, due, to a great extent, to reduction of the inflation rate in El Salvador and to an acceleration of the inflation rate in Guatemala and Costa Rica and, to a lesser extent, to some increase in the inflation of the industrial countries.

Table VII.2 provides three alternative measures of the real exchange rate for El Salvador.[39] The first and most commonly employed is the trade-weighted real effective exchange rate index, which is formulated as the nominal effective exchange rate index adjusted for changes in consumer prices in El Salvador relative to those abroad (i.e., El Salvador's major trading partners: United States, Germany, Japan, Guatemala, and Costa Rica).[40] The index indicates a real appreciation of about 50 percent in 1993 with respect to the 1980 level. After a real depreciation in 1990,[41] the colon has appreciated in real effective terms despite the adoption of a flexible exchange rate regime and a nominal effective depreciation, which means that the nominal depreciation was less than the inflation differential. This behavior of the real exchange rate is primarily attributable to increasing capital inflows (see Section D.2).

Using monthly data, Figure VI.3, in Chapter VI, provides evidence on the behavior of nominal and real exchange rates from 1980 to 1993. Three aspects emerge from the figure. First, the relative prices of El Salvador's major trading

---

38 The consumer prices of El Salvador's main trading partners are calculated as trade-weighted consumer prices of the United States, Germany, Japan, Guatemala, and Costa Rica, using the same methodology as in Chapter V (see Appendices V.1 and VII.2).

39 Appendix VII.2 contains the methodology used to calculate the real exchange rates.

40 A depreciation is represented by an increase in the index.

41 Actually, a decline in the rate of appreciation.

Table VII.2

Three Measures of Real Exchange Rate for El Salvador
(1980 = 1)

	1986	1987	1988	1989	1990	1991	1992	1993
1. TRADE - WEIGHTED EXCHANGE RATE								
Nominal Effective Exchange Rate Index*	1.61	1.57	1.58	1.63	2.26	2.34	2.47	2.51
Relative Prices**	0.64	0.52	0.46	0.42	0.40	0.41	0.40	0.37
Real Effective Exchange Rate Index*	0.91	0.76	0.66	0.62	0.75	0.73	0.72	0.66
Nominal Effective Depreciation/Appreciation***	0.38	0.36	0.37	0.39	0.56	0.57	0.59	0.60
Real Effective Depreciation/ Appreciation***	-0.09	-0.32	-0.50	-0.63	-0.33	-0.36	-0.38	-0.52
El Salvador CPI Change	31.95	24.90	19.80	17.60	24.00	14.40	11.20	17.30
Trade Patners CPI Change	4.96	0.65	6.62	8.16	16.14	16.99	8.76	8.02
2. BILATERAL EXCHANGE RATE								
Real Exchange Rate	0.85	0.70	0.61	0.61	0.69	0.64	0.60	0.54
Real Depreciation/ Appreciation	-0.17	-0.43	-0.64	-0.64	-0.44	-0.56	-0.65	-0.84
3. INTERNAL TERMS OF TRADE								
Relative Prices Traded/ Nontraded	0.83	0.70	0.71	0.66	0.64	0.63	0.59	0.58
Traded Goods Prices (annual change)	42.23	3.04	17.15	10.80	21.55	10.93	5.05	13.66
Nontraded Goods Prices (annual change)	33.32	21.17	15.66	19.88	25.07	12.85	12.29	15.88
Real Depreciation/ Appreciation	-0.21	-0.42	-0.41	-0.52	-0.56	-0.59	-0.70	-0.73

Sources: Central Reserve Bank of El Salvador, IMF, *International Financial Statistics* (basic data), and author's estimates (Appendix VII.2 contains the methodology used to calculate the three measures of the real exchange rate).

CPI: Consumer Price Index.

* An increase (decrease) indicates depreciation (appreciation).

** Major trade partners CPI to El Salvador's CPI.

*** Depreciation/Appreciation with respect to the base year (1980), negative numbers indicate appreciation.

partners′ CPI to El Salvador′s CPI declined consistently during the period. Second, the nominal effective exchange rate has remained rather stable with a slow rate of depreciation. From mid-1989, when a more flexible arrangement was adopted, to early 1991, the average monthly exchange rate depreciation was around 2 percent; and for the rest of the period this rate decreased to less than 1 percent and, in some months, even appreciated. Third, the long-run trend of the real exchange rate reflected an appreciation of the colon with respect to the 1980 level despite a tariff reform and a removal of the exchange controls (see footnote 42).

The second measure is a bilateral real exchange rate vis-à-vis the United States, which is the exchange rate times the U.S. wholesale price index (WPI), serving as a proxy for the price of tradables, divided by the El Salvador consumer price index as a proxy for nontradables.

The third measure of the real exchange rate is the relative price of tradable to nontradable goods. A pure tradable and nontradable index for El Salvador does not exist. Thus, they were constructed from the GDP deflator by sectors (see Appendix VII.2). The relative price of traded to nontraded goods (Table VII. 2) shows that the prices of nontradable goods have increased more rapidly than the prices of tradable goods, and that this tendency was not reversed with the adoption of a flexible exchange rate regime and the liberalization of the trade system. This may suggest that the equilibrium relative prices have changed. In other words, the equilibrium real exchange rate has appreciated to reflect the relative abundance of foreign exchange existing in recent years and the capital account liberalization.[42] Therefore, as long as large flows of workers' remittances and capital inflows are not reversed, one can expect that El Salvador's equilibrium real exchange rate will remain low.

2. *Transfers and Capital Flows*

Tables VI.3a and VI.3b provide information on the balance-of-payments accounts. In the current account, the private transfer inflows appear to be higher

42 The standard analysis of the effects of a tariff reform suggests that tariff reduction is typically accompanied by a depreciation of the equilibrium real exchange rate. A lower tariff will reduce the relative prices of importables, creating excess demand for those goods and excess supply of both nontradables and exportables.To restore equilibrium, relative prices of nontradables must fall. Thus, in response to tariff reduction, the equilibrium exchange rate tends to depreciate (see Aghevli, Khan, and Montiel, 1991, p. 9, and Edwards, 1991). By contrast, a capital account liberalization will require an equilibrium real exchange rate appreciation.

than total exports of goods. They have been around 13 percent of the GDP during the last three years. The private capital inflows appear to be positive: they increased from -2.9 percent of GDP in 1988 to 5 percent of GDP in 1990. Since then, private capital inflows have remained positive, around 1.6 percent of GDP. Substantial parts of the surplus in the private capital account may represent repatriation of previous capital flight. Private transfers and capital flows are also depicted for the 1980's and the 1990's in Figure VII.2. Various policy measures and events (domestic and external) contributed to reverse capital flight in El Salvador. Among them we can mention: capital account liberalization, exchange rate stability and positive interest rate differentials between domestic and U.S. interest rates, and improvement of the political environment as a result of the negotiation process between the government and the Farabundo Martí National Liberation Front, and later the signing of the Peace Accord in early 1992 that put an end to 12 years of civil conflict. While it is relatively easy to assess what factors caused the reversal in capital flight in El Salvador, it is very difficult to determine the relative importance of the causes of the reversal: the importance of external versus domestic causes.[43] In fact, the timing of the changes of external factors (falling of nominal interest rate and reduction of output growth in the United States) roughly coincide with the reorientation of El Salvador's economic policies. Interest rates and real GDP began to fall in the United States in 1989 (see Figures VII.4 and VII.5); and in El Salvador a new government assumed office in mid-1989 and introduced a comprehensive stabilization and structural reforms designed to create a more market-oriented and private-sector-led economy. However, while developments in the United States are important, they may not be the dominant causes of the inflows for the following reason: The intensity of the inflows varied during the four years of inflows and there is not an exact correlation between their intensity and the interest rate and GDP drop in the United States. Second, private capital inflows jumped in 1990 and peaked at about 5 percent of the GDP, which may suggest that inflows were attracted by the reorientation of domestic policies. The improvement in fiscal position, the nominal depreciation, which improved external competitiveness in 1990, as well

43 In an empirical study for ten Latin American countries, Calvo, Leiderman, and Reinhart (1993) conclude that foreign factors, particularly falling interest rates, recession, and balance-of-payment developments in the United States, were very significant factors driving investors to shift resources to Latin America. By contrast, in a recent paper that reviews the experiences of six countries that had recent surges in capital inflows (Chile, Colombia, Egypt, Mexico, Spain, and Thailand) Schadler et al. (1993) concluded that developments in foreign interest rate and growth, while important, cannot be seen as dominant causes of the inflows.

Figure VII.2
PRIVATE CAPITAL FLOWS
Percent of GDP

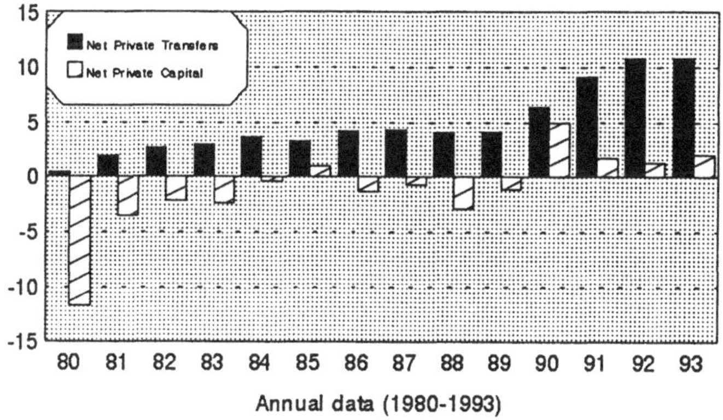

Source: Central Reserve Bank of El Salvador, *Quarterly Review*, various issues.

Figure VII.3
PUBLIC SECTOR CAPITAL INFLOWS
Percent of GDP

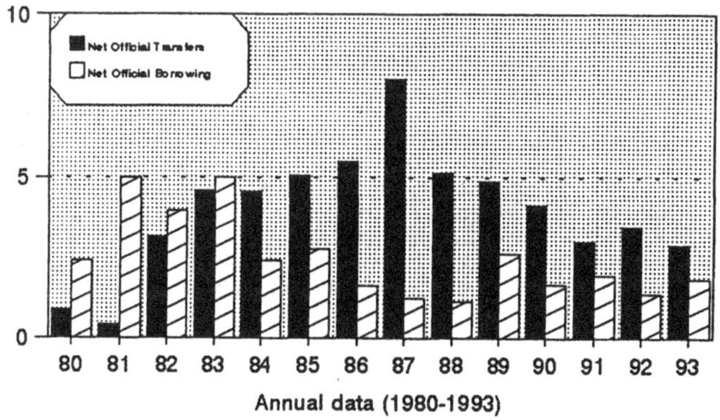

Source: Central Reserve Bank of El Salvador, *Quarterly Review*, various issues.

Figure VII.4
UNITED STATES INTEREST RATES

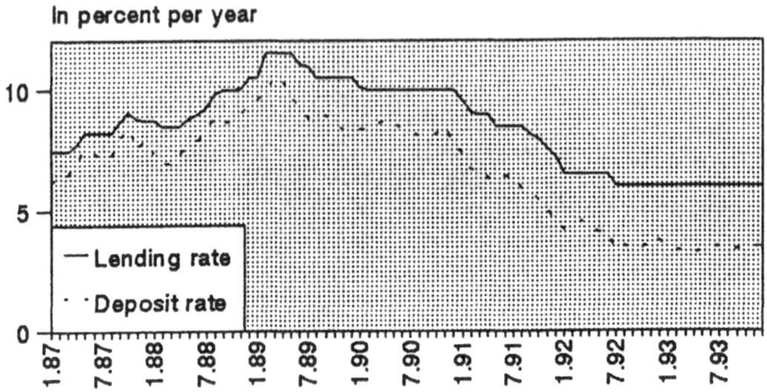

Monthly data (January 1987 - December 1993).

Source: International Monetary Fund, *International Financial Statistics*. Lending rate (line 60p), deposit rate (line 60l).

Figure VII.5
UNITED STATES OUTPUT GROWTH
Annual Change

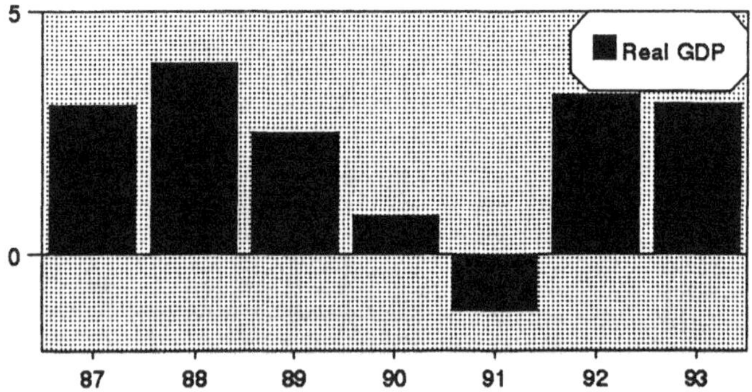

Annual data (1987-1993)

Source: International Monetary Fund, *International Financial Statistics*.

as the tightening of credit conditions and the beginning of the financial liberalization process may have been perceived by economic agents as the basis of sustainable growth, which could have increased the attractiveness of domestic investment and of domestic financial assets.[44]

Concerning the private transfers, of which most are workers' remittances, a similar amount probably flowed into the country before the exchange rate liberalization took place, since a substantial part of them were formerly exchanged on the black market for foreign currency. As noted in Chapter III, the official figures of private transfers were underestimated.

Additionally, Tables VI.3a and VI.3b report a slight increase in net external borrowing by the public sector. The increase was primarily due to borrowing by the public sector from multilateral organizations to finance the economic stabilization and reform program implemented since mid-1989. Also, it may represent official borrowing from private foreign banks as the country recovered its international creditworthiness as a result of implementing economic and political reforms that have recently taken place. By contrast, official transfers have gradually decreased, after having reached a peak level of 7.7 percent of the GDP in 1987, to about 3 percent of the GDP in 1993 (Figure VII.3).

The inflows of transfers and foreign capital contributed to the appreciation of the real exchange rate reported above (see Table VII.2) for two reasons: (a) the increased supply of foreign exchange caused appreciation of the nominal exchange rate (or a slower rate of depreciation),[45] (b) transfers and capital inflows allowed a higher level of absorption than would occur under normal circumstances, resulting in a greater consumption of both imports and nontraded goods. As already noted the increase in demand for nontraded goods put upward pressure on the price of nontraded goods, causing a further appreciation of the exchange rate. This drew resources out of the tradable sector into the nontradable sector, so that nontradable output rose and tradable output fell. The consequent decline in the tradable sector has come to be known as the *Dutch disease.*[46]

In the case of El Salvador, the presumption is that the agricultural sector, which is the most export-oriented sector, will decline following and infusion of foreign capital owing to the reallocation of resources in favor of the nontraded goods sector induced by the increase in the price of these goods.

---

44 Cáceres (1993) presents evidence of the causes of capital flight from Central America. In the case of El Salvador, capital flight showed a response to the real exchange rate. It would be logical to think that a reversal of that phenomenon could be influenced by an improvement of external competitiveness.

45 From January 1991 to December 1993 the average annual depreciation was 3.6 percent.

46 See Chapter IV.

However, examining the sectors' output (Tables VII.3 and II.2), it is not clear that agriculture has been hurt. Following the liberalization of the foreign exchange regime, agricultural production grew, except in 1991, when the sector's production fell by 0.05 percent per year owing to a severe drought. In addition, the share of agricultural production in total GDP has been quite stable during the period under study and it is similar to previous levels in the late 1970's, when capital inflows were not significant and the agricultural sector was experiencing a boom because of high international coffee prices.

Table VII.3

Sectorial Growth Rates

(percentages)

	1987	1988	1989	1990	1991	1992	1993
Agricultural Sector (export-oriented)	2.08	-0.95	0.47	7.44	-0.05	9.02	2.82
Manufacturing Sector (import-competing oriented sector)	2.99	3.01	2.48	2.99	4.87	6.01	7.60
Nontraded Good Sector*	2.84	2.25	0.86	1.94	4.59	3.35	5.04

Source: Central Reserve Bank of El Salvador, *Quarterly Review*, various issues, and author's calculations.

* Includes: Construction, electricity and water, mining, commerce, residential rents, personal services, public administration, financial services, and transport.

Additionally, the manufacturing sector, which produces import-competing goods, also experienced a relatively high growth. This suggests that the increase in demand for tradables following an inflow of capital may not be met only by imports at constant world prices, but also by home-produced manufactures that are close but not perfect substitutes for imports. Thus, the import-competing sector may expand its output with a large infusion of foreign exchange.[47]

47 An early analysis leading to this conclusion is provided by Benjamin, Devarajan, and Weiner (1989). Another situation in which this result, i.e., the import-competing sector may expand following an inflow of capital, may appear is in developing countries that impose exchange controls on current account transactions (see Chapter IV). The presence of foreign exchange controls implies that the market for importables behaves partly in the same manner as the market for nontraded goods. An increase in demand for importables (say, because of receiving a transfer) cannot be

How have the Salvadorean authorities responded to the appreciation of the real exchange rate? On the one hand, the Central Reserve Bank has intervened in the foreign market by buying foreign exchange (see Table VII.1), which has had very little impact on preventing a real appreciation of the colon (see Table VII.2). On the other hand, the Central Bank sought to absorb liquidity stemming from capital inflows by issuing sterilization bonds, increasing reserve requirements, and requiring banks and financial institutions to hold part of their deposits in Central Reserve Bank bonds (sterilized intervention). The latter policies have helped to moderate money growth, but capital inflows have been too strong to sterilize completely, so that rapid M2 growth continues despite those policies (see Tables VII.4 and VII.5).

By itself, real appreciation does not constitute grounds for intervention, and intervention is less advisable when the instrument is a nominal depreciation through foreign exchange market operations (i.e., the central bank's buying of foreign currency), which, as noted earlier, could be inflationary and would further appreciate the real exchange rate (through an increase in domestic prices).

Moreover, if the monetary authorities are reluctant to let the money supply grow by an amount corresponding to the accumulation of reserves and they decide to sterilize to keep the money supply under control, this may result in an ineffective policy in the long run;[48] and it may also be inconvenient for three reasons: First, sterilization risks intensifying the conditions that attract capital inflows: increasing domestic interest rates.[49] Second, maintaining high domestic interest rates and tight liquidity deprived the economy of the benefits of capital inflows: increasing investment and growth. Third, sterilization in the form of open market operation may be costly for the central bank; but increasing reserve requirements – although this may be profitable for the Central Reserve Bank

freely satisfied by imports because of the exchange controls. Thus, in order to clear the market for importables, the domestic price of these goods must rise to equate the domestic demand for imports and the supply of imports determined by the exchange controls authorities. This was the situation in El Salvador prior to the exchange regime reform (see Saca, 1990b). This cannot currently be the case, because El Salvador has removed all exchange controls on current and capital accounts.

48 Mussa (1981) concludes that sterilized intervention cannot have any permanent effect on the exchange rate. Moreover, Kenen (1982) concludes that when foreign and domestic bonds are perfect substitutes, sterilized intervention is ineffective in the long and short run.

49 An especially large increase in interest rates could be an even more probable outcome in an environment of financial liberalization and economic reforms, because residents could have increased their demand for money in response to a reorientation of economic policy.

because only a portion of the reserve requirement (10 percent) is remunerated – may discourage financial intermediation.[50]

In fact, there is no disease, since no sector appears to be hurt and the inflows of capital increase national income and welfare. They also improve the distribution of income, since the recipient families of remittances are from low middle-class to extreme poverty-class.[51]

Finally, while large inflows increase prices of nontraded goods and cause exchange rate appreciation, this does not preclude rapid growth of exports, as shown by El Salvador's export performance; especially nontraditional exports have grown rapidly during the last few years (Tables VI.3a and VI.3b).

3. Experience with Interest Rate Liberalization

Figure VII.6 shows the behavior of the Salvadorean deposit and lending interest rate and El Salvador's inflation rate. The deposit rate is the interest rate on time deposits with a maturity of up to 180-day. The lending rate is the rate of interest on credits with maturities of up to one year. As noted in Chapter II, the impact of interest rate liberalization was to move the nominal rate downward due to the excess liquidity resulting from capital inflows. However, even if the nominal interest rate had a downward tendency, the real interest rate was positive from the beginning of the interest rate liberalization process until the end of 1992, particularly during the first six months of full deregulation (from March to August 1992), due to a substantial reduction in inflation (see Figures VII.6 and II.1).[52] By the end of 1992, the inflation rate accelerated and, subsequently, the interest rate rose, but the increase in nominal rates was not sufficiently large and resulted in negative real interest rates during the first seven months of 1993. Then the inflation rate declined and nominal interest rates experienced a slight decline, resulting in positive real interest rates for the rest of the period.

Figure VII.7 provides evidence on the interest rate differential between El Salvador and the United States and the annual exchange rate changes.[53] Three main aspects emerge from Figure VII.7. First, during the period prior to the exchange reforms 1987-1988, the interest rate differential was positive, which

---

50 For an examination of the policy responses of six countries that had recent surge inflows, see Schadleret et al. (1993).

51 See Montes (1990).

52 The real interest rate is calculated as in footnote 33 of Chapter II.

53 In view of the fact that the lending and deposit rates are very close, only the deposit rate was plotted.

Figure VII.6
NOMINAL INTEREST RATES AND INFLATION

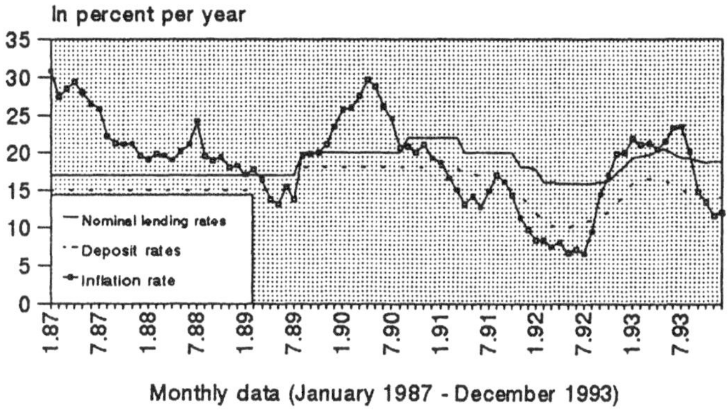

Source: International Monetary Fund, *International Financial Statistics*.
Lending rate: loans up to one year (line 60p), deposit rate: 180-day time deposits (line 60l).
Inflation rate is 12-month percent change in CPI (line 64).

Figure VII.7
INTEREST RATE DIFFERENTIALS

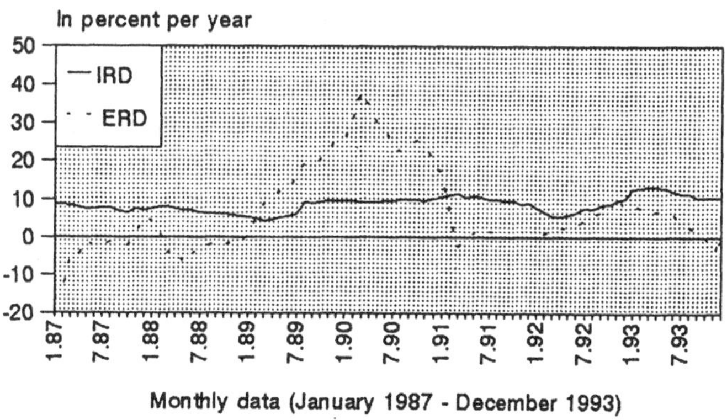

Source: International Monetary Fund, *International Financial Statistics*, and author's estimates.
IRD is domestic deposit interest rate minus U.S. deposit rate.
ERD is exchange rate depreciation/appreciation.

was enhanced by an appreciation of the black market exchange rate.[54] Second, during the period prior to the liberalization of the interest rate but with a more flexible exchange rate regime, the positive interest rate differentials were more than offset by an acceleration of exchange rate depreciation, resulting in a negative depreciation-adjusted interest rate differential.[55] Third, since the process of liberalization of the interest rate began, the depreciation-adjusted interest differential has been consistently positive. In addition to interest rate liberalization, some other factors have contributed to the last outcome. Among these are the decline in the U.S. interest rates and sizable capital inflows which led to a very slow exchange rate depreciation.

4. Credit and Monetary Aggregates

During the 1990's the Central Reserve Bank sought to absorb liquidity from transfers and capital inflows by increasing reserve requirements, open market operations, and requiring financial institutions to hold part of their deposits in the form of the Central Bank's sterilization bonds. However, as noted earlier, capital inflows were too strong, so the rate of growth of money supply was high, about 25 percent per year on average (Table VII.5).

Tables VII.4 and VII.5 provide a summary of the recent behavior of monetary aggregates. Three main aspects emerge with regard to monetary conditions. First, the monetary base is increasingly composed of foreign assets. Net international reserves of the Central Reserve Bank increased from 5.1 percent of GDP in 1987 to 9.2 percent of GDP in 1993. The increase in official reserves indicates that part of the capital inflows were met by foreign exchange market intervention which, in turn, increased the money supply. Second, domestic credit, especially to the public sector, has been contracted to partly offset the growth in international reserves. As one can see from the behavior of net domestic assets of the Central Reserve Bank, monetary policy has been quite tight. Third, the currency-to- deposit ratio has decreased, which is normal in an economy under a process of financial liberalization. However, the money multiplier continues to be at similar levels or even lower, because reserve requirements have been increased to strengthen monetary control.

---

54 It is assumed that before exchange rate liberalization, the relevant exchange rate for capital account transactions was the black market exchange rate.

55 The depreciation-adjusted interest rate differential is measured by the domestic interest rate minus the sum of the U.S. interest rate and the annual exchange rate depreciation.

Table VII.4

Monetary and Credit Indicators
(millions of colones)

	1987	1988	1989	1990	1991	1992	1993
CENTRAL RESERVE BANK							
Monetary Base	2492.0	2902.9	3252.1	4202.2	5143.0	6090.0	8574.5
(% of GDP)	10.8	10.6	10.1	10.2	10.8	11.1	12.9
Net Foreign Assets	-781.1	-761.9	-622.4	-291.1	681.6	1423.2	3544.5
(% of GDP)	-3.4	-2.8	-1.9	-0.7	1.4	2.6	5.3
of which:							
Net International Reserves	1180.5	972.0	1310.1	2954.4	3377.4	4452.3	6085.4
(% of GDP)	5.1	3.6	4.1	7.2	7.1	8.1	9.2
Net Domestic Assets	3273.2	3664.8	3874.5	4493.3	4461.4	4666.8	5030.0
(% of GDP)	14.1	13.4	12.0	10.9	9.3	8.5	7.6
COMMERCIAL BANKS							
Colones Deposits	5998.9	6864.1	7103.4	9342.9	11282.3	14737.8	18960.8
(% of GDP)	25.9	25.1	22.0	22.8	23.6	26.9	28.5
Dollars Deposits	253.0	274.0	283.9	582.5	385.2	764.4	819.1
(% of GDP)	1.1	1.0	0.9	1.4	0.8	1.4	1.2
Credit	5847.2	6523.1	7263.2	7907.9	9498.2	13003.8	15415.2
(% of GDP)	25.3	23.8	22.5	19.3	19.9	23.7	23.2
MONETARY AGGREGATES							
Currency	2812.3	3033.0	3384.9	4189.2	4451.7	5778.1	6408.5
(% of GDP)	12.2	11.1	10.5	10.2	9.3	10.5	9.6
Velocity (M1)	8.2	9.0	9.5	9.8	10.7	9.5	10.4
M2: Currency Plus Colones Deposits	7432.4	8312.1	8918.5	11276.2	13323.6	17308.4	21733.0
(% of GDP)	32.1	30.4	27.7	27.5	27.9	31.6	32.7
Velocity (M2)	3.1	3.3	3.6	3.6	3.6	3.2	3.1
M2 Plus Dollars Deposits	7685.4	8593.7	9451.5	12397.8	14521.4	18823.3	23466.5
(% of GDP)	33.2	31.4	29.3	30.2	30.4	34.3	35.3
Total Credit	9363.8	10463.6	12093.9	13576.4	15756.2	20151.8	22893.3
(% of GDP)	40.5	38.2	37.5	33.1	33.0	36.7	34.5
to Private Sector	5528.5	6218.4	6884.9	7494.3	8701.0	12491.3	14667.2
(% of GDP)	23.9	22.7	21.4	18.3	18.2	22.8	22.1
to Public Sector	3835.3	4245.1	5208.9	6082.1	7055.1	7660.5	8246.1
(% of GDP)	16.6	15.5	16.2	14.8	14.8	14.0	12.4

Source: Central Reserve Bank of El Salvador, *Quarterly Review*, various issues, and author's calculations.

Table VII.5

Growth Rate of Monetary Variables and Money Multiplier
(average annual percent change, unless otherwise indicated)

	1987	1988	1989	1990	1991	1992	1993
MONETARY VARIABLES							
Monetary Base							
Central Bank NIR	25.26	16.49	12.03	29.22	22.39	18.41	40.80
Central Bank NDA	32.58	-17.66	34.78	125.51	14.32	31.83	36.68
Central Bank NDA	-7.57	11.97	5.72	15.97	-0.71	4.60	7.78
(including reserve requirements)	-24.34	0.91	13.12	-7.08	-13.71	-10.21	-81.98
Narrow Money Supply (M1)	0.57	7.85	11.60	23.76	6.26	29.80	10.91
Broad Money Supply (M2)	7.57	11.72	7.18	28.87	15.60	31.83	24.79
Total Credit	8.36	11.75	15.58	12.26	16.06	27.90	13.60
MONEY MULTIPLIER*	3.03	2.92	2.80	2.80	2.91	3.22	2.92
Currency / Deposits	0.21	0.19	0.23	0.19	0.17	0.16	0.13
Bank Reserves / Deposits	0.19	0.22	0.21	0.24	0.23	0.20	0.25
BROAD MONEY MULTIPLIER**	3.08	2.96	2.91	2.95	2.82	3.09	2.74

Source: Central Reserve Bank of El Salvador, *Quarterly Review*, various issues, and author's calculations.
* The money multiplier is calculated as $m = (c+1)/(c+r)$, where c denotes the currency-to-deposit ratio and r denotes the bank-reserve-to-deposits ratio.
** Ratio of broad money to reserve money.
NIR: Net International Reserves, NDA: Net Domestic Assets.

Before concluding this section, it is important to note that the increase in the monetary aggregates in the 1990's is substantially due to an increase in the demand for money. As noted before, inflows of remittances surged in the early 1980's; however, most of them were not exchanged through the banking system. Also, the demand for real cash balances decreased as a result of a currency substitution process experienced in El Salvador in the late 1980's.[56] Thus, inflows did not represent a corresponding increase in money growth and, in fact, the rate of growth of monetary aggregate fell in 1987-1989. By contrast, in the 1990's the monetary effects of inflows are different for two reasons: First, the exchange rate policy and the financial reform played a key role in attracting remittance

56 For details of the currency substitution process in El Salvador, see Saca (1990a).

inflows through the banking system and in increasing the proportion of interest-bearing deposits. Second, as is discussed below, reorientation of the domestic policies probably played an important role in attracting the inflows to feed growth (through higher investment), therefore increasing aggregate spending, which in turn increased the demand for nominal money balances.

5. Domestic Activity, Savings, and Investment

Transfers (official and private) played a key role in stabilizing the economy after 1983. The fall in GDP during the first years of the civil war (real GDP fell by 24 percent between 1979 and 1982) stopped in 1983, when most components of aggregate demand ceased to decline. Private investment grew after 1982. However, real output growth during most of the 1980's was moderate (1 to 2 percent per year) and aggregate demand growth came purely from domestic sources and the contribution of the external sector was negative. By contrast, in the 1990's output growth accelerated, and aggregate demand growth was led by exports, followed by private and public investment (see Table VII.6), which indicates that the reorientation of economic policy may have driven resources to the traded goods sector.

Investment, as well as savings, increased and the deficit in the current account narrowed (Table VII.6).

E. Implications for Monetary Policy

When analyzing the recent economic experience of the Salvadorean economy and the issues that the Central Reserve Bank is facing, three main questions seem to need answering: (1) Do unification and exchange rate flexibility create any problems? (2) What are the monetary policy implications of financial liberalization? (3) Has exchange rate unification or financial liberalization made monetary control difficult?

1. Exchange Rate and Monetary Policy

From the analysis in Section D, it is clear that, in recent years, capital inflows have been a major shock to the Salvadorean economy, although with many beneficial effects. Capital inflows led to an increase in spending, which is a real

Table VII.6

Economic Activity, Savings and Investment

	1970-1974	1975-1979	1980-1984	1985-1989	1990	1991	1992	1993
REAL ECONOMIC GROWTH (in percent)								
Real GDP Growth	5.0	3.9	-4.3	1.6	6.5	3.5	4.6	5.0
Real Gross Domestic Investment	11.6	6.5	-13.0	7.8	-5.3	18.9	23.8	9.7
Public	14.3	10.0	-9.7	5.2	-20.1	17.1	42.8	5.1
Private	10.5	4.8	-16.2	8.9	0.7	19.4	17.8	11.5
Real Consumption	4.1	4.0	-3.8	1.5	3.7	3.1	-16.6	3.1
Public	5.1	8.2	0.6	2.8	1.0	6.8	0.2	-0.5
Private	4.0	3.4	-4.6	1.3	4.3	2.3	2.7	3.1
Real Export of Goods & Services	5.0	9.2	-8.0	-6.4	23.8	-1.6	11.2	12.6
SAVINGS AND INVESTMENT (in percent of GDP)								
Savings	n.a.	n.a.	10.5	9.2	5.2	8.8	11.0	12.7
Public Sector	n.a.	n.a.	-0.2	0.4	-0.3	-0.7	0.2	0.7
Private Sector	n.a.	n.a.	10.8	8.8	5.5	9.5	10.7	12.0
Investment	15.4	20.4	12.5	13.0	11.8	13.5	15.7	16.1
Public Sector	4.2	6.6	5.7	3.1	2.3	2.5	3.4	3.3
Pivate Sector	11.2	13.8	6.8	9.9	9.5	10.9	12.2	12.8
Current Account*	-10.8	0.7	-6.3	-9.9	-6.7	-5.0	-5.8	-4.2

Source: Central Reserve Bank of El Salvador, *Monetary and Financial Program*, various issues.
* Excluding official transfers. There is a statistical discrepancy between the current account of the balance-of-payments and the difference between the savings and investment in the national accounts.

disturbance. In this particular case, a flexible exchange rate, rather than one pegged to a single currency, is desirable to curb the possibly destabilizing effects of capital inflows.[57] Thus, unification and the adoption of a flexible exchange rate regime have contributed to attract inflows through the banking system and enhanced the beneficial effects of capital inflows (higher exports, domestic investment and growth). Moreover, monetary management has been relatively easier than it would have been under a fixed exchange rate regime. Under such a

57 See the discussion on the choice of the appropriate exchange rate regime of Chapter VI.

regime, the Central Reserve Bank would have had more difficulties in controlling monetary conditions.[58] For example, an inflow of capital would increase the money supply and reinforce the effect on prices and the real exchange rate of the increase in spending following an inflow of capital.[59] Under these circumstances, control over the money supply would require that the authorities sterilize the inflow of reserves completely. However, sterilization may be not advisable for the reasons discussed above.

By contrast, under a uniform flexible exchange rate regime an inflow of capital would lead to a nominal appreciation of the domestic currency in response to the increased supply in foreign exchange. This appreciation at least partly offsets the spending effect of the boom by curbing the demand for domestically tradable goods and reducing inflationary pressures.

Thus, the monetary restraint required under a flexible exchange rate may be less than under a fixed exchange rate regime.

2. *Monetary Policy Implications of Financial Liberalization*

The financial liberalization undertaken in El Salvador since late 1989 has probably changed the environment in which monetary policy operates. The structural changes in the financial system could create instability in the money supply process and in the money demand; and could also have affected the channels of transmission of monetary policy. This section examines these issues in the light of the experience of El Salvador.

a. Money Supply Process

The analysis of the effects of financial liberalization on the money supply process will cover two main aspects. First, it will assess the effects on the determinants of the money supply and on the underlying factors of the money supply's components. Second, it will assess the effects on monetary control.

i. Determinants of the Money Supply

The growth of money supply can be decomposed into the growth of high-powered money and changes in the money multiplier. High-powered money

58 A very clear exposition on the controllability of the money supply under a fixed exchange rate regime is by Willms (1971).

59 In this case, real appreciation would be entirely the result of domestic inflation.

growth continues to be the primary determinant in the growth of the money supply in El Salvador (Table VII.5). The money multiplier, calculated in its two alternative definitions,[60] has not increased, as was expected, although its structure has changed. The currency-to-deposit ratio has decreased, reflecting that positive real interest rates and the increasing availability of financial assets have shifted public desire towards keeping funds in interest-yielding deposits. Similarly, a higher level of interest may induce a shift from demand deposits with a higher reserve requirement (30 percent) to higher-yielding deposits, which have a lower reserve requirement (20 percent), which in turn lowers banks' effective reserve-to-deposit ratio. This, however, is not reflected in the effective reserve requirement ratio (i.e., the actual banks' reserve-to-deposit ratio). Rather, it has increased (Table VII.5). The reasons are as follows: first, the legal reserve requirement for both types of deposits has increased (Table VII.7). Second, the legal reserve requirement on savings and time deposits has been unified for both types of financial institutions: commercial banks and savings and loans associations. Prior to financial liberalization the savings and loans associations' reserve requirement on savings and time deposits was lower than the reserve requirement on the same type of deposits at the commercial banks (Table VII.7).

Table VII.7

Legal Reserve Requirements
(deposits in colones)

Type of Deposits	Prior Financial Liberalization		From July 91 to March 93		From March 93	
	Banks	SA*	Banks	SA*	Banks	SA*
Demand deposits	23	-	25	-	30	-
Savings deposits	23	10	15	15	20	20
Time deposits	15	10	15	15	20	20

Source: Central Reserve Bank of El Salvador; data provided by the Department of Monetary Operations.

* Savings and loans associations.

The increase in the legal reserve requirements prevented the rise in the money multiplier normally experienced in the wake of financial liberalization.[61]

60 See footnote 15 in Section B.
61 See Akhtar (1983a, and 1983b).

With respect to the factors underlying the high-power money, reserve movements have been a major source of reserve money growth in the last few years (see Table VII.8). The Central Reserve Bank of El Salvador has accumulated reserves not only because of its intervention in the foreign exchange market (i.e., buying foreign exchange to avoid appreciation of the colon), but also because of surrender requirements on coffee export receipts and the foreign exchange from official aid and external borrowing by the public sector.[62]

ii. Monetary Control

The main factors affecting the reserve money can be classified into nonpolicy factors (i.e., those that are outside the control of the Central Reserve Bank), and policy factors (i.e., those that are used as tools of monetary policy). As noted above, net international reserves have been the primary determinant of the reserve money growth during the last few years (Table VII.8). Under a flexible exchange rate regime, a change in official international reserves is policy-determined. To smooth the monetary effects of the reserve inflows, the Central Reserve Bank could have sold the foreign exchange. However, this would have appreciated the exchange rate and could have implied a potential contradiction between control of money and one of the Central Reserve Bank's objectives (i.e., avoiding appreciation of the colon).[63,64] Instead, under these circumstances, the Central Reserve Bank sought to control liquidity, placing greater reliance on reserve requirements.[65] This policy, however, is not advisable for two reasons: First, reserve requirements typically act as a tax on financial intermediation through the banking system. Second, over time, with the development of new financial innovations,[66] monetary control through reserve requirements could turn out to be ineffective because banks could look for forms other than deposits

62 In May 1994, the surrender requirements on coffee exports were eliminated.

63 See the discussion in Section C.

64 Note that in Table VII.8, I have classified net international reserve of the Central Reserve Bank as a nonpolicy factor. This is so for two reasons: (1) the Central Reserve Bank accumulated reserves from other sources and not only from its intervention in the foreign exchange market, and (2) the Central Reserve Bank's policy objective constrains it to use this instrument accordingly.

65 Although open market operation has increased its role to manage reserve money in 1993, reserve requirements continue to be the main instrument in controlling liquidity (see Table VII.8).

66 Financial innovations could take many forms of a widespread use of new financial instruments, or the emergence of new financial markets, institutions and practice (see, for example, Podolski, 1986, p. 107, and Hester, 1981, pp. 146-168).

to borrow funds in order to reduce their reserve obligations. For example, funds borrowed through repurchase agreements do not have reserve requirements. In fact, most of the transactions of El Salvador's Stock Exchange in 1993 were repurchase agreements (about 70 percent of the transactions) at the initiative of the commercial banks seeking to reduce their reserve requirements. Thus, it would be preferable to use open market operations for the purpose of monetary control.

Table VII.8

Factors Affecting the Monetary Base*

(change as percent of the monetary base at the end of the previous period)

	1987	1988	1989	1990	1991	1992	1993
NO POLICY FACTORS							
Net International Reserves	14.58	-8.37	11.65	50.56	10.07	20.9	26.82
Medium and Long Term							
Foreign Liabilities	24.16	9.14	-6.84	-40.37	13.08	-6.48	8.02
Net Credit to the Public Sector							
Net Claims on Private Sector	11.80	18.11	30.56	26.04	13.08	15.98	5.66
Net Other Assets	-0.09	-0.99	0.02	-0.31	-0.30	1.58	-0.48
	-31.86	0.10	-38.40	27.56	28.86	-9.70	15.80
POLICY FACTORS							
Credit to Banks							
Direct Policy Instruments**	14.09	6.56	28.67	4.78	-27.49	2.90	1.22
Open Market Operations	0.00	0.00	0.00	-16.23	0.77	-7.94	-3.48
	-4.51	3.23	0.21	-0.57	0.39	-0.61	-13.20
MONETARY BASE							
(sources)							
	25.26	16.49	12.03	29.22	22.39	18.41	40.80
Memorandum Items							
Reserve Requirement	-21.09	-14.94	2.53	-24.34	-17.12	-9.57	-35.42
Banks	-21.09	-14.94	2.53	-24.34	-6.64	-7.88	-29.61
Financing Institutions	0.00	0.00	0.00	0.00	-10.48	-1.69	-5.81

Source: Central Reserve Bank of El Salvador, *Quarterly Review*, various issues, and author's calculations.

* Positive sign indicates an increase in assets or a decline in liabilities, that is, an expansionary factor; negative sign indicates a decrease in assets or an increase in liabilities, that is, a contractionary factor.

** Obligatory holding by commercial banks and financial institutions (financieras) of sterilization bonds.

b. Money as a Leading Indicator of Inflation and Income

In the conduct of monetary policy, the Central Reserve Bank of El Salvador has used a two-stage strategy which presupposes that monetary aggregates play an important leading role in the determination of income and inflation. Thus, the formulation of monetary policy is based on the assumption of a stable and predictable relationship between monetary aggregates, economic activity, prices, and the interest rate. As noted in Section B, financial liberalization creates a potential for instability in money demand. It may lead to a shift in the level of money holding and change the elasticity of money demand. However, tests of the stability and predictive power of the demand for money function for El Salvador are not addressed here because the time period of the financial liberalization is too short to permit determining the effect of financial liberalization on money demand elasticities using econometric tests. Instead, the aim of this section is to examine the data on monetary aggregates, income, and the inflation rate to see if there is any change in the relationships between those variables and to which extent those changes can be attributed to the financial liberalization process.

During the 1960's and 1970's and even most of 1980's, growth in M1 and M2 were good leading indicators of growth in nominal GDP (Figures VII.8a and VII.8b). This behavior is also shown in terms of income velocity of monetary aggregates. The income velocity of M1 and M2 were rather stable until the mid-1980's. Then income velocity (M1) started to grow rapidly as real demand for domestic money declined, pushing inflation up in 1985 (see Figure VII.9).[67]

Concerning the relationship between money and inflation, it seems that M1 was a good leading indicator of inflation (Figure VII.10a).

In the 1990's, with the liberalization of the interest rate and the implementation of financial reforms, the income velocity (M1) has remained high and rather unstable, but the income velocity of M2 began to decline as the public shifted funds into interest rate bearing deposits. Moreover, it seems to be that the early relationship between money and nominal GDP as well as between money and inflation was not reestablished. Thus, monetary aggregates appeared not to be good leading indicators of economic activity and inflation. This appears to be confirmed using monthly data (see Figures VII.11a, VII.11b and VII.11c).[68]

---

67 On the currency substitution process experienced in El Salvador in the late 1980's, see Saca (1990a).

68 In order to use monthly data to capture the short-run movements of the variables, the index of economic activity was used as a proxy of GDP.

Figure VII.8a
MONEY and NOMINAL GDP
Growth in M1 (lagged one year) and nominal GDP

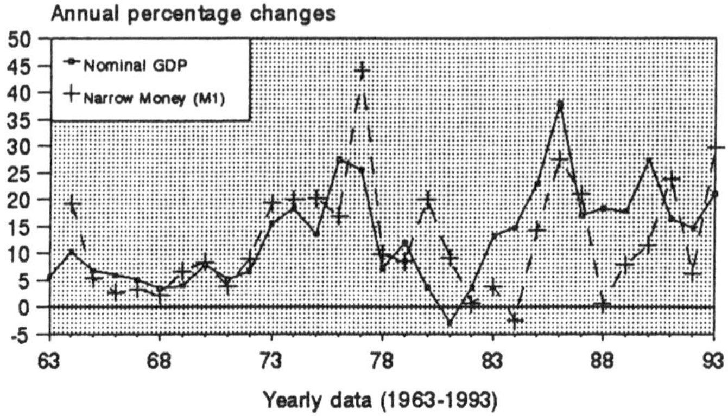

Source: Central Reserve Bank of El Salvador, *Quarterly Review*, various issues.

Figure VII.8b
MONEY and NOMINAL GDP
Growth in M2 (lagged one year) and nominal GDP

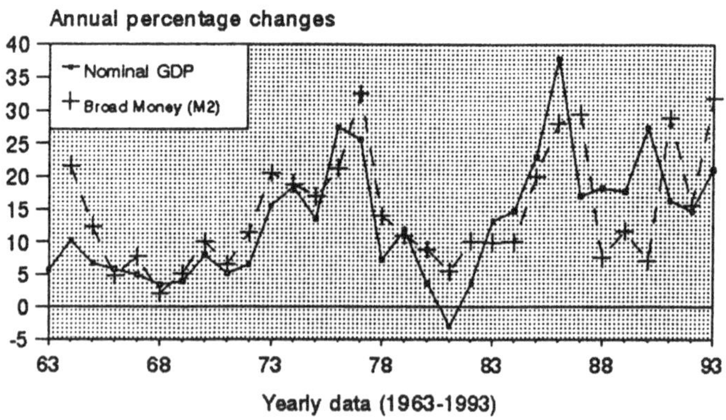

Source: Central Reserve Bank of El Salvador, *Quarterly Review*, various issues.

Figure VII.9
INCOME VELOCITY

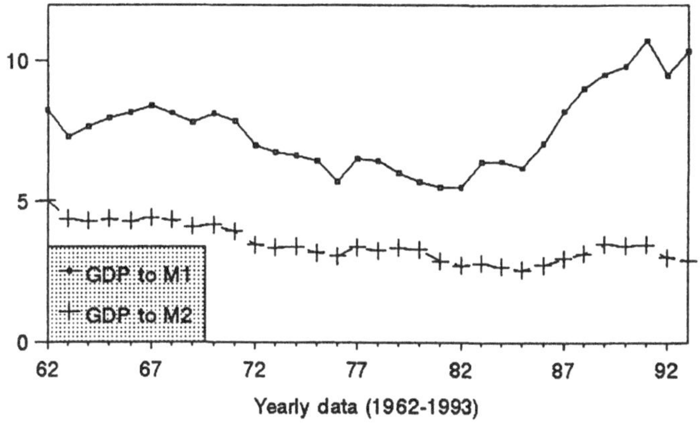

Source: Central Reserve Bank of El Salvador, *Quarterly Review*, various issues.

Figure VII.10a
MONEY and INFLATION
(growth in M1 lagged one year)

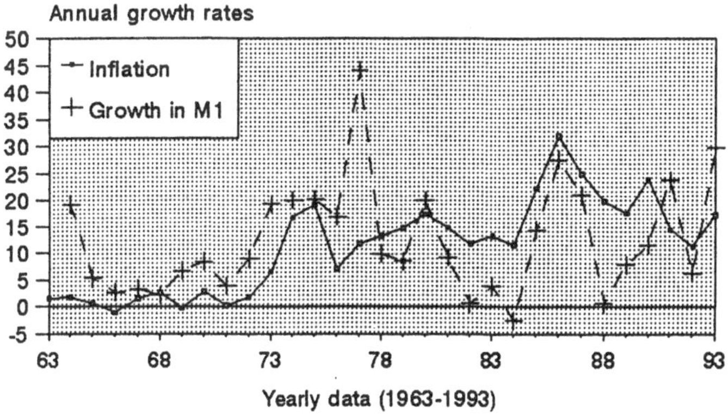

Source: Central Reserve Bank of El Salvador, *Quarterly Review*, various issues.

Figure VII.10b
MONEY and INFLATION
(growth in M2 lagged one year)

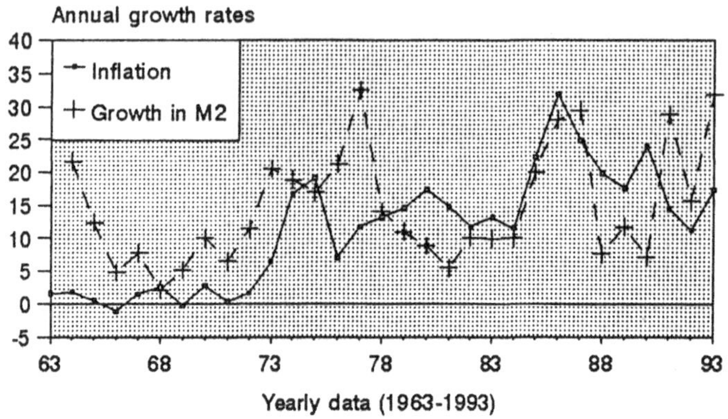

Source: Central Reserve Bank of El Salvador, *Quarterly Review*, various issues.

Figure VII.11a
MONEY AND ECONOMIC ACTIVITY

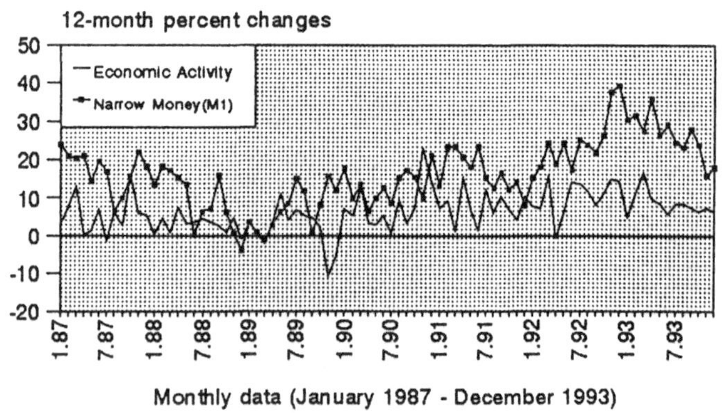

Source: Central Reserve Bank of El Salvador, *Quarterly Review*, various issues.
The data on the economic activity index was provided by the Department of National Accounts of the Central Reserve Bank of El Salvador.

Figure VII.12
TRANSMISSION MECHANISMS
Central Reserve Bank Domestic Credit and Economic Activity

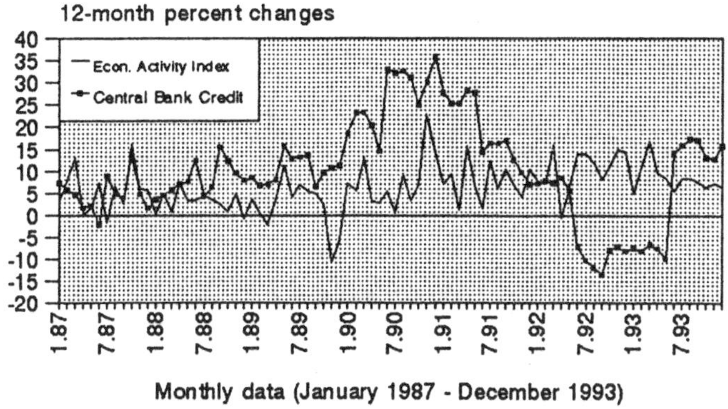

Source: Central Reserve Bank, *Quarterly Review;* and the monthly data on the index of economic activity was provided by the Department of National Accounts of the Central Reserve Bank.

Figure VII.11b
MONEY AND INFLATION
(M1 lagged six months)

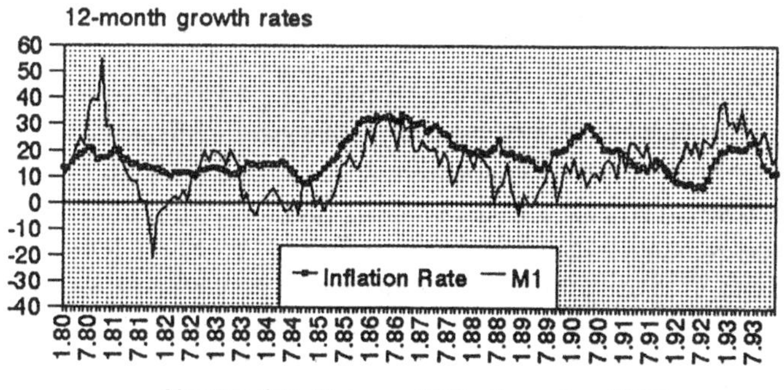

Source: International Monetary Fund, *International Financial Statistics*.
M1 is taken from line 34.

Figure VII.11c
MONEY AND INFLATION
(M2 lagged six months)

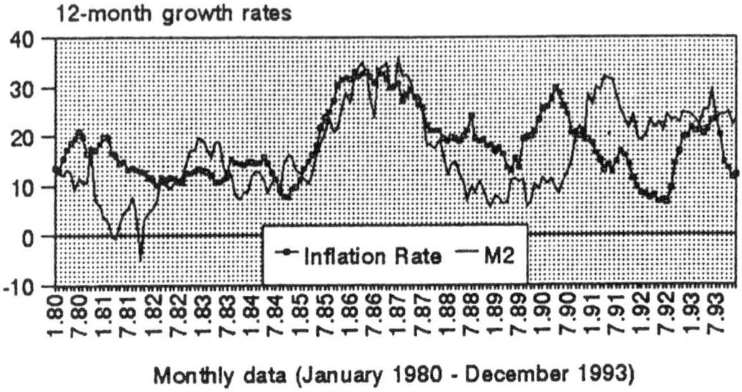

Source: International Monetary Fund, *International Financial Statistics*.
M2 is taken from lines 34 plus 35. Inflation rate is 12 month change in CPI (line 64) from the corresponding month in the previous year.

However, it would be going too far to conclude from this evidence that there are no links between money, economic activity, and inflation; and the main shortcoming is that the time period of the financial reforms is too short to draw definite conclusions. Further research on these issues should be done.

c. Channels of Transmission of Monetary Policy

As pointed out in Section C, directed credit to selective sectors is no longer the main channel of transmission of monetary policy in El Salvador.[69] The financial reform undertaken in late 1989 together with the liberalization of interest rates and the adoption of a flexible exchange rate regime gave a greater role to interest rates and the exchange rate to transmit the effects of monetary policy.

The effects of interest rates and exchange rates on aggregate demand are well known. An increase in the real interest rate increases the cost of capital and reduces investment, which in turn lowers production.

Real exchange rate movements influence economic activity primarily through their effect on the international competitiveness of domestic production.

69 In fact, the relationship between economic activity and central bank credit seemed to break down, possibly as a result of reduction in the rediscount credit of the Central Reserve Bank (see Figure VII.12).

An appreciation of the real exchange rate would shift demand away from domestic goods toward foreign products.

However, in view of the fact that the period since the financial and exchange rate liberalization has been very short, and in view of the limited available evidence, there is not much to say empirically about how the transmission mechanisms of monetary policy may have changed.

This section can be concluded by recommending that the monetary authorities should keep observing the economy and be ready to modify their actions in case the relationship between their instruments and the ultimate targets of policy change over time.

3. Concluding Remarks

At the end of the past decade, El Salvador began a comprehensive adjustment process in all economic areas. The exchange rate and financial reforms were part of the overall adjustment process and this posed new challenges to the Central Reserve Bank in the conduct of monetary policy. Specifically, the Central Reserve Bank should review the way in which monetary policy is formulated and implemented. First, the objectives of monetary policy should be reconsidered: insistence upon unrealistic and incompatible goals may lead to a poor functioning of the policy. Second, financial liberalization may have altered or may alter the relationship between money, income, and the interest rate, which may render ineffective the strategy of using monetary aggregates as an intermediate target. In this regard, as was pointed out above, the monetary authorities should keep observing the economy and be ready to modify their actions in case the relationship between their instruments and the ultimate targets of policy has changed or changes over time. Third, in the new financial environment, monetary control is more complicated, particularly because new indirect instruments of monetary control (i.e., open market operations) are still not well developed and also because of the thinness of money and capital markets.

Appendix VII.1

The Equilibrium Real Exchange Rate

This appendix summarizes some theoretical aspects of the determination of the equilibrium real exchange rate that were used as a framework to analyze the problems associated with setting the real exchange rate as an objective of the monetary authority in Section C.1.

Basically, in the literature there are two theories of the equilibrium real exchange rate. The most popular and traditional theory is based on the notion of relative purchasing power parity (PPP). The PPP theory states that the "true" value of currencies should be "intimately" linked to their internal purchasing power, that is, the equilibrium exchange rate is equal to the relative price levels of the home country and its major trading partners.[70]

The application of the PPP theory involves the estimation of the real effective exchange rate index, which is formulated as the nominal effective exchange rate index adjusted for movements in prices or costs at home relative to those abroad.[71] Any deviation in the actual real effective exchange rate index from its level in a base period, which is assumed to exhibit external equilibrium and is considered the equilibrium real exchange rate, provides a measure of the change in competitiveness. A decrease in a country's real effective exchange rate index over its level in a base period, when the external position was considered adequate, implies a real effective appreciation.[72] Competitiveness can be restored to its base period level through a change in the nominal exchange rate, a change in the level of domestic prices, or costs relative to those abroad.

An alternative and more recent theory is one which considers nontraded goods, and which defines the real exchange rate as the relative price of tradable to nontradable goods. This definition provides a measure of the internal competitiveness of the traded goods sector relative to the nontraded goods sector (i.e., the ability of the traded goods sector to compete with the nontraded goods sector for scarce factors of production).[73] If the domestic price of traded goods rises relative to the price of nontraded goods, resources will be reallocated toward the traded goods sector. Under this approach the equilibrium real exchange rate corresponds to the relative price of traded to nontraded goods that, for given sustainable values of other relevant variables – such as taxes, international prices, and technology – simultaneously yields internal and external equilibrium. Internal equilibrium implies that a nontraded goods market clears continuously, while external equilibrium implies that a current account deficit is financed with capital inflows.

---

70 See, for example, Officer (1976), Genberg (1978), and Katseli-Papaefstratiou (1979).

71 For a comprehensive review of the concept of the real effective exchange rate, see Maciejewski (1983).

72 The International Monetary Fund has adopted an opposite definition in which a real appreciation is reflected by an increase in the real effective exchange rate index.

73 See Johnson (1985) and Edward (1989).

Appendix VII.2

Calculating the Real Exchange Rate (Methodology of Table VII.2)

1. Trade-weighted Real Exchange Rate Index

Using the same methodology outlined in Appendix V.1 of Chapter V, this index was calculated as the relative prices of foreign and domestic goods weighted in terms of the share of bilateral trade with El Salvador's major trading partners (Costa Rica, Guatemala, Germany, Japan, and the United States). The base period was 1980.[74] Formally:

$$r = (ee\ P^*)/P,$$

where:

$ee = \quad \Sigma\, w_i(e)(e^*)$

$P^* = \quad \Sigma\, w_i\ (CPI_i).$

All variables are defined as in Appendix V.1, the only difference is that these calculations also include El Salvador's major trading partners in the CACM, namely, Costa Rica and Guatemala.

This methodology was also used in Figure VI.3 of Chapter VI using monthly data.

2. Bilateral Real Exchange Rate

The bilateral real exchange rate vis-à-vis the United States is used here as an indicator of the relative price of tradables to nontradables, and is calculated as follows: the exchange rate (colones per U.S. dollar) times the U.S. WPI, serving as a proxy for the price of tradables, and the El Salvador CPI as a proxy for nontradables:

$$r_b = (e\ P_{US})/P$$

r_b : bilateral real exchange rate vis-à-vis the United States

e : nominal exchange rate index

P_{US} : U.S. wholesale price index (WPI)

P : El Salvador consumer price index (CPI).

---

74 1980 was selected as the base period because, in that year, the balance of trade was at a "satisfactory" level. It was the last year that El Salvador experienced a surplus in the trade balance.

3. Internal Terms of Trade: P_T/P_N

The tradable and nontradable price indices were constructed from the GDP deflator by sectors published by the Central Reserve Bank of El Salvador, *Quarterly Review*, various issues. The GDP deflator contains eleven sectors which were grouped into two categories, namely, traded (T) and nontraded (N) using the classification and weights presented in Table 1:

$$P_T = \Sigma\, \alpha_{jT} P_j$$

$$P_N = \Sigma\, \alpha_{jN} P_j\,,$$

where

α_{jT} is the sector's share in total production of traded goods, $\Sigma\, \alpha_{jT} = 1.00$,

α_{jN} is the sector's share in total production of nontraded goods, $\Sigma\, \alpha_{jN} = 1.00$,

P_j GDP deflator of the jth sector.

Table 1

Classification and Weights of Economic Sectors

SECTORS	WEIGHTS (BASE 1980)	CLASSIFICATION
Agriculture	0.2557	T
Mining	0.0012	N
Manufacture	0.1782	T
Construction	0.0338	N
Electricity & Water	0.0321	N
Transport	0.0589	N
Commerce	0.1900	N
Residential Rent	0.0395	N
Personal Services	0.0754	N
Public Administration	0.0754	N
Financial Services	0.0312	N

T are Traded goods.
N are Nontraded goods.

Chapter VIII

Conclusions

Widespread exchange and trade restrictions in developing countries have led to the emergence of illegal markets for foreign currencies. For about one and a half decades the literature devoted considerable attention to the study of theses markets. More recently, attention has turned to issues related with the unification of the foreign exchange markets due to many developing countries having undertaken unification of their foreign exchange markets. This study has examined the behavior of an economy under both situations, namely, a multiple exchange rate regime with exchange rate rationing, and the abandonment of that system and adoption of a uniform flexible exchange rate regime.

Detailed findings of this study were summarized in the concluding remarks of every chapter; they need not be repeated here. Outlining the most important conclusions and suggestions for future research should be adequate.

A review of the theoretical literature as well as of the experience of El Salvador allowed this study to identify a series of difficulties in maintaining a system of dual exchange rates, and the disappointment in the efficiency of such regimes in attaining the objectives for which they were adopted (e.g., as a device for solving balance-of-payments problems and for insulating domestic prices from exchange rate movements). The empirical evidence for El Salvador shows that a dual exchange rate system with a black market for foreign exchange does not insulate domestic prices from exchange rate movements.

The determinants of the black market exchange rate and its interactions between the black market and the macroeconomic developments in the economy were investigated using both traditional econometric methods and cointegration and vector autoregression analysis.

The black market exchange rate appears to be primarily determined by the exchange rate, monetary and interest rate policies and also by expectations of exchange developments and policy changes. However, the empirical tests do not support the view of the existence of a long-run relationship between those variables and the black market exchange rate, suggesting that the black market exchange rate is a weakly exogenous variable that moves far apart from other macroeconomic variables. This could be interpreted to mean that the black market exchange rate is a variable which appears as a result of goverment intervention in the foreign exchange market, and this variable may drift apart from its long-run value according to government intervention and seasonal factors. Thus, this variable would converge to its long-run equilibrium only when economic forces such as a market mechanism would cause it to move together with other macroeconomic variables.

In addition, the black market exchange rate has an impact on a number of macroeconomic variables, namely, the official exchange rate, domestic prices, the money supply, and the interest rates.

Concerning the unification of foreign exchange markets, the overall experience of El Salvador with the process was positive, particularly the pace and the macroeconomic effects of exchange rate unification performed according to theoretical expectations. The process was gradual and the exchange rate reform was widely expected. In the transition period the black market exchange rate kept depreciating. No jumps occurred when the reform was actually implemented, and the black market premium dropped to zero. The effects on prices had already taken place.

In contrast, in the post-reform period the Central Reserve Bank has encountered serious problems in controlling the money supply in the new context of exchange and financial liberalization. In official circles, the appropriateness of a flexible exchange rate regime of a managed type for El Salvador is beginning to be questioned.

On the last issue, this study has provided only some insight into the working of monetary policy under the new environment of reforms. It is obvious that a number of issues are still unanswered and that we still have a lot to learn. There are at least two issues that deserve particular attention in the future. One is the effects of financial liberalization on the money demand. Financial liberalization may have altered the relationship between money, income, and interest rates, which may render ineffective the strategy of using monetary aggregates as an intermediate target. Research on selecting the appropriate monetary targets and on the channels of transmission of monetary policy in the new context of financial liberalization could improve the knowledge of the authorities in conducting monetary policy.

The second major area towards which further research should be directed is related to the appropriate exchange rate regime for El Salvador, using the criteria for choosing an optimal exchange rate regime proposed in the theoretical literature. These criteria are mainly the nature of shocks to the economy and economic structural characteristics. In this context an empirical study to identify the type of shocks that the Salvadorean economy experiences more frequently would be necessary. Additionally, an econometric model of the economy which models the effects of the different types of shocks under alternative exchange rate regimes would also be useful.

References

Adams, Charles, and Jeremy Greenwood (1985) "Dual Exchange Rate Systems and Capital Controls: An Investigation." *Journal of International Economics* **18**, 43-63.

Adams, Charles, and Daniel Gros (1986). "The Consequences of Real Exchange Rate Rules for Inflation: Some Illustrative Examples." IMF *Staff Papers* **33** (September), 439-476.

Agénor, Pierre-Richard (1991). "A Monetary Model of the Parallel Market for Foreign Exchange." *Journal of Economic Studies* **18**, 4, 4-18.

Agénor, Pierre-Richard, and Robert P. Flood (1992). "Unification of Foreign Exchange Markets." IMF *Staff Papers* **39**, 4, 923-947.

Agénor, Pierre-Richard (1990). "Stabilization Policies in Developing Countries with a Parallel Market for Foreign Exchange." IMF *Staff Papers* **37**, 3 (September), 560-592.

Agénor, Pierre-Richard (1992). *Parallel Currency Markets in Developing Countries: Theory, Evidence, and Policy Implications*. Essays in International Finance 188. Princeton University Press.

Aghevli, Bijan B., Mohsin S. Khan, and Peter J. Montiel (1991). *Exchange Rate Policy in Developing Countries: Some Analytical Issues*. IMF Occasional Paper 78. Washington DC: International Monetary Fund.

Aizenman, Joshua, Jacob A. Frenkel (1985) "Optimal Wage Indexation, Foreign Exchange Intervetion, and Monetary Policy." *The American Economic Review* **75**, 3 402-423.

Aizenman, Joshua (1985). "Ajustment to Monetary Policy and Devaluation Under Two-Tier and Fixed Exchange Rate Regimes." *Journal of Development Economics* **18**, 153-169.

Akhtar, M. A. (1983a). "Financial Innovation and Monetary Policy: A Framework for Analysis." Meeting of central bank economists at the Bank for International Settlements. November.

Akhtar, M. A. (1983b). *Financial Innovations and their Implications for Monetary Policy: An International Perspective*. BIS Economic Papers 9. Basle: Bank for International Settlements.

Argy,Victor, Warwick Mckibbin, and Eric Siegloff (1989). *Exchange-Rate Regimes for a Small Economy in a Multi-Country World*. Princeton Studies in International Finance. No. 67. Princeton University Press.

Argy, Victor, and Paul De Grauwe,eds.(1990). *Choosing an Exchange Rate Regime: The Challenge for Smaller Industrial Countries.* International Monetary Fund, Washington D.C.

Artus, Jacques R., and Andrew D. Crockett (1978). *Floating Exchange Rates and the Need for Surveillance.* Essays in International Finance 127. Princeton University Press.

Bailey, Martin J. (1956). "The Welfare Cost of Inflationary Finance." *Journal of Political Economy* **LXIV**, 2, 93-110.

Banerjee, Anindya, Juan Dolado, and Ricardo Mestre (1992) "On Some Simple Tests for Cointegration: The Cost of Simplicity" Unpublished paper.

Batten, Dallas S., Michael P. Blackwell, In-Su Kim, Simon E. Nocera, and Yuzuru Ozeki (1990). *The Conduct of Monetary Policy in the Major Industrial Countries: Instruments and Operating Procedures.* IMF Occasional Paper 70. Washington DC: International Monetary Fund.

Bautista, Romeo M. (1988). "Foreign Borrowing as Dutch Disease: A Quantitative Analysis for the Philippines." *International Economic Journal* **2**, 3, 35-49.

Benavie, Arthur (1983). "Achieving External and Internal Targets with Exchange-Rate and Interest-rate Intervetion" *Journal of International Money and Finance* **2**, 75-85.

Benjamin, Nancy C., Shantayanan Devarajan, and Robert J. Weiner (1989). "The Dutch Disease in a Developing Country: Oil Reserves in Cameroon". *Journal of Development Economics* **30**, 71-92.

Bewley, R.A.(1979). "The Direct Estimation of Equilibrium Response in a Linear Dynamic Model". *Economics Letters* 3, 357-361.

Bhagwati, Jagdish (1978). *Foreign Exchange Regimes and Economic Development: Anatomy and Consequences of Exchange Controls Regime.* New York: National Bureau of Economic Research.

Bhandari, Jagdeep S., and Carlos A. Vegh (1990). "Dual Exchange Markets Under Incomplete Separation: An Optimizing Model." IMF *Staff Papers* **37**, 1, 146-167.

Bhandari, Jagdeep S., and Bernard Decaluwe (1987). "A Stochastic Model of Incomplete Separation Between Commercial and Financial Exchange Rate Markets." *Journal of International Economics* **22**, 25-55.

Bhandari, Jagdeep S. (1985). *Exhange Rate Management under Uncertainty. The MIT Press, Cambrige, Massachusetts.*

Bhandari, Jagdeep S. (1988). "Exchange Rate Reform and Structural Disturbances in a Dual Exchange Economy". IMF Working Paper WP/88/99.

Biswas, Basudeb, and Sukumar Nandi (1984). "A Monetarist Approach to Black Market Exchange Rate Determination: An Econometric Study." *Arthaniti* **XXIII**, 31-41.

Black, Stanley W. (1976). "Exchange Policies for Less Developed Countries in a World of Floating Rates." In *The International Monetary System and the Developing Nations*. Bureau for Program and Policy Coordination, Agency for International Development, Washington/ D.C.

Blanchard, Oliver J., and Stanley Fischer (1989). *Lectures on Macroeconomics*. The MIT Press, Cambridge, Massachusetts.

Blejer, Mario (1978a). " Exchange restrictions and the monetary approach to the exchange rate." In Jacob A. Frenkel and Harry G. Johnson (eds.), *The Economics of Flexible Exchange Rates*. Reading, MA.: Addison-Wesley, 117-128.

Blejer, Mario (1978b). "Black Market Exchange Rate Expectation and the domesticic demand for money: Some empirical results." *Journal of Monetary Economics* **4**, 767-773.

Blundell-Wignall, Adrian, and Frank Browne (1991). "Macroeconomic Consequences of Financial Liberalization: A Summary Report." OECD Working Paper 98. February.

Blundell-Wignall, Adrian, Frank Browne, and Paolo Manasse (1990). "Monetary Policy in the Wake of Financial Liberalization." OECD Working Paper 77. April.

Boulding, Kenneth (1937). "A note on the theory of the black market." *Canadian Journal of Economics & Political Science* **13** (February), 115-118.

Boyer, Russell S. (1978) "Optimal Foreign Exchange Market Intervention." *Journal of Political Economy* **86**, 6 1045-1055.

Branson, William, and Louka Katseli-Papaefstratiou (1981). "Exchange Rate Policy for Developing Countries." In Grassman and Lundberg *The World Economic Order: Past and Prospects*.

Bronfenbrenner, M. (1947): "Price Control Under Imperfect Competition." *The American Economic Review* **37**, 107-120.

Browning, Edgar, and William P. Culbertson Jr. (1974). "A Theory of Black Markets Under Price Control: Competition and Monopoly." *Western Economic Journal* **12**, 175-189.

Bryant, Ralph C. (1982). "Federal Reserve Control of the Money Stock." *Journal of Money, Credit and Banking* **14**, 4, 597-625.

Bryant, Ralph C. (1980). *Money and Monetary Policy in Interdependent Nations*. Washington DC: Brookings Institution.

Cáceres, Luis R. (1993). "Capital Flight from Central American Countries". *Saving and Development* **17**, 2, 137-152.

Calvo, Guillermo A., Leonardo Leiderman, and Carmen M. Reinhart (1993). "Capital Inflows and Real Exchange Rate Appreciation in Latin America." IMF *Staff Papers* **40**, 1 (March), 108-151.

Calvo, Guillermo A. (1991). "The Perils of Sterilization." IMF *Staff Papers* **38**, 4, 921-926.

Campbell, John Y., and Pierre Perron (1991) "Pitfalls and Opportunities: What Macroeconomists Should Knows about Unit Roots". *NBER Macroeconomics Annual 1991*. The MIT Press Cambridge, Massachusetts.151-219.

Canto, Victor A. (1985). "Monetary Policy, 'Dollarization', and Parallel Market Exchange Rates: The case of the Dominican Republic." *Journal of International Money and Finance* **4**, 4 (December), 507-521.

Central Reserve Bank of El Salvador (1993). "Evaluacion de la Politica Cambiaria: Julio 1989-Diciembre 1992". Unpublished document (March).

Comisión Económica para América Latina y el Caribe (CEPAL) (1991). "Remesas y Economía Familiar en El Salvador, Guatemala y Nicaragua." Document prepared for the Seminar on International Remittances and Poverty in Central America. México, D.F. June 6-7 1991.

Clements, K. and L. Sjaastad (1984). *How Protection Taxes Exporters*. London: Trade Policy Research Centre.

Corden,W.M. (1982). "Booming Sector and Dutch Disease Economics: A Survey". Working Papers in Economics and Econometrics. The Australian National University.

Corden, W.M. (1984). "Booming Sector and Dutch Disease Economics : Survey and Consolidation". *Oxford Economic Papers* **36**, 359-380.

Corden, W.M. and Peter Neary (1982). "Booming Sector and Deindustrialization in a Small Open Economy", *Economic Journal* **92**, 825-848.

Craine, Roger; Arthur Havenner (1981). "Choosing a Monetary Instrument. The Case of Supply-Side Shocks." *Journal of Economic Dynamics and Control* **3**, 217-234.

Cuevas, Carlos E., Douglas H. Graham, and Julia A. Paxton (1991). "El Sector Financiero Informal en El Salvador." Fundacion Salvadoreña Para el Desarrollo Economico y Social (FUSADES) Working Paper 29.

Cukierman, Alex, and Nissan Liviatan (1992). "The Dynamics of Optimal Gradual Stabilizations." *The World Bank Economic Review* **6**, 3, 439-458.

Culbertson, William P. (1989). "Empirical Regularities in Black Markets for Currency." *World Development* **17**, 12, 1907-1919.

Culbertson, William P. (1975). "Purchasing power parity and black market exchange rate." *Economic Inquiry* **13** (May), 287-296.

Cumby, Robert E. (1984). "Monetary Policy Under Dual Exchange Rate." *Journal of International Money and Finance* **3**, 195-208.

Cuthbertson, K. (1988) "The Demand for M1: A Forward Looking Buffer Stock Model." *Oxford Economics Papers* **40**, 110-131.

de Sebastian, Luis (1979). *Inflation, Money and the Balance of Payments in El Salvador*. Dissertation. Institut Universitaire de Hautes Etudes International, Geneva.

de Vries, Margaret G. (1965). "Multiple Exchange Rates: Expectations and Experiences." IMF *Staff Papers* **22**, 282-311.

de Macedo, Jorge B. (1982). "Exchange Rate Behavior with Currency Inconvertibility." *Journal of International Economics* **12**, 65-81.

de Macedo, Jorge B. (1987). "Currency Inconvertibility, Trade Taxes and Smuggling." *Journal of Development Economics* **27**, 109-125.

de Macedo, Jorge B. (1979). "Exchange Rate in Portugal 1973-1978: A Portfolio Model of an Inconvertible Currency." Economic Growth Center Discussion Paper No 324. Yale University.

Devarajan, Shantayanan, Christine Jones, and Michael Roemer (1989). "Markets Under Price Controls in Partial and General Equilibrium." *World Development* **17**, 12, 1881-1893.

Diario Oficial de la República de El Salvador (1991). *Ley Orgánica del Banco Central de Reserva de El Salvador*. **311**, 80 (May).

Diario Oficial de la República de El Salvador (1990). *Ley Orgánica de la Superintendencia del Sistema Financiero*. **309**, 278 (December).

Dickey, David, Dennis W. Jansen, and Daniel L. Thornton (1991) "A Primer on Cointegration with an Application to Money and Income". *Review*,Federal Reserve Bank of St. Louis **73**, 2 (March/April), 58-78.

Dornbusch, Rüdiger (1976). "Expectation and Exchange Rate Dynamics." *Journal of Political Economy* **84**, 6, 1161-1176.

Dornbusch, Rüdiger (1980). *Open Economy Macroeconomics*. Basic Books, Inc. Publishers, New York.

Dornbusch, Rüdiger, Daniel V. Dantas, Clarice Pechman, Roberto de Rezende Rocha, and Demetrio Simões (1983). "The Black Market for Dollars in Brazil." NBER Reprint 364, 25-40.

Dornbusch, Rüdiger, and Stanley Fischer *Macroeconomics*. McGraw-Hill Publishing Company, New York.

Edwards, Sebastian (1989). *Real Exchange Rates, Devaluation and Adjustment: Exchange Rate Policy in Developing Countries*. MIT Press, Cambridge, Massachusetts.

Edwards, Sebastian (1991). "Capital and Current Account Liberalization and Real Exchange Rates in Developing Countries". In Emil-Maria Claassen (ed.)., *Exchange Rate Policies in Developing and Post-Socialist Countries*. San Francisco, California: ICS Press.

Enders, Klaus, and Horst Herberg (1983). "The Dutch Disease: Causes, Consequences, Cures and Calmatives." *Weltwirtschaftliches Archiv* **3**, 473-497.

Engle, Robert and C.W.J. Granger (1987). Cointegration and Error Correction: Representation Estimation, and Testing." *Econometrica* **55**, 2, 251-276.

Engle, Robert F. and C.W.J. Granger (1991), eds. *Long-Run Economic Relationships*. Oxford University Press.

Fleming, J.Marcus. (1962). "Domestic Financial Policies Under Fixed and Under Floating Exchange Rates." IMF *Staff Papers* 369-381.

Fleming, J.Marcus (1971). "Dual Exchange Rates for Current and Capital Transactions: A Theoretical Examination". In his Esseys in International Economics. Cambridge, Harvard University Press.

Flood, Robert P., and Nancy P. Marion (1983). "Exchange Rate Regimes in Transition: Italy 1974." *Journal of International Money and Finance* **2**, 279-294.

Flood, P., Bhandari,J.S., Horne, J.P. (1989) "Evolution of Exchange Rate Regimes." *IMF Staff Papers* **36**, 4, 810-835.

Flood, Robert P. (1979). "Capital Mobility and the Choice of Exchange Rate System." *International Economic Review* 20, 2, 405-416.

Flood, Robert P. (1978). "Exchange Rate Expectations in Dual Exchange Market." *Journal of International Economics* **8**, 65-77.

Frenkel, Jacob A. (1982) "Aspects of the Optimal management of Exchange Rates." *Journal of International Economics* **13**, 231-256.

Frenkel, Jacob A. and Assaff Razin (1987). "The Mundell-Fleming Model, A Quarter Century Later: A Unified Exposition". IMF *Staff Papers* **34**, 4, 567-620.

Frenkel, Jacob A., and Michael L. Mussa (1985). "Asset Market Exchange Rate and the Balance of Payments." In R.W. Jones, and P.B. Kenen (eds.), *Handbook of International Economics* **II**. Elsevier.

Frenkel, Jacob A., and Harry, G. Johnson (1976),eds. *The Monetary Approach to the Balance of Payments to the Balance of Payments*. University of Toronto Press, Toronto.

Frenkel, Michael (1990). "Exchange Rate Dynamics in Black Markets." *Journal of Economics* **51**, 2, 159-176.

Friedman, Benjamin M. (1975). "Targets, Instruments, and Indicators of Monetary Policy." *Journal of Monetary Economics* **1**, 443-473.

Friedman, Benjamin M. (1977). "The Ineffiency of Short-Run Monetary Targets for Monetary Policy." *Brookings Papers on Economic Activity* **2**, 293-346.

Friedman, Benjamin M. (1983a). "Using a Credit Aggregate Target to Implement Monetary Policy in the Financial Environment of the Future." In

Monetary Policy Issues in the 1980's. Symposium sponsored by the Federal Reserve of Kansas City.

Friedman, Benjamin M. (1983b). "Monetary Policy Management." In William Miller (ed.), *Regrowing the American Economy.* The American Assembly, Columbia University, 72-99.

Friedman, Milton (1971). "Government Revenue from Inflation." *Journal of Political Economy* **79**, 4, 846-856.

Froot, Kenneth A. (1988). "Credibility, Real Interest Rates, and the Optimal Speed of Trade Liberalization." *Journal of International Economics* **25**, 71-93.

Froot, Kenneth A., and Maurice Obstfeld (1991). "Exchange-rate Dynamics Under Stochastic Regime Shifts." *Journal of International Economics* **31**, 203-229.

Galbis, Vicente (1993). "Experience with Floating Interbank Exchange Rate Systems in Five Developing Economies." IMF Working Paper WP/36.

Gardner, Grant W. (1985). "Money, Prices, and the Current Account in a Dual Exchange Regime." *Journal of International Economics* **18,** 321-338.

Gardner, Grant W. (1983). "The Choice of Monetary Policy Instruments in an Open Economy." *Journal of International Money and Finance* **2**, 347-354.

Genberg, Hans (1978). "Purchasing Power Parity under Fixed and Flexible Exchange Rates". *Journal of International Economics* **8**, 247-276.

Genberg, Hans (1981). "Purchasing Power Parity as a Rule for a Crawling Peg." In John Williamson (ed.), *Exchange Rate Rules: The Theory, Performances and Prospects of the Crawling Peg*. London: MacMillan.

Genberg, Hans (1989). "Exchange Rate Management and Macroeconomic Policy: A National Perspective." *Scandinavian Journal of Economics* **91**, 2, 439-469.

Genberg, Hans, and Jean-Pierre Roth (1979). "Exchange-Rate Stabilization Policy and Monetary Target with Endogenous Expectations." *Schweiz Zeitschrift für Volkswirtschaft und Statistik* **3**, 527-522.

Genberg, Hans, Michael K. Salemi, and Alexander Swoboda (1987). "The Relative Importance of Foreign and Domestic Disturbances for Aggregate Fluctuations in the Open Economy." *Journal of Monetary Economics* **19**, 45-67.

Genberg, Hans, Carlos Rodriguez, and Larry Sjaastad (1985). *Politica Comercial en El Salvador*. Ministerio de Planificacion y Coordinacion del Desarrollo Economico y Social. San Salvador.

Genberg, Hans, and Alexander Swoboda (1985). *External Influences on the Swiss Economy under Fixed and Flexible Exchange Rates*. Verlag Rüegger, Grüsch.

Ghei, Nita, and Miguel A. Kiguel (1992). "Dual and Multiple Exchange Rate Systems in Developing Countries." World Bank Working Paper WPS 881. April.

Gilbert, R. Alton (1985). "Operating Procedures for Conducting Monetary Policy". *Review*, Federal Reserve Bank of St. Louis **67**, 13-21.

Giovannini, Alberto (1994). "Monetary Policy, Liquidity, and Foreign Exchange Markets." *Journal of Monetary Economics* **33**, 63-86.

Gönensay, Emre (1966). "The Theory of Black Market Prices." *Economica* **33**, 130 (May), 219-225.

Goodhart, Charles (1989) "The Conduct of Monetary Policy." *The Economic Journal* **99**, 293-346.

Goodhart, Charles (1986). "Financial Innovation and Monetary Control." *Oxford Review of Economic Policy* **2**, 4, 79-102.

Granger, C.W.J. and P. Newbold (1974). "Spurious Regressions in Econometrics". *Journal of Econometrics* 2, 111-120.

Greenwood, J., and K. P. Kimbrough (1987). "Foreign Exchange Controls in a Black Market Economy." *Journal of Development Economics* **26**, 1, 129-143.

Gros, Daniel (1988). "Dual Exchange Rates in the Presence of Incomplete Market Separation: Long-Run Effectiveness and Policy Implications." IMF *Staff Papers* **35**, 437-460.

Grosse, Robert (1992). "Colombia's Black Market in Foreign Exchange." *World Development* **20**, 8, 1193-1207. IMF Working Paper WP/93/36. April.

Guidotti, Pablo (1988). "Insulation Properties Under Dual Exchange Rates." *Canadian Journal of Economics* **XXI**, 4 (November), 799-813.

Guidotti, Pablo, and Carlos Vegh (1988). "Macoreconomic Interdependence Under Capital Controls: A Two Country Model of Dual Exchange Rates." IMF Working Paper WP/88/74.

Gupta, Sanjeev (1980). "An Application of the Monetary Approach to Black Market Exchange Rate." *Weltwirtschafliches Archiv* **116**, 2, 235-252.

Gupta, Sanjeev (1981). "A note on the Efficiency on Black Markets in Foreign Currencies." *Journal of Finance* **36**, 705-710.

Halm, G, ed (1970). *Approaches to Greater Flexibility of Exchange Rates, The Bürgenstock Papers*. Princeton University Press, NJ.

Hamilton, James D. (1994). *Time Series Analysis*. Princeton University Press, Princeton, New Jersey.

Hansen, Gerd (1993). *Quantitative Wirtshaftsforschung*. Verlag Franz Vahlen München.

Hansen, Gerd. (1994). "Cointegration and Monetary Model of the Exchange Rate." In: Jürgen Kaehler and Peter Kugler (eds), *Econometric Analysis of Financial Markets*. New York: Physica-Verlag. 47-63.

Hansen, Gerd and Jeong-Ryeol Kim (1995)." Money and Inflation in Germany: A Cointegration Analysis". Arbeit aus dem Institut für Statistik und Ökonometrie der Christian-Albrechts-Universität zu Kiel, Nr. 78/1995.

Harberger, Arnold C., and Daniel L. Wisecarver (1990). "Guidelines for Development: Suggestions for Economic Policy in El Salvador." Fundacion Salvadoreña Para el Desarrollo Economico y Social (FUSADES) Working Paper 12. San Salvador, El Salvador.

Helpman, Elhanan, and Leonardo Leiderman (1991). "Exchange Rate Systems: New Perspectives." In Zvi-Eckstein (ed.), *Aspects of Central Bank Policy Making*. Berlin: Springer-Verlag.205-239.

Hester, Donald D. (1981). "Innovations and Monetary Control." *Brookings Papers on Economic Activity* **1**, 141-199.

Interamerican Management Consulting Corporation (1989). "El Sector Financiero de El Salvador." Unpublished document.

International Monetary Fund (1991). "El Salvador - Review Under Stand-By Arrangement." Unpublished document. January.

International Monetary Fund (1990). "El Salvador Staff Report for 1990, Article IV Consultation and Request for Stand-By Arrangement". Unpublished document, August 8.

International Monetary Fund (1992). "El Salvador: Coordinacíon de Objectivos, Recapitlaización y Control Monetario del Banco Central de Reserva - Problemas y Recomendaciones." Unpublished document. June.

International Monetary Fund (1994a). "El Salvador - Request for the Extension and Modification of the Stand-by Arrangement." Unpublished document. February.

International Monetary Fund (1994b). "El Salvador - Staff Report for the 1994 Article IV Consultation and Midterm Review Under the Stand-By Arrangement." Unpublished document. September.

International Monetary Fund (1977). *The Monetary Approach to the Balance of Payments*. International Monetary Fund, Washington DC

International Monetary Fund. *Annual Report on Exchange Arrangements and Exchange Restrictions*. Annual publications (1983-1991). Washington DC.

Johnson, G.G. et al. (1985). *Formulation of Exchange Rate Policies in Adjustement Programs*. IMF Occasional Paper 36. Washington DC: International Monetary Fund.

Johnson, Harry (1970). "The Case for Flexible Exchange Rates, 1969". In Halm, George (ed), *Approaches to Greater Flexibility of Exchange Rates, The Burgenstock Papers*. Princeton University Press, Princeton NJ, 91-111.

Jones, Christine, and Michael Roemer (1989). "Editors' Introduction: Modeling and Measuring Parallel Markets in Developing Countries." *World Development* **17**, 12, 1861-1970.

Kamin, Steven B. (1993). "Devaluation, Exchange Controls, and Black Markets for Foreign Exchange in Developing Countries." *Journal of Development Economics* **40**, 151-169.

Kareken. John H., Thomas Muench, Neil Wallace (1973) "Optimal Open Market Strategy: The Use of Information variables." *The american Economic Review* **63**, 1 156-172.

Katseli-Papaefstratiou, Louka T.(1979) "The Remergence of Purchasing Power Parity Doctrine in the 1970's". Economic Growth Center, Yale University, May 1979.

Kenen, Peter B. (1982). "Effects of Intervention and Sterilization in the Short Run and the Long Run." In Richard N. Cooper, Peter B. Kenen, Jorge B. de Macedo and Jacques Van Ypersele (eds.), *The International Monetary System Under Flexible Exchange Rates.* Billinger Publisher, Cambridge Massachusett.

Khan, Mohsin S. (1986). "Developing Country Exchange Rate Policy Responses to Exogenous Shocks." *American Economic Review Papers and Proceedings* **76**, 2, 84-87.

Khan, Mohsin S., and J. Saúl Lizondo (1987). "Devaluation, Fiscal Deficits, and the Real Exchange Rate." *The World Bank Economic Review* **1**, 2, 357-374.

Khan, Mohsin, and Peter Montiel (1987) "Real Exchange Rate Dynamics in a Small

Primary-Exporting Country" IMF *Staff Papers* **34**, 681-710.

Kharas, Homi, and Brian Pinto (1989). "Exchange Rate Rules Black Market Premia and Fiscal Deficits: The Bolivian Hyperinflation." *Review of Economic Studies* **56**, 435-448.

Kiguel, Miguel, and Lizondo J. Saúl (1990). "Adoption and Abandonment of Dual Exchange Rate Systems." *Revista de Analisis Economico* **5**, 1, 3-23.

Kindleberger, Charles P. (1969). "The Case For Fixed Exchange Rates, 1969." In *The International Adjustement Mechanism.* Proceedings of the Monetary Conference. Melvin Village, New Hampshire, October 8-10, 1969. Sponsored by the Federal Reserve Bank of Boston, Boston..

Kouri, P. (1975). *Essays in the theory of flexible exchange rates.* Ph.D. dissertation. Massachusetts Institute of Technology.

Kouri, P. (1976). "The Exchange Rate and the Balance of Payments in the Short Run and in the Long Run: A Monetary Approach." *The Scandinavian Journal of Economics* **78**, 229-248.

Krueger, Anne (1978). *Foreign Trade Regimes and Economic Development: Liberalization Attempts and Consequences.* National Bureau of Economic Research. New York.

Krueger, Anne (1983). *Exchange Rate Determination.* London: Cambridge University Press.

Krugman, Paul (1979). "A Model of Balance-of-Payments Crises". Journal of Money, Credit, and Banking 11, 3, 311-325.

Lanyi, Anthony (1975). "Separate Exchange Markets for Capital and Current Transactions." IMF *Staff Papers* **XXII**, 3 (November), 714-749.

Lindauer, David L. (1987). "Government wage and employment policy: An analytical treatment with special reference to Africa." Country Policy Department Discussion Paper 1987-3 (March). Washington, DC World Bank.

Lindauer, David L. (1989). "Parellel,Fragmented, or Black? Defining Market Structure in Developing Economies." *World Development* **17**, 12, 1871-1880.

Lizondo, J. Saúl (1987b). "Exchange Rate Differential and Balance of Payments Under Dual

Exchange Markets." *Journal of Development Economics* **26**, 37-53.

Lizondo, J. Saúl (1990). "Multiple Exchange Rates and Black Market Exchange Rates: A Non-Technical Survey of Theoretical Results". University of Tucuman.Unpublished.

Lizondo, J. Saúl (1991). "Alternative Dual Exchange Market Regimes: Some Steady-State Comparisons." IMF *Staff Papers* **38**, 3 (September), 560-581.

Lizondo, J. Saúl (1987a). "Unification of Dual Exchange Markets." *Journal of International Economics* **22**, 57-77.

Loehr, William (1991) "Recent Reforms in Trade and Payments in El Salvador", February. Unpublished document.

Maciejewski, Edouard B. (1983). "'Real' Effective Exchange Rate Indices: A Re-Examination of the Major Conceptual and Methodological Issues." IMF *Staff Papers* **30**, 491-541.

Marion, Nancy P. (1981). "Insulation Properties of a Two-tier Exchange Market in a Portfolio Balance Model. *Economica* **48**, 61-70.

Martin, Lawrence, and Arvind Panagariya (1984). "Smuggling, Trade, and Price Disparity: A Crime-Theoretic Approach." *Journal of International Economics* **17**, 201-217.

May, Ernesto (1985). "Exchange Controls and Parallel Market Economies in Sub-Saharan Africa: Focus on Ghana." World Bank Staff Working Papers 711. Washington DC.

McCallum, Bennett T. (1989). "Targets, Indicators, and Instruments of Monetary Policy." NBER Working Paper 3047. July.

McDermott, John H. (1989). "Foreign-Exchange Rationing and Employment in Industrializing Countries." *Journal of International Economics* **27**, 245-264.

McDonald, Donogh C. (1985). "Trade Data Discrepancies and the Incentive to Smuggle: An Empirical Analysis." IMF *Staff Papers* **32**, 668-692.

McKinnon, Ronald (1976). "International Transfers and Non-traded Commodities: The Adjustment Problem". In Leipziger, ed. The International Monetary System and the Developing Nations. Agency for International Development, Washington D.C. , 157-174.

McKinnon, Ronald (1981). "Financial repression and liberalisation problem within less-developed countries." In Sven Grassman and Erik Lundberg (eds.), *The World Economic Order: Past and Prospects*. New York: St Martin's Press. 365-390.

Michaely, Michael (1954). "Communications: A geometrical analysis of black market behavour." *American Economic Review* **54**, 4 (September), 627-637.

Montes, Segundo (1987a). *El Salvador 1987, Salvadoreños Refugiados en los Estados Unidos*. Instituto de Investigaciones Universidad Centroamericana José Simeón Cañas. San Salvador.

Montes, Segundo (1987b). "La Crisis Salvadoreña y las Consecuencias de una Repatriación Masiva de Refugiados en los Estados Unidos." *Boletín de Ciencias Económicas y Sociales* **1**, 5-15.

Montes, Segundo (1990). El Salvador 1989: *Las Remesas que envían los Salvadoreños de Estados Unidos*: *Consecuencias Sociales y Económicas.* Uca-editores, San Salvador.

Montiel, Peter J., and Jonathan D. Ostry (1991). "Macroeconomic Implications of Real Exchange Rate Targeting in Developing Countries." IMF *Staff Papers* **38**, 4, 872-900.

Montiel, Peter J., Pierre-Richard Agénor, and Nadeem U. Haque (1993). *Informal Financial Markets in Developing Countries: A Macroeconomic Analysis.* Oxford UK & Cambridge USA: Blackwell.

Mundell, R. A. (1963). "Capital Mobility and Stabilization Policy Under Fixed and Flexible Exchange Rates." *Canadian Journal of Economics and Political Sciences* **XXIX**, 4 (November), 475-485.

Mundell, Robert A. (1968). *International Economics*. Macmillan, New York.

Mussa, Michael L. (1984). "The Theory of Exchange Rate Determination." In Bilson and Marston (eds.), *Exchange Rate Theory and Practice*. University of Chicago Press.

Mussa, Michael L. (1981). The Role of Official Intervention. Group of Thirty Occasional Papers 6. New York.

Neary, Peter, and Sweder Wijnbergen (1986). *Natural Resources and the Macroeconomy*. Basil Blackwell, Oxford, England.

Niehans, Jürg (1975). "Some Doubts about the Efficacy of Monetary Policy Under Flexible Exchange Rates." *Journal of International Economics* **5**, 275-281.

Nowak, Michael (1985). "Black Market for Foreign Exchange." *Finance and Development* **22**, 1 (March), 20-23.

Nowak, Michael (1984). "Quantitative Controls and Unofficial Markets in Foreign Exchange: A Theoretical Framework." IMF *Staff Papers* **31**, 404-431.

Obstfeld, Maurice (1982). "Can We Sterilize? Theory and Evidence." *American Economic Review Papers and Proceedings* **72**, 2, 45-50.

Obstfeld, Maurice (1984). "Balance-of-Payment Crises and Devaluation". *Journal of Money, Credit, and Banking* **16**, 2, 208-217.

Officer, Lawrence H. (1976). "The Purchasing Power Parity Theory of the Exchange Rate: A Review Article." IMF, *Staff papers* **23**, 1-60.

Olgun, Hasan (1984). "An Analysis of the Black Market Exchange Rate in Developing Economy - The Case of Turkey." *Weltwirtschafliches Archiv* **120**, 2, 329-347.

Phylaktis, Kate (1992). "The Black Market for Dollars in Chile." *Journal of Development Economics* **37**, 155-172.

Pick, Franz (1986-1987). *Pick's Currency Yearbook*, New York.

Pinto, Brian (1991a). "Unification of Official and Black Market Exchange Rates in Sub-Saharan Africa." In Emil-Maria Claassen (ed.), *Exchange Rate Policies in Developing and Post-Socialist Countries*. San Francisco, California: ICS Press.

Pinto, Brian (1991b). "Black Markets for Foreign Exchange, Real Exchange Rates and Inflation." *Journal of International Economics* **30**, 121-135.

Pinto, Brian (1987). "Nigeria During and After the Oil Boom: A Policy Comparison with Indonesia." *The World Bank Economic Review* **1**, 3, 419-445.

Pinto, Brain (1990). "Black Market Premia, Exchange Rate Unification, and Inflation in Sub-Saharan Africa." *The World Bank Economic Review* **3**, 3, 321-338.

Pitt, Mark (1981). "Smuggling and Price Disparity." *Journal of International Economics* **11**, 447-458.

Pitt, Mark (1984). "Smuggling and the Black Market for Foreign Exchange." *Journal of International Economics* **16** (May), 243-257.

Podolski, T.M. (1986). *Financial Innovation and the Money Supply*. Padstow, GB: T J Press Ltd.

Poole, William (1970). "Optimal Choice of Monetary Policy Instruments in a Simple Stochastic Macro Model." *Quarterly Journal of Economics* **84**, 197-216.

Quirk, Peter J., Benedicte V. Christensen, Kyung-Mo Huh, and Tshihiko Sasaki (1987). *Floating Exchange Rates in Developing Countries: Experience with Auction and Interbank Markets.* IMF Occasional Paper 53. Washington DC: International Monetary Fund.

Rhomberg, Rudolf R. (1976). "Indices of Effective Exchange Rates." IMF *Staff Papers* **30**,1 (March), 88-112.

Rodriguez, Carlos A. (1993). "Money and Credit Under Currency Substitution." IMF *Staff Papers* **40**, 2, 414-426.

Rodrik, Dani (1988). "Promises, Promises: Credible Policy Reform Via Signaling." NBER Working Paper 2600. May

Rodrik, Dani (1989). "Credibility of Trade Reform - a Policy Maker's Guide." *The World Economy* **12**, 1-16.

Roemer, Michael, and Christine Jones (1991). Eds. *Markets in Developing Countries: Parallel, Fragmented and Black.* International Center for Economic Growth. Harvard Institute for International Development. San Francisco, California: ICS Press.

Saca, Nolvia N. (1982). *The Real Exchange Rate of El Salvador.* Mémoire du Diplôme. Institut Universitaire de Hautes Etudes Internationales, Geneva.

Saca, Nolvia N. (1989). "The Black Market Exchange Rate: The Case of El Salvador". Kiel Advanced Studies Working Paper 177. Kiel Institute of World Economics.

Saca, Nolvia N. (1990a). "The Black Market Exchange Rate and the Demand for Money: The Case of El Salvador". Kiel Advanced Studies Working Paper 181. Kiel Institute of World Economics.

Saca, Nolvia N. (1990b). "Exchange Controls, Transfers, and Export Competitiveness: Theory and Some Evidence from El Salvador". Kiel Institute of World Economics (Unpublished paper).

Salter, W.E.G. (1959). "Internal and External Balance: The role of Price and Expenditure Effects". *Economic Record* 35, 1211-1222.

Sargent, T. (1979). "Estimating Vector Autoregressions using Methods not Based on Explicit Economic Theories". *Quarterly Review*, Federal Reserve Bank of Minneapolis.

Schadler, Susan, Maria Carkovic, Adam Bennett, and Robert Kahn (1993). *Recent Experiences with Surges in Capital Inflows.* IMF Occasional Paper 108. Washington DC: International Monetary Fund.

Sellon, Gordon H., and Ronald L. Teigen (1981). "The Choice of Short-Run Targets for Monetary Policy." *Economic Review*. Federal Reserve Bank of Kansas City, **66**, 3-16.

Sheikh, Munir A. (1976). "Black markets for foreign exchange capital flows and smuggling." *Journal of Development Economics* **3**, 9-26.

Sherwood, Joyce (1956). "Revenue Features of Multiple Exchange Rate Systems: Some Case Studies." IMF *Staff Papers* **5**, 74-107.

Sijben, Jac J. (1988). "Financial Innovations, Monetary Policy and Financial Stability." *Kredit und Kapital* **1**, 43-66.

Simpson, Thomas d. (1984) "Changes in the Financial System: Implications for Monetary Policy." *Brookings Papers on Economics Activity* **1**, 249-272.

Sims, C. (1980). "Macroeconomics and Reality". *Econometrica* **48**, 1-47.

Swoboda, Alexander (1974). "The Dual Exchange System and Monetary Independance." In R.Z. Aliber (ed.), *National Monetary Policies and the International Financial System*. Chicago: University of Chicago Press. 258-270.

Tanzi, Vito and Mario Blejer (1982) "Inflation, Interest Rate Policy, and Currency Substitutions in Developing Economies: A Discussion of Some Major Issues". *World Development* **10**,9, 781-789.

Tanzi, Vito (1978). Inflation, Real Tax Revenue, and the case for Inflationary Finance: Theory with an Application to Argentina". IMF *Staff Papers* **25**, 417-451.

Thottathil, Pelis (1988). "The Internal Transfers of Income from Exporters to Importers within a Foreign Exchange Control Regime: an Indian Case." *Applied Economics* **20**, 1211-1222.

Tseng, Wanda, and Robert Corker (1991). *Financial Liberalization, Money Demand, and Monetary Policy in Asian Countries*. IMF Occasional Paper 84. Washington DC: International Monetary Fund.

Turnovsky, Stephen J. (1976). "The Relative Stability of Alternative Exchange Rate Systems in the Presence of Random Disturbances." *Journal of Money, Credit, and Banking (February)* , 29-50.

Turnovsky, Stephen J. (1985). "Optimal Exchange Market Intervention: Two Alternative Classes of Rules".In Bhandari, Jagdeeps S. (ed), *Exchange Rate Management under Uncertainty*. The MIT Press Cambridge, Massachusetts.

Urbain, Jean-Pierre (1993). *Exogeneity in Error Correction Models*. Lecture Notes in Economics and Mathematical Systems 398. Springer-Verlag, Berlin.

Van Wijnbergen, Sweder (1985). "Trade Reform, Aggregate Investment and Capital Flight." *Economics Letters* **19**, 369-372.

Wallich, Henry C. (1984) "Recent Techniques of Monetary Policy." *Economics Review* 21-29.

Watson, Mark W. (1993). "Vector Autoregression and Cointegration." Federal Reserve Bank of Chicago Working Paper WP-93-14. December.
Wickham, Peter (1985). "The Choice of Exchange Rate Regime in Developing Countries: A Survey of the Literature." IMF *Staff Papers* **32** (June), 248-288.
Williamson, John (1982). "A Survey of the Literature on the Optimal Peg." *Journal of Development Economics* **11**, 39-61.
Willms, Manfred (1971). "Controlling Money in an Open Economy: The German Case". *Review*, Federal Reserve Bank of St. Louis **53**, 4, 10-27.
Willms, Manfred (1993). "The Money Supply Approach: Empirical Evidence for Germany". *In Fundations of European Central Bank Policy*. Heildelberg. Studies in Contemporaty Economics.
World Bank (1987). *World Development Report*. New York: Oxford University Press
World Bank (1989). *World Development Report*. New York: Oxford University Press.
World Bank (1989a). "EL Salvador: Country Economic Memorandum." Report 7818-ES. Unpublished document.
World Bank (1989b). "Trade Liberalization and Economic Integration in Central America." World Bank Report 7625-CAM.
World Bank (1991). "Report and Recommendation of the President of the International Bank for Reconstruction and Development to the Executive Directors on a Proposed Structural Adjustment Loan to the Republic of El Salvador." Report P-5447-ES. Unpublished document
World Bank (1994). "World Development Indicators." In *World Development Report*. New York: Oxford University Press.
Younger, Stephen D. (1992). "Aid and the Dutch Disease: Macroeconomic Management When Everybody Loves You." *World Development* **20**, 11, 1587-1597.

FSC
www.fsc.org
MIX
Papier | Fördert gute Waldnutzung
FSC® C083411

Kolibri 360 GmbH
Ferdinand-Jühlke-Straße 7
99095 Erfurt, Deutschland
produktsicherheit@kolibri360.de

Druck:
CPI Druckdienstleistungen GmbH
im Auftrag der
Kolibri 360 GmbH
Ferdinand-Jühlke-Str. 7
99095 Erfurt